THE STAUNTON STREAK

THE
STAUNTON STREAK

PAUL HATCHER'S BASKETBALL DYNASTY

Introduction by Jarrett Hatcher

PATRICK HITE

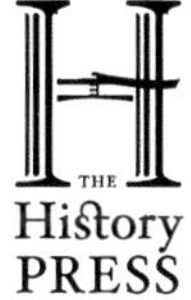

Published by The History Press
Charleston, SC
www.historypress.net

First published 2016

Manufactured in the United States

ISBN 978.1.46713.566.5

Library of Congress Control Number: 2016936017

Notice: The information in this book is true and complete to the best of our knowledge. It is offered without guarantee on the part of the author or The History Press. The author and The History Press disclaim all liability in connection with the use of this book.

For my wonderful parents, Wayne and Mary Ann.
Thanks for all of the love and support you've shown.

Contents

Acknowledgements

For several months near the end of 2015, I came to cherish Sunday evenings. That was the day I went to Paul and Judy Hatcher's house to interview them, along with their eldest son, Jarrett, for this book.

Most weeks we sat on the screened-in porch in the Hatchers' backyard. On the evenings when Paul felt it was too cold to sit there, we would meet in the living room. The first few weeks we discussed the eighty-five-game winning streak, but as the weeks progressed, we got into many other aspects of Paul's coaching career, his youth in Bassett Forks, the Hatchers' marriage, their life together and so much more. One evening we even spent some time talking about the squirrels that inhabit his backyard.

Paul has a remarkable memory. He would rattle off scores—and I verified they were correct—from games played decades earlier. He recalled players who hadn't been on his team for years, and he remembered specific moments and plays, some of which excited him so much that he got out of his chair and demonstrated them for me.

Jarrett joined us almost every week, and from time to time, Judy would also. Even when she didn't want to sit on the porch with us, she brought us cookies and drinks. I enjoyed that part, too. Brandon Hatcher even joined us once. It was great seeing the entire family together.

My thanks to all of the Hatchers for giving their time and being so open to this project. In addition to sitting for the many interviews, Paul let me borrow all of the newspaper articles about his games that he has kept over the years. He had stories saved from every game played during the winning streak, saving me the trouble of going to the library or sifting through the *News Leader*'s archives.

Jarrett and Paul helped me get in touch with many of the people interviewed for this book. Much thanks to both for that help.

Without Jarrett, this project would have never happened. We have been talking about writing a book on Paul for years, and in the summer of 2015, we finally decided it was time. Jarrett was instrumental in getting his family on board with the project and answering so many of my questions along the way. The two of us spent many hours on the phone during this project, and I have been grateful for his assistance throughout.

Brandon deserves a huge thank-you for scanning many of the photos you see in this book. His help was invaluable.

Special thanks also to The History Press and my acquisitions editor, J. Banks Smither, for agreeing to publish this book and helping me every step along the way. Banks endured all of my e-mails asking him questions that he had probably already answered before. He didn't complain once (at least not to me, although it's possible he tossed a few swear words toward the computer screen whenever another e-mail from me popped into his inbox).

Thank you to all of those who agreed to be interviewed for this book, either in person, on the telephone or, in one or two cases, via e-mail. I am especially grateful to the players who were part of the streak that I had a chance to speak with: Tyler Crawford, Jason Jordan, Keary Bonner, Eli Crawford, Ryan Crawford and Keon Scott. Also, former Hatcher players Kevin Madden, Mouse Patterson, Mark Newlen, Tony Randolph and Mike Madden were extremely helpful. Thank you to all of them.

Former Martinsville coach Troy Wells spent a lot of time with me on the telephone during the holiday season discussing his team's games against Lee, and for that I am very appreciative. Ralph Sampson must get tired of people asking him for his time, but he never showed it when I asked him before a basketball game at Lee High to talk to me for this project. Thank you to both of them.

Waynesboro coach C. Jay DeWitt, former Fort Defiance coach Charley Butcher and former Broadway coach Gary Leake were all wonderful in answering questions about very specific games against Lee High in their coaching careers. Thanks to all three.

Hubert F. Grim III and Jim Sacco were the sports editors of the two major daily newspapers in the area—the *News Leader* and the *News Virginian*, respectively—during the streak, and both gave of their time to talk about covering Lee High basketball and Paul Hatcher over the years. Thank you to both.

The *News Leader*, especially executive editor Dave Fritz, was very accommodating to me for this project, allowing me access to the newspaper's photograph archives and granting me permission to use any photos I needed for the book. Dave didn't need to do that, and I'm grateful for his help.

Thank you to the *News Leader*'s photographer, Mike Tripp, for agreeing to take a photograph in the Paul Hatcher Gym that I needed. He was photographing a basketball game for the newspaper at the time, and I appreciate his willingness to take a photo to be used in this book.

Much thanks to Jim Britt at WSVA Radio in Harrisonburg for digging up some cassette tapes of Lee High games that he and Karl Magenhofer called during the streak. I had to dust off my cassette player from the basement—and endure my eleven-year-old daughter's mocking of old technology—to listen to them, but actually hearing the games again brought back fond memories.

Robert Anderson, the high school sports editor of the *Roanoke Times*, also deserves a big thank-you for helping me with research on the Western District. One of the few things Paul Hatcher couldn't remember was which teams made up the district in the early 1970s. To be fair, Paul remembered thirteen of the fourteen teams. Robert came to our rescue by looking through microfilm to figure out that one remaining team: Amherst County. Thanks Robert.

Thank you also to Jim Quist for agreeing to read a very early rough draft of the manuscript and providing valuable feedback. It's good to have friends who are willing to help when asked.

Last, but certainly not least, is a giant thank-you to my family—Kari, Alexa and Ainsley—for putting up with my constant obsession with this project, including all of the research, editing and writing that was involved. My wife, Kari, also proofread the manuscript and saved me, her technophobic husband, from several computer disasters. Thank you doesn't seem sufficient for what she has meant to me this past quarter of a century. I am grateful to her for sticking by my side and being my best friend and the love of my life.

This has been a very entertaining and worthwhile project on which to work. I hope you enjoy reading it as much as I enjoyed writing it.

INTRODUCTION

By Jarrett Hatcher

This book is the culmination of the last twelve years of talking and discussing the best three years I have ever spent as a coach. I started sketching out this book on a legal pad the day after Lee High won the state title in 2004. It seemed like such a Hollywood story. Little did I know that it would be the first act in a three-part play, with one exception: the good guys do not really win in the end. Dad and I stressed to our teams over the years the idea of the journey and not the destination. There were so many fascinating stories and subplots during this journey.

It is mind-boggling to think of winning eighty-five games in a row. Several years ago, Patrick and I discussed writing a book on my dad and Lee basketball, but life got in the way. In the summer of 2015, an opportunity for us to commit to the book presented itself, and we jumped at the chance. It has been a wonderful trip down memory lane, with memories not just of the streak but also of my entire life.

When my parents brought me home from the hospital, my father put a Wilson Jet basketball in my crib. I was the stereotypical coach's son in every way possible. My first time in public was at a Lee High summer-league game, and as a toddler, I was taught the lessons of taking a charge by my dad. I lived and died with Lee High basketball. I have been a manager, a stat guy, a videographer, a water boy, a player, the jayvee coach, the assistant coach, the interim coach and, now, the head varsity coach.

I was not the most talented player at Lee. In fact, my dad cut me several times. It was the best life lesson I have ever received. It taught me to earn things, it taught me perseverance and it taught me to never give up on your goals and dreams. My dream and goal as an adult was to win a state title with my father and to be the first to congratulate him.

As a kid, I drew up plays and gave them to my dad, who always told me he used them and they worked. I cheered Lee victories and cried after the losses. When the games were too far away, I listened on the radio. I read every article, listened to every interview and watched my dad at practice. My brother Brandon and I were his biggest fans. While Brandon would sometimes be running around the gym or climbing the bleachers, I paid attention on the bench. I watched my dad after great wins and after tough losses. It was the best on-the-job training a coach could have.

There are moments, both positive and negative, that really stick out. The look of devastation on Dad's face after the 1983 JFK-Suffolk loss was unbearable. I would see that look at times when Mom was sick. The pain I felt watching Dad in the office the night the streak ended and that discussion with him will always be with me. Standing in the freezing cold drinking coffee behind the Waffle House in Troutville after losing three games in Roanoke during Tyler Crawford's freshman season was a low point, but the payoff was coming. The joke Dad and I make when things are not going our way is: "We need to go to the Waffle House."

In the 2004 state championship game, we were up big in the fourth quarter with about two minutes to go. With about twenty seconds left and up thirty-seven points, Dad grabbed my arm and said, "I think we got 'em." I believe he was the only person in the Siegel Center who did not know the game was over long before that moment. That is my dad in a nutshell—keep working until it is over.

I had no idea that I would end up being on the bench with my dad for over four hundred victories and two state titles. Taking the job as the jayvee coach at Lee is the best decision I have ever made in my life. I am grateful to Ron Ball, the athletic director at the time, for taking a chance on a then twenty-year-old college junior. I thank him whenever I see him. It gave me the chance to go to work every day with my hero, role model, best friend and the person who has influenced me more than anyone in my life.

As I write this, I am in the middle of my fifth season as the head coach at Robert E. Lee. I ended up being the successor to the coach with the most wins in the history of Virginia public schools in any sport. I know firsthand exactly how hard it is to be successful. My dad won eighty-five games in a row, and I have yet to win eighty-five games as a head coach. I never wanted to be the head coach, and I always wanted to be the head coach.

The shadow and the legacy that my dad left were impossible for anyone to follow. When I took the jayvee job, the deal was that I would never be his successor. I was fine with that, until my dad told me I should pursue the job. I have found that listening to my dad is usually a good thing.

I seldom go anywhere that someone doesn't come up to me and ask about my dad. He is a legend and an icon. He is so humble and sweet. I have never met a person with more integrity or class. He is also the single-most competitive person I have ever been around. His intense and serious demeanor on the court are a great contrast to the fun-loving, smart-aleck, compassionate father who held a family together in crisis. My father is witty and sly. He is also rigid, unyielding and uncompromising of his principles. He is a thoughtful and caring husband and father who is loyal to a fault. My father possesses a strong faith and is very devout. I am not saying that he was always that way in the heat of the moment or in the locker room at halftime. (Just kidding, Dad.)

Coaching takes people away from their families and can be a strain on the spouse and children. My father did a great job of helping blend the two together. Our family time was bus rides to games, time spent at practice and wonderful scouting trips. My dad took my brother and me on the road to give my mom a break. I have so many wonderful memories of sitting beside my dad on the bus on the way to games. I learned so many lessons on those bus rides and on the scouting trips with Dad.

My brother, Brandon, and I are blessed with great parents. Ultimately, basketball was the glue for our family. It was the most important thing in all of our lives. I have a mom who was devoted to her husband and willing to make great sacrifices for forty-three years. We always sat at the table for dinner even if it was game day and the bus was leaving soon. Mom and Dad made an effort to make all of our birthdays and holidays special. My brother was born during the 1975 regional tournament. There were many years we celebrated his birthday with cake or cupcakes in a locker room somewhere.

Our family does not always talk basketball. My parents pushed us to have other interests and hobbies. My dad's passions range from NASCAR to Shakespeare. My parents attend many plays at Staunton's Blackfriars Theater. Dad is such a fan of the Bard that we had an inbounds play called Shakespeare. My dad is a voracious reader, as is my mother. We talk books as much as basketball these days. And he loves golf. He introduced Brandon and me to the game at a young age. We spent our winters in the gym and every summer evening on the golf course. We would walk a few holes and have putting and chipping contests. The winner always got to buy a Mountain Dew from the drink machine. My favorite summer memories are riding home on Bells Lane with my dad in his Firebird and splitting a Mountain Dew with my brother.

As my brother and I grew older and both began to help Dad as coaches, our family beach trip became the unofficial start of basketball season. My aunt Joyce and uncle Jack always let us use their beach house in Cherry Grove, South Carolina, for our vacations. We always took game film with us, watching the previous season's games and some of Dad's favorites from past seasons. We would plan and discuss changes to what we wanted to do. We would sit on the porch, and I would get Dad talking about favorite games or stories. As we approached Tyler Crawford's senior year, we talked openly about winning a state title. Knee deep in the water, we agreed that we would put a picture on the wall.

The following spring, I had planned a golf trip to Cherry Grove over Easter. Brandon and two of our buddies, Matt Peterson and Jason Davis, rented a condo for a week. As it turned out, my parents came to the beach as well. Dad and I took a walk down the beach one morning, about one month removed from the state title. We talked about golf, and we talked about the season. I got very emotional and hugged my dad, telling him we did it, we won. Then I asked, "Now what?" Dad just looked at me with his sly grin and said, "We try and win the next game."

1
The Promise

Paul Hatcher was settled in and ready for the trip home when Tyler Crawford asked the Robert E. Lee High School basketball coach if he would mind getting off the bus for a moment.

Earlier in the day, Hatcher's team had beaten its Valley District rival Spotswood, but this wasn't just another regular season game between the two schools. It was five days after Christmas, and Lee High and Spotswood had played in what was then known as the MCI Center, home to the NBA's Washington Wizards.

The game was part of the NBA's "Play at the Pros" promotion. In exchange for playing at the professional basketball arena, both schools had to sell advance tickets to the NBA contest. Lee brought close to eight hundred fans to see its game, which was preceded by a contest between the girls' teams from both high schools and followed by the Wizards and the Miami Heat.

There were a lot of noteworthy accomplishments by this Lee High basketball team, including back-to-back state championships and Hatcher's 778 wins, which was already the state record for Virginia public high school basketball coaches and would continue to grow for a few more years.

At the moment, however, the main storyline following this team dealt with a winning streak. After the forty-five-point win over Spotswood in Washington, D.C., that winning streak stood at sixty-two games.

Clintwood High School, located in Dickenson County less than ten miles from the Virginia-Kentucky border, held the Virginia High School League

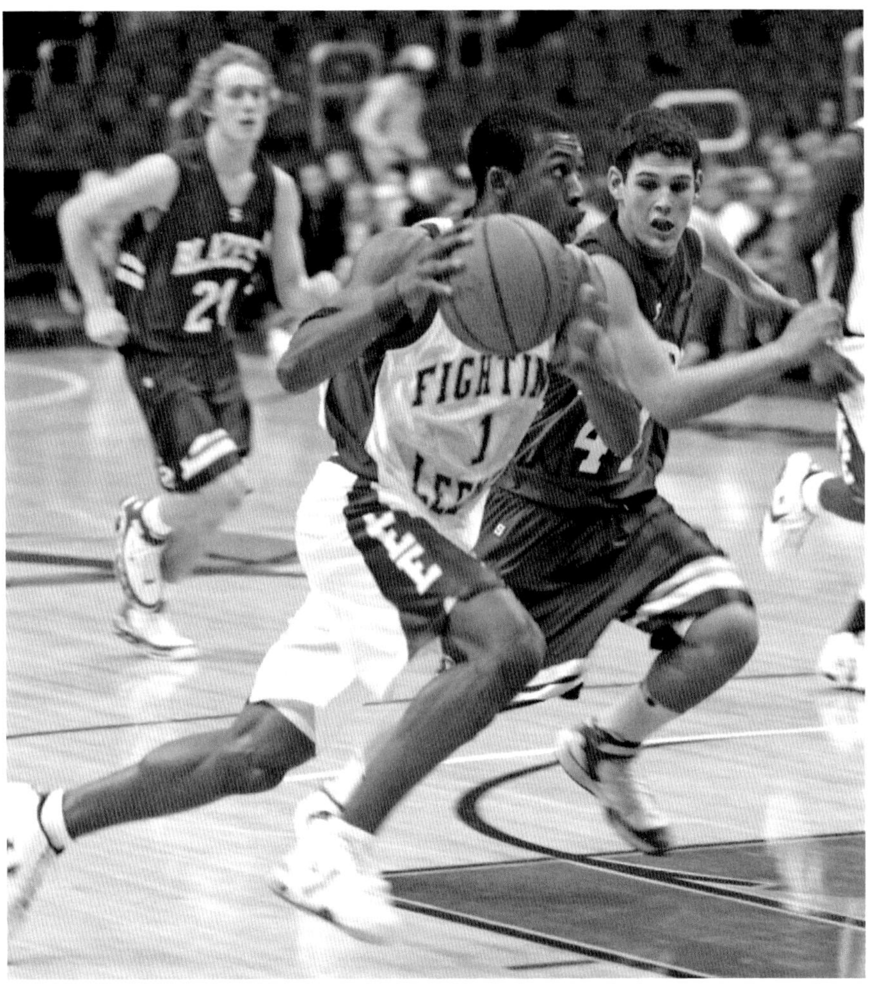

Ryan Crawford and his Lee High teammates played Spotswood in Washington, D.C.'s MCI Center on December 30, 2005. *Mike Tripp/the* News Leader.

record with sixty-six wins. The record was set over parts of three seasons and included state championships in 1950 and 1951, the second coming against Lee High. Those were the only two state titles in the history of the school, which will forever remain the case. Following the 2013–14 school year, Clintwood shut its doors and consolidated with Haysi, another Dickenson County school.

Clintwood's record, however, was in jeopardy. If Lee could win its next five games, it would own the longest winning streak in Virginia high school basketball history.

The local newspaper, the *News Leader*, had mentioned the streak from time to time in game stories, but it wasn't until win number fifty-nine that the word "streak" appeared in a headline, and in that case, it was a subhead. Finally, when Lee won its sixtieth game in a row, the *News Leader*'s headline was "Win Streak Stands at 60."

By the time Lee High beat Spotswood and the winning streak had reached sixty-two games, there was plenty of excitement in the community about the very real possibility that the Leemen would break the state record. Hatcher, though, wasn't approaching games any differently now than he had throughout his career.

"It's the same every year whether you've got a streak going or not," said Hatcher. "You're trying to win the next game. That's all we ever did."

In fact, Hatcher had been through this before. This wasn't the first Lee High winning streak to make the VHSL record book. From the 1983–84 season through the following season, 1984–85, the Leemen won fifty-two straight games, which is still seventh all-time in the state. Actually, after Lee lost in the 1985 state semifinal game to Martinsville, it won the first twenty-five games the next season before once again losing in the state semifinals, this time to Brunswick.

"That's kind of gone unnoticed," said Hatcher. "We won fifty-two, lost one, then won twenty-five straight. So that's seventy-seven out of seventy-eight. I was pretty proud of that, but nobody even mentions that."

Now, Hatcher's team was in the midst of another winning streak, but after a long day in the nation's capital, Hatcher wasn't concerned about the streak at that very moment. He simply wanted to get back to the small town he and his high school called home: Staunton, Virginia.

He did, however, delay that departure just a few minutes to meet with Crawford, one of his former players. Crawford was, by then, a sophomore at Georgetown University, where he played for the Hoyas basketball team. He wanted three of his college teammates—Roy Hibbert, Jeff Green and Jonathan Wallace—to meet his high school coach. Earlier in the day, the four had watched the Leemen destroy Spotswood on the basketball court.

When Hatcher stepped off the bus, the first thing Crawford did was give his old coach a hug. That sent Jarrett Hatcher, the coach's son and assistant coach, straight down memory lane to five years earlier in 2000.

Crawford was a Lee High freshman in 2000. During the school's Christmas break, the basketball team had played—and lost—three straight games in three consecutive days in Roanoke, about an hour and a half south of Staunton. Salem, Cave Spring and Osborne Park beat them, and the atmosphere in Lee High's locker room was about what you would expect after a disastrous road trip.

Paul Hatcher got a report that there was a problem. One of his players had lost his temper and was yelling at the other players. Hatcher was already in a bad mood. Losing did that to him. Now, one of his players was causing problems in the locker room. Jarrett Hatcher tried to calm the player down, to no avail. His teammates tried to calm him down, but that didn't work either.

"I don't need y'all!" the player shouted to no one in particular. "I don't need any of y'all!"

Paul Hatcher simply looked at him and said, "You need a ride home."

As the player stormed out of the locker room, he turned and told his coach he didn't even need that; he'd find a way home. To which Hatcher responded that he could do just that because he couldn't ride the bus back to Staunton.

"You didn't have any fight on the floor, don't show me no fight in here," Hatcher said of the incident, which resulted in the player getting kicked off not only the bus but also the team.

It wasn't the first time he had kicked a player off his team, although it hadn't happened very often since Hatcher took over as head coach in 1968. If it needed to happen, though, Hatcher wasn't reluctant. He had even kicked off starters during two of his state championship runs.

"He never put winning above doing what was right," said his wife, Judy Hatcher. "That's incredible."

Hatcher usually didn't suspend players. He felt that might put off a problem for a week or two, but it didn't remedy the problem. The coach's philosophy was to dismiss a player if needed, and that player was welcome to come out the next year to try out for the team again.

But in the locker room in Roanoke that December day in 2000, almost as soon as Hatcher told the player he couldn't ride home, he knew it might cost him his job. He couldn't leave a high school student stranded an hour and a half from home. So he quickly found Chris Lassiter, one of his former players and by then a writer for the *News Leader*, who was at the game. Lassiter agreed to drive the student home.

The incident made an impact on Crawford, who decided right then and there that he would never be like his ex-teammate. He wanted to be a team leader, someone teammates could look up to. He loved his coach and had no tolerance for those who felt otherwise. Crawford felt a connection to Hatcher.

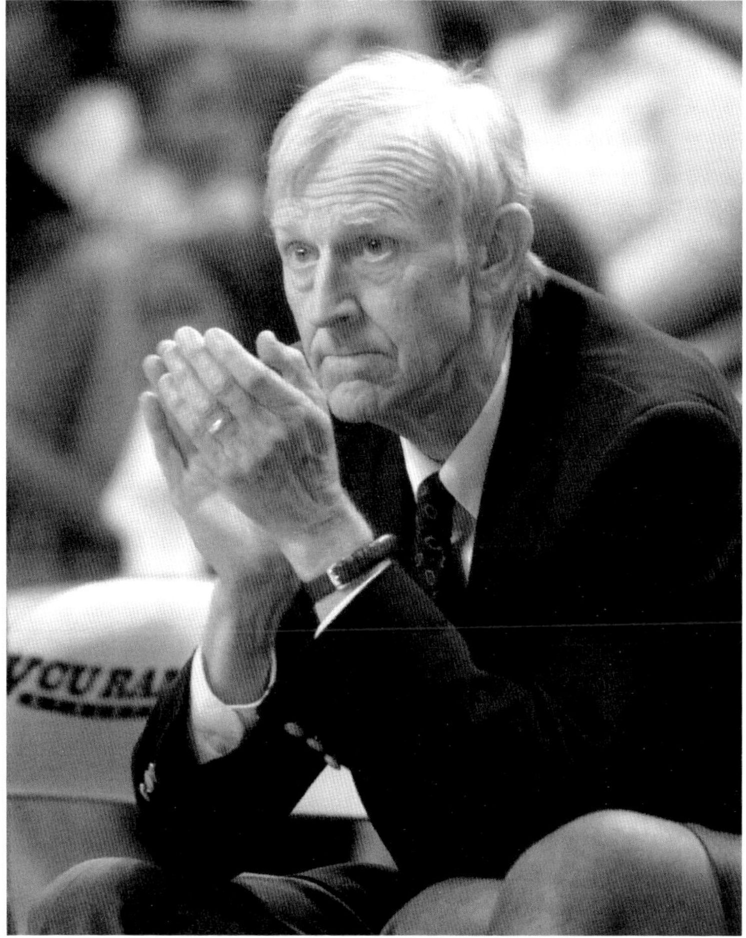

Paul Hatcher won 897 games and four state championships in forty-three years as Lee High's head basketball coach. His teams won a staggering 85 games in a row from 2003 to 2006. *Vincent Lerz/the* News Leader.

"I got along really well with Paul Hatcher because I feel like we had the same mindset," said Crawford. "He didn't like to lose. I watched him kind of grit his teeth together when he lost and things happened. I felt the same way."

Hatcher had been gritting his teeth a lot early that 2000–01 season. The loss dropped Lee High to 3-4, but things would turn around. Whether it was addition by subtraction with the dismissal of the player or something else, the Leemen ripped off eighteen straight wins after the three losses in Roanoke.

At the time, though, the coach wasn't sure exactly how things would turn out. He was pretty dejected as he prepared to head for home. With the players already on the bus for the third trip home from Roanoke in three days, Hatcher was walking toward the bus to get on when Crawford came down the steps.

"Coach, you look like you need a hug," said Crawford, wrapping his arms around Hatcher.

Five years later, there was Crawford, once again hugging his coach as the Leemen prepared for a bus trip home.

A STAR IS BORN

As Tyler Crawford walked off the court at Virginia Commonwealth University's Siegel Center on March 13, 2004, one of the first people he saw on the sidelines was Jarrett Hatcher. He gave his assistant coach a big, sweaty hug and said, "I always make good on my promises."

Lee High had just crushed previously unbeaten Greensville County 96–57 to win the Virginia High School League Group AA boys basketball state championship. It marked the twenty-fourth win in a row for Lee, capping off a 30-1 season and giving the team's legendary coach, Paul Hatcher, his 740th win and third state title in thirty-six years of coaching.

The win, and the twenty-three before it, were the first leg in what would become a remarkable three-year journey for Lee High, but at the time, no one was thinking about just how far the program could extend that winning streak, although winning another state title or two was certainly being discussed, at least by the players.

After beating Greensville and gathering in the locker room at the Siegel Center in Richmond, the players dared to look ahead. Unlike their coaches or longtime fans of the Lee program who knew just how quickly expectations of victory can turn into an upset loss, this group of teen athletes had no fear of projecting future success.

Lawrence Lightfoot looked at his teammates and said, "We're coming back next year."

Sophomore Eli Crawford, the younger cousin of Tyler Crawford, responded, "No, we're coming back the next two years."

The Lee players then started rapping, "We're going going, back, back to Richmond, Richmond" just like the Notorious B.I.G. had rapped "Going Back to Cali."

Paul Hatcher didn't have a problem that his players were already looking ahead, but at the same time, he knew it was a long time before next March, and a lot of basketball would be played in that span.

The concern among the Hatchers, especially Jarrett, was that a bulk of the roster was made up of sophomores who knew they would be around for two more years. The assistant coach could potentially see Lee High stumbling along the path to a repeat the following season, perhaps lacking some of the hunger the players had had during this championship run. He envisioned a scenario where next year's team failed to win a championship but bounced back the following year to win it with a senior-laden roster.

For Tyler Crawford, it didn't matter. He knew he wasn't going back, back to Richmond. This was it for the senior. In less than three months, he would graduate from Lee High and head to Washington, D.C., where he had signed to play for Georgetown University.

Watching Tyler Crawford in youth basketball leagues, it wasn't hard to tell he was very good and could be a special player. He started playing as a five-year-old, and his family has a video of him dunking on a Playskool basketball goal and breaking it. Those watching him, however, always assumed that, in high school, he would one day follow in the footsteps of Dell Curry.

Curry is the best basketball player in the history of Fort Defiance, a high school situated just north of Staunton. Curry helped the school win a state championship as a sophomore in 1980 and eventually went on to play at Virginia Tech, where he is generally regarded as the greatest player in school history. After Tech, Curry played in the NBA for sixteen years, and his son, Stephen Curry, currently plays for the Golden State Warriors and has become one of the league's biggest stars.

Crawford grew up in Verona, a small Augusta County community just north of Staunton, and was on track to play at Fort Defiance just like his older brother did. Just like Dell Curry did.

But plans change. Following his seventh-grade year, Crawford attended Lee High's summer basketball camp. One of the camp counselors, Chris Davis, was talking to Crawford about the items on the gym wall. There are only two items of recognition on the walls at Paul Hatcher Gym, named for the coach in 1990.

On the southeast side of the gym are state championship banners for any team fortunate enough to have won one. As of 2015, Lee boys' basketball was responsible for six of the eighteen banners, with four of those six coming under Hatcher. The banners all have white lettering and trim on a blue background (blue and white are the school's colors). On the northwest side of the gym are framed, blown-up photos of a few of the teams that won those state titles. The six boys' basketball state champions are honored with their photos on the wall, as are two girls' basketball teams, two volleyball teams and the golf team.

That suits Hatcher just fine. No banners for district or regional championships. Hatcher's philosophy was always that you played to win the state championship. Anything less and the team didn't achieve its goal. Winning was everything.

"The only reason you play is to win," said Hatcher. "Why would you go to Broadway on a cold winter's January night other than to win the game?"

Chris Davis had played on the 1990 state title team. At camp, Davis teased the rising eighth-grader Crawford that he would never win a state title going to a county school. Crawford surprised Davis with his response. He said his family was moving from Verona to Stuarts Draft, another community in Augusta County, but that he and his younger brother were going to come to Shelburne Middle School in Staunton because his family was going to pay tuition, which was allowed by the Virginia High School League.

So, instead of following in Dell Curry's footsteps, Crawford was about to be the next great player at Lee High. That was a move that didn't sit well with the Fort Defiance community. One Fort Defiance fan and a former teacher at the school said there was always a rivalry between Lee High and Fort Defiance, one school in the city and one in neighboring Augusta County, but she said the animosity grew, at least from the perspective of the Fort Defiance faithful, after Crawford transferred.

Charley Butcher, the Fort Defiance coach during much of Crawford's time at Lee, said he was never aware of any animosity toward the player, although he admits just because he didn't see it doesn't mean it wasn't present.

"Tyler was a phenomenal basketball player and was surrounded by other top-quality players and was coached by a legend, hence the streak," said Butcher. "But I can honestly say I never once heard any animosity. I did hear, 'Man I wish he was at Fort playing for us,' and that was from some of the Fort faithful, as well as the little voice in my head. But who wouldn't want him to play for their team?"

Crawford doesn't care if there was animosity or not. He did what was best for him, and he insists the move to Staunton schools was more about education than basketball.

"People think I went to Lee High solely for basketball, like I was recruited, yada, yada, yada," said Crawford. "No."

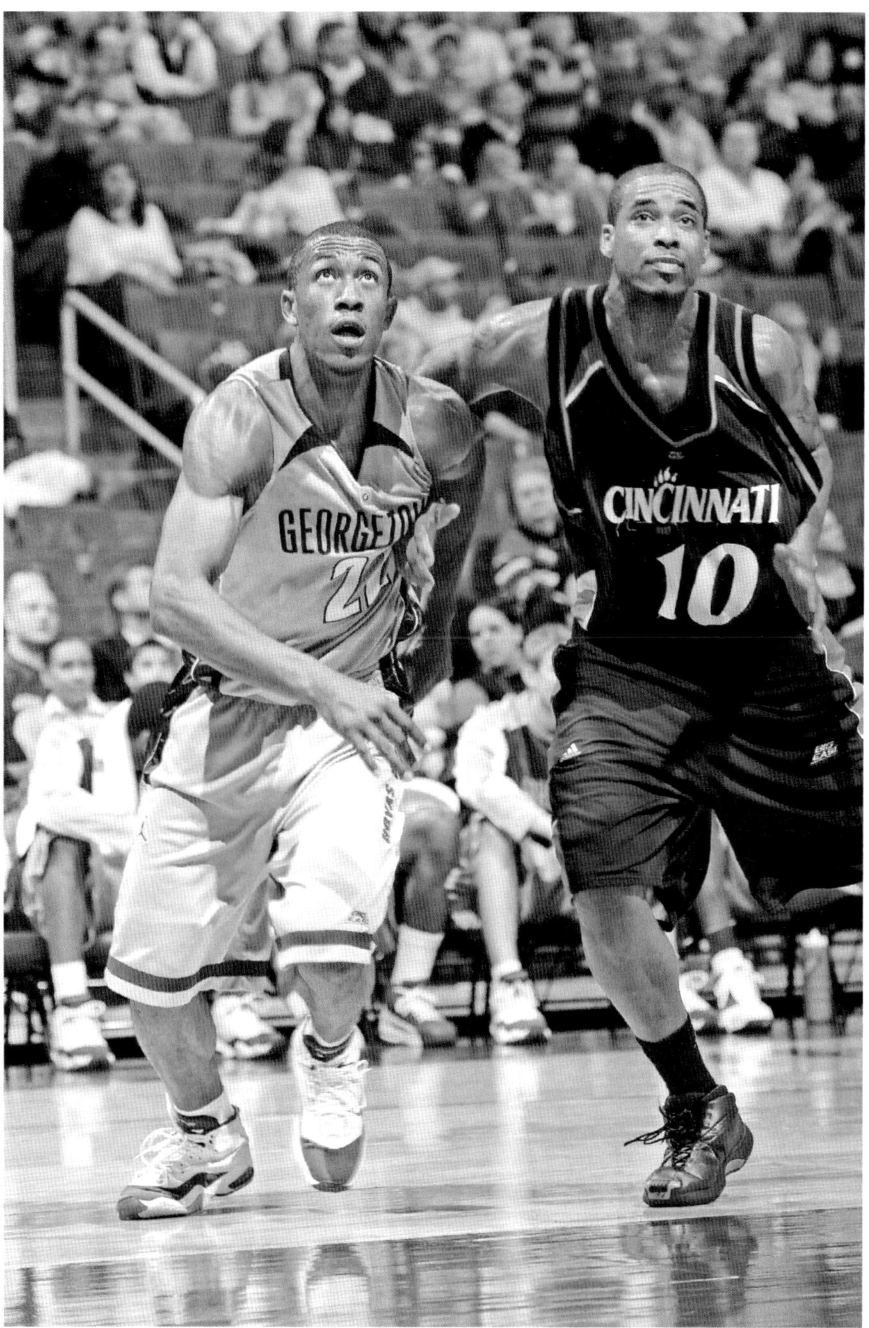

Tyler Crawford played college basketball at Georgetown, following a high school career in which he became the second all-time leading scorer at Lee High. *Photo courtesy of Georgetown University.*

Crawford struggled in math and ended up getting tutored by Robin Zombro, a teacher in the Staunton City Schools.

"She really helped me like math," said Crawford. "Just getting to know all the teachers in Staunton was one of the reasons [he transferred to Lee High]. I went to Lee High for the teachers. It wasn't for the basketball."

Still, it didn't hurt that he was going to play for a school that was a perennial state championship contender and for a coach who was regarded as the best in the state. Sitting in his Staunton home in late 2015, Crawford pointed to a photo of him playing at Georgetown; then he gestured toward his wife, whom he met at Georgetown, and said neither would have happened if he hadn't gone to Lee High.

He admits he didn't play as much at Georgetown as he thought he deserved to play, never averaging more than eight minutes a game in his four seasons. Still, he met good friends and his soul mate at the school. After college, he played professionally in Slovenia and Serbia and even got to work out with the Seattle Supersonics for a week before finally realizing it was time to give up on playing basketball.

"Do I feel like I should be doing what a lot of my buddies are doing? Yes," said Crawford. "Am I? No. Am I upset about it? Sometimes. It's bittersweet. Like, I miss the game a lot because that's all I've ever seen myself doing."

Still, the way his life has worked out—he's now married and is a deputy with the Augusta County Sheriff's Office—he said it's everything he's ever prayed for, and he would never want to go back and change it even if he could. Crawford owes a lot of that to playing at Lee. When he transferred there, he saw immediate improvement in his game.

"When I was there [Fort Defiance], I don't like talking about stuff, but physically, I was better than everybody else," said Crawford. "I was faster, I was stronger. Playing basketball, like, I could do all those things better than everybody else. When I got to Lee High, it was like, 'Oh, we've got some faster people, we've got some stronger people. So I've got to use my IQ to beat some of these people down.'"

In addition to his talent and intellect, Crawford also worked hard. Hatcher said he never had a player who worked harder than Crawford. Two Saturday mornings a month, Hatcher, who was also Lee High's driver's education teacher, taught a defensive driving improvement course at the school. Usually the coach could expect to see Crawford on those mornings, asking for the gym keys. He would stay in the gym the rest of the day, by himself, shooting, running after the ball and dribbling to the other end, where he would repeat the drill.

"He would come to you and say, 'Coach, what do I need to do, what do I need to do?' You'd tell him, and he'd go work on it for hours," said Hatcher.

Crawford said he saw a lot of himself in Paul Hatcher, especially in the way they approached the game. That's one of the reasons he worked so hard.

"He took such a big pride in being good or being great," said Crawford. "I never wanted to let that down. I knew that if I gave it my all, he would always appreciate it."

When Crawford was a freshman, Lee lost in the regional semifinals to Handley High School in Winchester, Virginia, but the next season, Hatcher would lead the Leemen to the state tournament for the twelfth time in his coaching tenure. Crawford scored twenty-seven points in a state quarterfinal win over York. With the game tied at fifty-seven, Crawford took the ball at the top of the key in the game's final seconds, drove the lane, hit a short jumper and was fouled. He completed the three-point play, giving him eleven points in the fourth quarter. His teammate Derrick Fields stole a York pass to seal the win.

The next game, in the state semifinals, didn't work out quite as nicely for Lee High, but maybe it didn't go as poorly as many thought it would either. Jarrett Hatcher and his younger brother, Brandon, had scouted Lee's next opponent, Martinsville, earlier in the season. Jarrett turned to a friend who had accompanied the brothers to the game and predicted Lee would lose by fifty.

"They were incredible," said Jarrett. "They had guards, they had size, they had quickness and shooters."

When Rache Waller hit a three-pointer in the fourth quarter, it appeared Jarrett Hatcher's hunch might be correct, as Martinsville took a ten-point lead. Then Paul Hatcher did something that caught everyone by surprise, even his own fans. He had his team start playing a zone defense. Conventional wisdom would be for Martinsville to just hold the ball and take the win if Lee was going to give it to them. But something—perhaps years of experience or Hatcher's innate knowledge of basketball—told the coach that his opponent wouldn't just hold it.

"They got antsy, and they turned it over," Hatcher said, rubbing his hands together. "Then somebody shot one they shouldn't have shot, and next thing you know we're in it."

The legendary coach was sometimes criticized for running the same plays over and over year after year and winning games simply because Lee had more talent, but it's moves like going to the zone when down double digits that dispel that way of thinking.

"He's sneaky with stuff," said Jarrett Hatcher.

Brandon Hatcher said his dad's practices were amazing. Paul Hatcher was involved in every aspect and had every minute accounted for. For the entire practice, he was teaching.

"It was always the thing around town, 'All they've got to do is roll the balls out. They've got talent, just roll the balls out and they win,'" said Brandon. "That used to always frustrate me because I used to see how much time was put into it. It was analyzing game film sitting at the beach in July. A lot of coaches weren't doing that."

Before anyone in the building realized what was happening, Lee went from down ten to up one, but when a Lee player missed the front end of a one-and-one, it opened the door for Martinsville, who scored to take a 60–59 lead. Lee got one more chance, but Derrick Fields's shot just before the buzzer was blocked, and Lee lost.

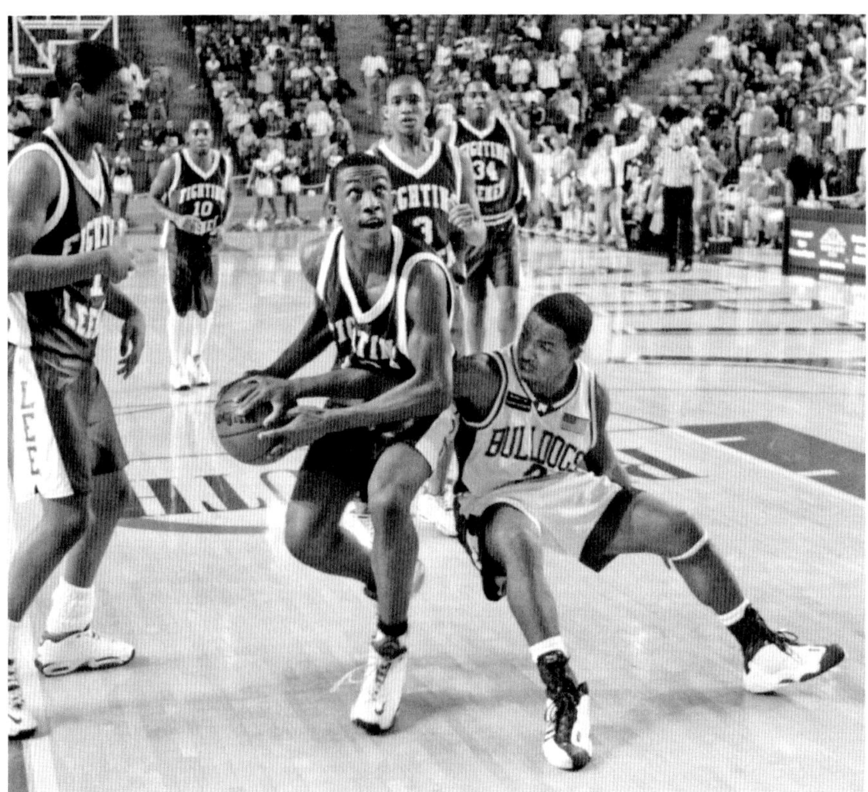

Tyler Crawford couldn't lead his team to victory in the 2002 Group AA state semifinals against Martinsville. *Vincent Lerz/the* News Leader.

The plan on the last play was to throw the ball to Crawford, but it went to Fields instead. Not ideal, but Hatcher is certain the block wasn't clean.

"I thought he got clobbered," said Hatcher, who is quick to tell you he has never been a fan of officials. "Well, he did get clobbered. And nothing."

To this day, Jarrett Hatcher can't stand to hear "Who Let the Dogs Out?" by the Baha Men, the anthem of choice for the Martinsville Bulldogs. The song blared throughout Liberty University's Vines Center after that game.

No one took the loss as tough as the head coach, though. It was so painful for Paul Hatcher that he ducked out of the building to avoid the media after the game. Jarrett Hatcher was left in charge of consoling the sobbing players and talking to the members of the media gathered outside the locker room.

It was so hard for Hatcher for a couple of reasons. First, the loss marked the sixth time in the state semifinals or finals that Lee High had lost by three points or less. It was the third one-point loss in the state semifinals, and all three times the team that beat Lee went on to win the state title. Paul Hatcher feels certain that with one more basket in each of those three losses, he would have had three more state championships on his résumé.

Hatcher won four state championships in his career but lost in the championship game five times, including three times before he finally won one.

"That's the worst feeling in the world," said Hatcher. "People make a big deal about state runner-up, but there were times I wouldn't go out there and get the [trophy]. I didn't want that. That's not what I came for."

He said he would have rather lost in the district semifinals than in the state finals. Either way, the season ended the same—with a loss—and if it had ended in the district tournament, he could have an extra month to spend time on something else.

Even now, retired since 2011, Hatcher focuses more on the tough losses than he celebrates the wins: four state championships and 897 victories. When he was coaching, he'd come home after a loss and tell his wife to put on a pot of coffee. Judy Hatcher knew that meant they'd be up half the night, with Paul breaking down every play from the game. Ten cups of coffee later, it would be 3:30 a.m., and the two would finally head to bed with the alarm set to go off in less than three hours.

"I've seen him take deaths better than he took losses," said Judy Hatcher

The coach always learned something from losses—he had only 174 in his career—but he would rather have avoided those lessons. Now that he's a head coach, Jarrett Hatcher is just like his dad. He'll stay up for hours replaying wins, even longer thinking about losses. Sleepless nights during basketball season are plentiful.

"I guess we're just screwed up that way as a family," said Jarrett.

Paul Hatcher said he knows he should feel fortunate to have won as many games as he did, but he can't stop himself from thinking about the ones he could have won. When he retired, three games short of 900 wins, a lot of people asked him why he didn't stay around another year to get those three extra wins. His response was always that he had 174 chances to get those three. If he couldn't do it, why stick around longer to try?

Brandon is one of those who would have loved his dad to stick around for nine hundred wins, but he understands why he didn't.

"It just goes to show that the accolades and accomplishments is not why he did it," said Brandon. "That's not what kept him motivated. What kept him motivated was beating the other guy. That's what he wanted to do."

Another reason the loss was so painful was the opponent: Martinsville.

Hatcher grew up in Bassett Forks, Virginia, and went to Bassett High School. His school's biggest rival, just fifteen miles away, was Martinsville. Years later, he's still tied to that rivalry. As a high school junior, Hatcher's first start for the basketball team came against Martinsville. Bassett won in overtime. And as a high school coach in Staunton, he faced the Martinsville Bulldogs six times, winning three of them, including one for his first state championship in 1984.

Bassett was usually good when Hatcher was growing up but most of the time not good enough to get past Martinsville in the district. Martinsville won its first state title in 1958, when Hatcher was a high school freshman. The next year, with Hatcher on the jayvee team, Bassett won the state championship.

Bassett got back to the state semifinals the next year, Hatcher's junior season, but lost to Varina. It didn't reach another state tournament until 2006. Meanwhile, Martinsville was just getting started with that 1958 title.

Under Paul Hatcher, Lee High was one of the most successful high school basketball programs in Virginia, but the title for most successful would probably go to Martinsville. After winning that first title, Martinsville won fourteen more through 2016, a state record. Martinsville has also been in twenty-seven state tournaments, another state record, seven ahead of both Lee High and Newport News, which are tied for second.

So beating Martinsville was special for Hatcher, but it might have been even bigger for his mom, Vilma. She hated the Bulldogs.

"At least she lived long enough to see us whip them," said Hatcher.

In 2002, though, the tables were turned, with Martinsville getting the win. After Jarrett Hatcher finished with the media, he returned to the locker room. He saw Crawford still sitting there in his uniform, crying. The game had ended an hour earlier.

"We are going to win one," Crawford told his assistant coach. "We are going to win one. We are going to win one for Coach."

Eventually, he would get that title, and Jarrett Hatcher believes that 2002 loss was a motivating factor. Crawford isn't so sure, however.

"Let's not get it twisted; the loss sucked," said Crawford. "Motivating me the rest of my high school career? I was always motivated."

Lee High lost to Turner Ashby in the regional tournament during Crawford's junior year, but that summer Crawford made a promise to Jarrett Hatcher as the two were standing at the elbow on the Paul Hatcher Gym floor looking at the two state title photos on the wall.

"We are putting a picture on the wall," Crawford said. "We are going to win a state title. I promise you."

With Lee's win over Greensville in 2004, Crawford made good on that promise.

2
Last Loss

The 2003–04 season began with a loss. Well, not officially, but Lee High and Handley played a six-period scrimmage, and Lee lost by one. That didn't sit well with the coach.

His players had been talking about winning a state title since the offseason started. That was fine with the coach as long as they backed it up. He told them he'd be happy to go along for the ride if they wanted to win the title. Losing in the opening scrimmage wasn't the way to go about that, though.

"Are you just talking a good game or do you want to get to Richmond?" Hatcher asked his players.

If he had had his way, the players would have had practice right after the scrimmage. Instead, the jayvee team was scheduled to scrimmage, so the coach told his players to come back that afternoon for a practice. Jarrett Hatcher argued that it was counterproductive, but his dad had spoken. He wanted to see what the team was made of.

The team had three starters back from the previous season, and all but two players on the roster had varsity experience, allowing preseason practices to move along at a faster pace. The players already knew what to expect from Paul Hatcher.

Of course, Tyler Crawford was back after averaging 23.2 points and thirteen rebounds a game as a junior. Daryl Taylor, who would go down in Lee High basketball lore later in the season, and Jason Jordan were also returning as starters. The remaining two starters were Travis Stuart, who had split point guard duties the season before but would get the job to himself this season, and Eli Crawford, who was up from an undefeated jayvee team.

Jordan played football as a freshman but gave it up before his sophomore year. He wanted to concentrate on basketball. According to Jordan, something was missing the year before—"I felt like we didn't have enough heart," he said—but the first tryout of the '03–'04 season, with all the players on the court, had Jordan thinking that the team could be special.

It was the final year for Tyler Crawford. For all the success he'd had individually, including moving into fifth place on the school's all-time scoring list in just three seasons, the team had been to only one state tournament and had never played in a state championship game since his arrival. Crawford didn't want that—no state titles—to be his legacy.

"It was like the last chance," he said. "During my entire time there, I never wanted to make it about 'me, me, me,' but personally, inside, Tyler Crawford was going out on top."

Did his teammates feel like they had to win one for Crawford? Jordan said they felt pressure, but it was the same pressure every Lee basketball player feels. It wasn't just about one player.

"It was pressure playing for Paul Hatcher," said Jordan. "The way Paul Hatcher coaches, he would never single Tyler out. He never told Tyler take over this game and shoot. He coaches everyone the same, and it's a matter of doing what he asks. And he demands so much respect, it's hard not to do what he asks."

Hatcher never catered to his star players. Mark Newlen graduated from Lee in 1973. He was Lee's first star on a Hatcher-coached team. As a freshman, Newlen played jayvee ball most of the season but was called up to varsity for the last few postseason games. He remembers sitting the bench for a majority of those games but did play a little. He became a much bigger part of the varsity team as a sophomore, though, eventually finishing his high school career with 1,506 points. He was named to the Dixie Dozen as one of the twelve best players in the South.

Newlen was recruited by several big-name schools. His first college visit was to the University of Tennessee after his sophomore season, but several Atlantic Coast Conference schools were also interested. North Carolina State's Norm Sloan came to watch Newlen play. So did North Carolina's Dean Smith. The Tar Heels were Newlen's first choice, but he also liked Wake Forest, William & Mary, Virginia Tech, Davidson and Virginia.

Newlen said Smith was up front with him about recruiting, telling him that Carolina wanted two guards for his class and Newlen was fourth in line.

So if anything fell through with two of the top three, Newlen would get an offer. That didn't happen, and Newlen ended up in Charlottesville instead of Chapel Hill, signing with the University of Virginia.

One of Hatcher's rules about which he was adamant was punctuality. School ended at 3:08 p.m. when Newlen was a student at Lee High. Hatcher expected the players to be on the floor and dressed for practice by 3:30 p.m. The catch was that the players practiced at the junior high school, about two miles away.

Hatcher remembers one practice when Newlen was late. Newlen explained to his coach that he had car trouble, which Hatcher believed. It didn't matter. If you're late, you're late, and the excuse made no difference. It didn't make a difference that Newlen was a star on the team, one drawing lots of attention from major college programs. He was late, and he had to run after practice. Hatcher remembers that, later, Newlen thanked him for not showing any favoritism.

The players on the 2003–04 team bought into Hatcher's philosophy of treating everyone the same. All for one and one for all. The motto of the team was "Us 11." It simply meant that the work to win a state championship happened not when the gym was full of fans but when the team was working together, practicing in the gym. There were eleven players on the varsity roster that year—"Us 11," a phrase that Tyler Crawford wrote on his arm before every practice that season.

Before the regular season began, Lee played a benefit game in Richmond. The game matched the two winningest coaches in the state, Paul Hatcher and Hopewell High School's Bill Littlepage. Interestingly enough, both coaches are graduates of Bridgewater College. Entering the game, Hatcher had 710 victories, and Littlepage stood at 697. Once all was said and done and the two retired, Littlepage in 2007 and Hatcher in 2011, they still held the top two spots in the Virginia High School League record book: Hatcher at 897 and Littlepage at 755.

Lee was a Group AA school, and Hopewell was one level up, at Group AAA. Hatcher and Littlepage had never coached against each other. That changed on November 25, 2003, at Varina High School, when the two played in a game that didn't count in the regular season standings. Varina's coach, Stu Richardson, came up with the idea.

"Those two guys are as old as dirt," Richardson was quoted as saying in the *News Leader*. "We had to get them together on the court at least once."

Hatcher used the game, which Lee won 70–50, to teach a lesson. If there was one issue Tyler Crawford struggled with over his career, it was foul

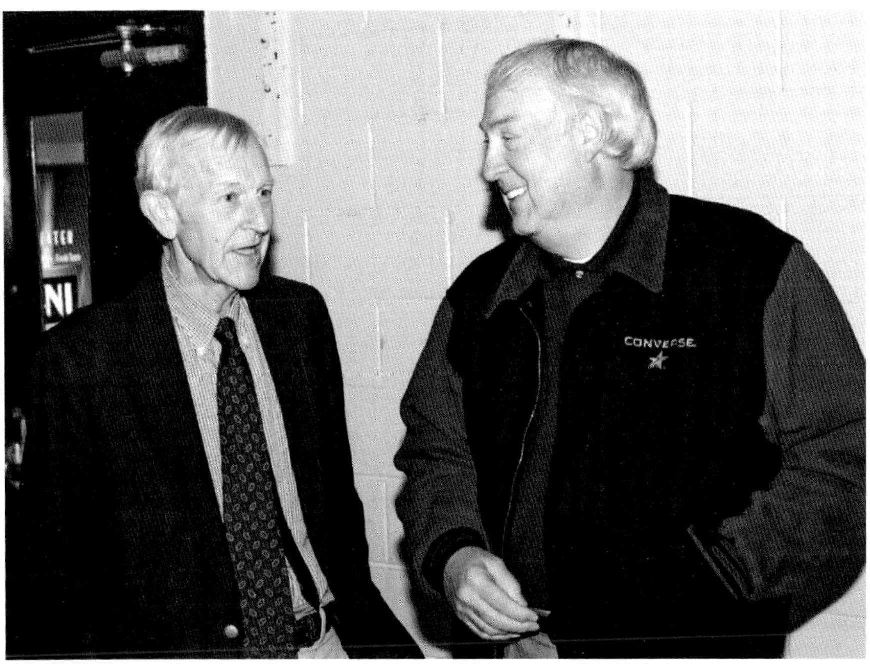

Lee's Paul Hatcher and Hopewell's Bill Littlepage, the two winningest coaches in VHSL boys' basketball history, coached against each other for the only time in a 2004 benefit game. *Mark Miller/the* News Leader.

trouble. Since he was young, Crawford had always been bigger than those he played against. He would just get a rebound and take off for the other end.

"If there was one guy in front of him or two guys in front of him or three guys in front of him, it didn't matter," said Hatcher. "He's going to wipe you out. We had a really hard time trying to get him into the pump fakes and the hesitations and all those kinds of things."

Hatcher had always taken his players out of the game once they got two fouls early. He'd remind them not to get another and then let them back on the floor.

"A lot of coaches will take them out after two fouls and leave them out the whole half," said Hatcher. "I've got a good player, and he might play for three days and never get another foul. Get him in the game but remind him—take him out for a minute or two and say, 'Hey, this is the situation.'"

Against Hopewell, Crawford got in early foul trouble with three fouls in the first quarter. Instead of taking his star player out, however, Hatcher just left Crawford on the floor. Hatcher thought it would be a good lesson for Crawford to learn to play with fouls and to realize he didn't always have to go 100 percent. That lesson was not learned that particular day. Crawford fouled out in the second quarter.

The Hopewell coaches approached Hatcher at halftime and said they were okay if Crawford played the second half. The game didn't count, and people were there to see the future Georgetown player. Crawford was out on the floor again in the second half and finished with fourteen points and eleven rebounds in the win.

"I was ultra-aggressive, man," said Crawford of his foul troubles, which would come up again later in the season. "Even in workouts. That's just how I am."

Before the game, the Lee players had a chance to visit Virginia Commonwealth University's Siegel Center, which would be the site of the state semifinals and final in March. Mike Ellis was an assistant athletics director at VCU and agreed to show the Leemen around the building. Ellis had been a student manager at the University of North Carolina. There, he was a roommate of Kevin Madden, who is Lee High's all-time leading scorer and played for the Tar Heels for four seasons.

Hatcher emphasized to his team that the building they were touring was where they wanted to be in March.

"[Paul Hatcher] told us, 'This is where it all ends for us guys.'" said Eli Crawford. "Hopefully the next time we come down here, we're hoisting the trophy."

Before Lee could win a trophy, though, there was an entire season ahead of it.

After beating Hopewell in the benefit game, Lee High rolled over its first six regular season opponents, winning the games by an average of 41.7 points per game. The closest game was a 38-point win over Turner Ashby in the second game of the season, a game that was a measure of revenge for Lee. TA had ended Lee's season the year before in the regional tournament. To be fair, it wasn't the same Turner Ashby team as a year earlier, with most of the key players from that squad gone due to graduation. Still, it felt good for the Lee players to roll over their rival so easily.

Lee started the game by scoring the first twenty-one points and led 43–7 at halftime. Turner Ashby, though, outscored Lee by three in the third quarter. Paul Hatcher was having none of that. In between quarters, he told his players that they didn't have what it took to be state champions. He said the 1989–90 team, which went unbeaten in winning the state championship, would have led by at least fifty after three quarters. That team never took its foot off the gas.

"He pushed them with that kind of stuff all year long," said Jarrett Hatcher.

The motivation may have worked. In the next game, Lee beat Stuarts Draft by forty-two, including outscoring their opponent 24–8 in the third quarter after leading by twenty at halftime. And in the next win over Spotswood, Lee stretched an eighteen-point halftime lead to thirty-two by the end of the third quarter and forty-seven by the end of the game.

The sixth win was against Charlottesville in the opener of the Daily Progress/Dick's Sporting Goods Holiday Boys' Classic at Albemarle High School. Paul Hatcher never cared for three-day regular season tournaments or tournaments over the Christmas break. A lot of years, Hatcher would just scrimmage teams during that break in December.

But the coach did like giving his teams a chance to play in college arenas. Over the years, Lee High played at Virginia Tech's Cassell Coliseum, the University of Virginia's University Hall, the Roanoke Civic Center, the Salem Civic Center, Liberty University's Vines Center, James Madison University's Godwin Hall and Convocation Center, the Norfolk Scope, the Pit at Virginia Military Institute, Virginia Commonwealth University's Siegel Center and the MCI Center in Washington, D.C.

"We tried to go and do and give these kids good experiences," said Hatcher. "Let people see them play. We played in most all the arenas over the years."

In the mid-1970s, Lee and Turner Ashby played a game at Bridgewater College over Christmas break. Until the last few years of Hatcher's tenure at Lee, the rule was the team could take a charter bus to away games if it traveled more than fifty miles. So Hatcher would get out his map and make sure that every non-district away game he scheduled was more than fifty miles from Staunton. He liked riding charter buses. So did his players.

"I just felt like that was important," said Hatcher. "It's more than getting on a school bus and riding across the county."

One of the reasons he scheduled the games in the Christmas tournament in 2003 was because the championship and third-place games would be played at University Hall in Charlottesville. Winning the game against Charlottesville High School ensured that Lee would get a game at U-Hall, win or lose in the semifinals.

Unfortunately for Lee, it was lose.

Lee shot a season-low 41 percent from the field and committed twenty-seven turnovers in a 66–63 loss to Group AAA Culpeper. It didn't help that Tyler Crawford had hurt his ankle in the previous game and hobbled around most of the game against Culpeper. He finished six of seventeen from the

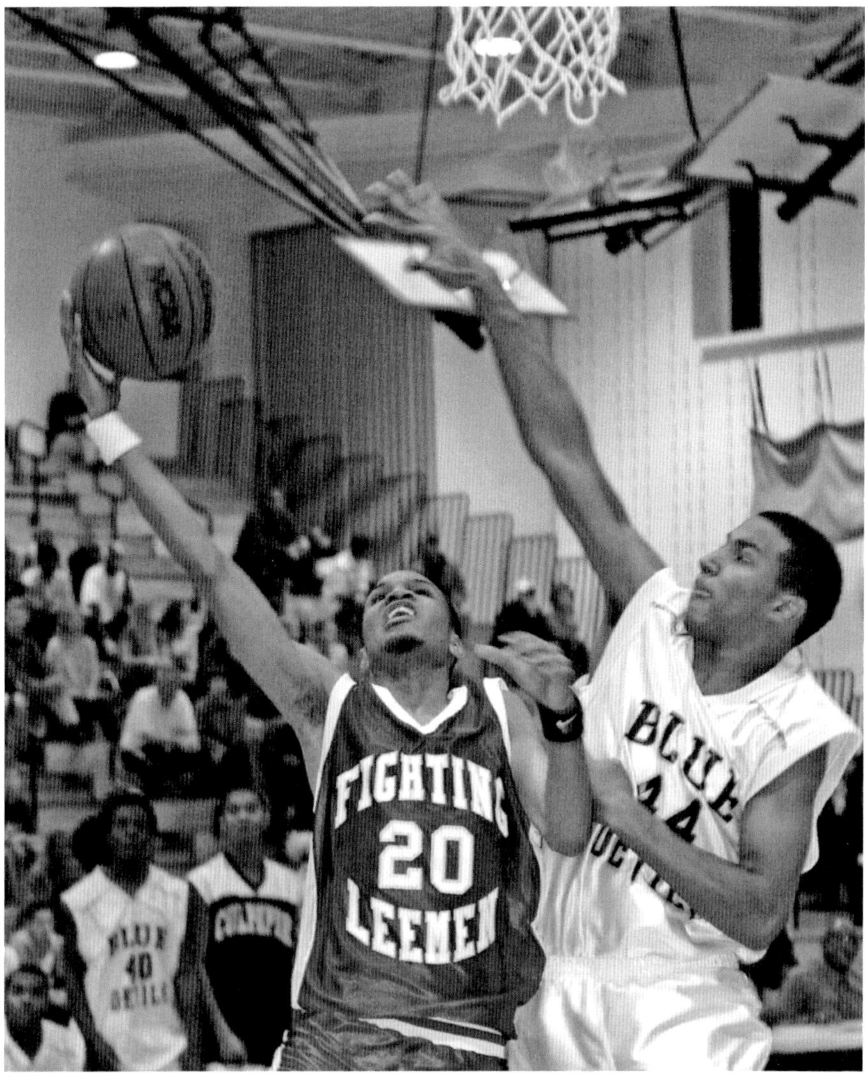

Robert E. Lee's Daryl Taylor attempts a shot against Culpeper's Frankie Bowles. Culpeper was the last team to beat Lee before the eighty-five-game winning streak. *Mark Miller/the* News Leader.

field with fourteen points in the loss, although he added thirteen rebounds and eight assists.

"That game was probably one of my most disappointing personally to myself," said Crawford. "I was caught up talking trash to people in the stands rather than being focused. I caused us to lose that game. I remember

I was doing pull-up threes, and I was doing dumb stuff in that game. It put us in a predicament and caused us to lose. It was all my fault."

The bus ride back to Staunton was very quiet. No one was happy. However, that loss would be the last one Lee High basketball would suffer for more than two years.

Like Father Like Son

For his first thirty-five years as head coach, Paul Hatcher never had an assistant coach. His freshman and jayvee coaches would sit on the bench with him during games and help him in practice when available.

Robert E. Lee High School has been in existence since 1926 but didn't move to its current location until 1983. That year, it moved into the building previously occupied by a junior high school. Even before the move, the Lee High varsity basketball team played and practiced at the junior high. Meanwhile, the jayvee team practiced at the high school. That meant, from 1968 until 1983, Hatcher didn't have anyone to help him during practice. He went it solo, something that didn't bother him. He couldn't imagine someone else giving his players instructions. That was his job.

"I don't see how these football guys can do it," said Hatcher. "They call a timeout, and they stand there outside the huddle and watch the offensive [coordinator] or the defensive [coordinator]…I'm thinking, I want to get in there, I'm in charge here."

Rigid. That's one of Jarrett Hatcher's favorite words to describe his dad. It's a pretty good word for the coach. Paul Hatcher knew how he wanted to run his program. He was very particular when it came to choosing a freshman or jayvee coach. As for a varsity assistant, he didn't want one unless he could find the perfect candidate. The right person or none at all was his stance. Luckily for him, that candidate ended up being someone he knew pretty well.

Jarrett Hatcher has never known life without Lee High basketball being part of it. When he was still too young to go to every game and was in bed before his dad returned home, Jarrett was up early the next morning, in the bathroom as his dad shaved, asking him the score.

When he was in fourth grade, Jarrett finally got to go with his dad to a game at home against Broadway. Later in his life, Broadway would be the first game in which Jarrett played, coached and, as head coach, won.

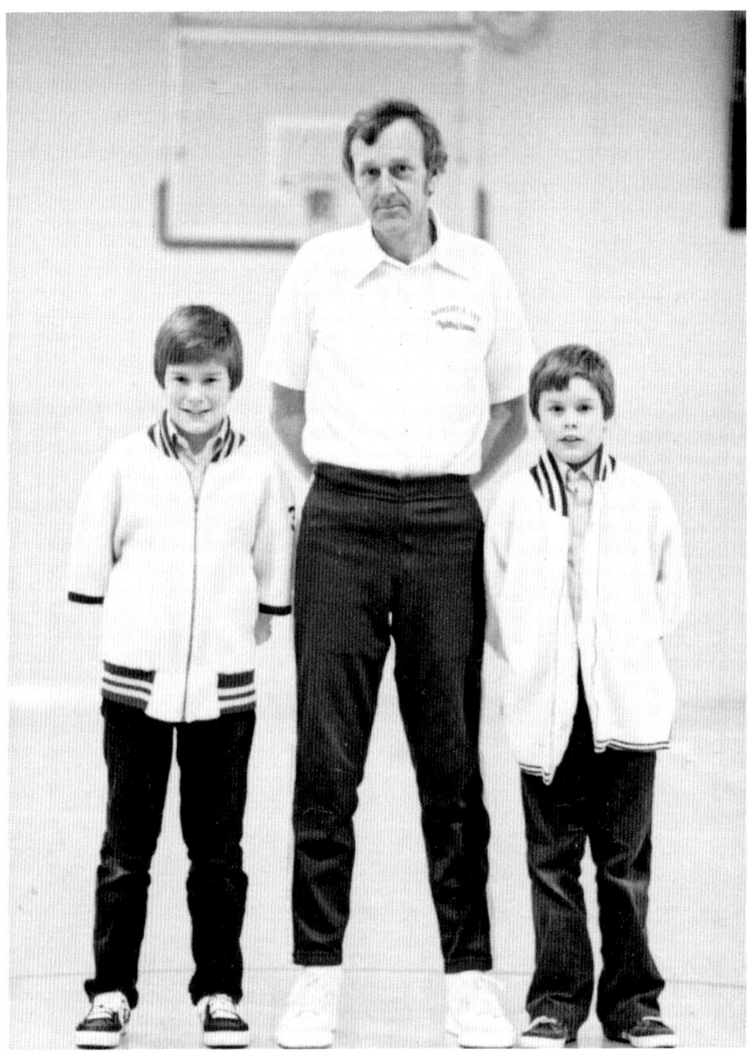

Jarrett (left) and Brandon Hatcher became managers for their dad's team while still in elementary school. *Paul Hatcher's collection.*

"I like Broadway," he said.

By the time he was in sixth grade and his younger brother, Brandon, was in second, the brothers went with their dad to all the games, serving as the team's managers.

"I would probably manage half the game and run around the bleachers the other half," said Brandon. "Couple of times I had to go to the emergency room because I split my head open under the bleachers."

Brandon was on the sidelines from second grade all the way through high school, until he left for college. He attended Chowan University in Murfreesboro, North Carolina, but even there he would occasionally scout games for his dad near the Carolina-Virginia border. When he graduated from college in 1998, he returned to Staunton and resumed helping his dad on the sidelines.

Brandon will tell you he was less the Xs and Os guy than his older brother and dad were and more the organizational coach. He never had the patience to worry about drawing up plays. His dad could see things that he missed.

"He was looking at a whole different aspect of it as a coach," said Brandon. "I am looking at it more like a fan."

Instead, Brandon compared his role with Lee High basketball to that of a college's director of basketball operations. He would make sure the equipment, including jerseys, was packed and the team managers were doing what they were supposed to do. When the team would travel overnight, Brandon had a sheet with each player's room number and would make certain everyone was where they needed to be that night. During games, he also kept stats, as well as giving any coaching input he felt was helpful.

"I would do the stuff that could keep their minds back on basketball," said Brandon.

Brandon's other job was security. With so many fans attending games involving Lee High, it was sometimes difficult to get out of the gym. Brandon would find his dad as soon as he shook hands with the opposing coach and get him out of the gym and to the bus if Lee was on the road or to his dad's office at Paul Hatcher Gym.

"I never went back on the floor at Lee High after a game," said Paul Hatcher. "I went to my office, and some of those rookie reporters couldn't find me. But I got out of the way, I got away from the players, away from everything. At away games, I looked for back doors to get out. Sometimes you had to go back through the gym, but if I could get to a backdoor to go, I would do it. You just open yourself up—I don't care if you win, lose, there was always some problem, somebody was upset. People complained about everything. Brandon got me out of there."

Brandon never considered following in his dad's footsteps as a coach, though. Jarrett will tell you he didn't either, but growing up, he appeared to be much more the typical coach's son than his younger brother. Eventually, Jarrett played for his dad and, while a student at Bridgewater College, helped him coach.

"I was hard on Jarrett," said Paul Hatcher. "I was hard on Jarrett as a player and that type of thing. I had to treat him like I treated the rest of them, see. That wouldn't be fair."

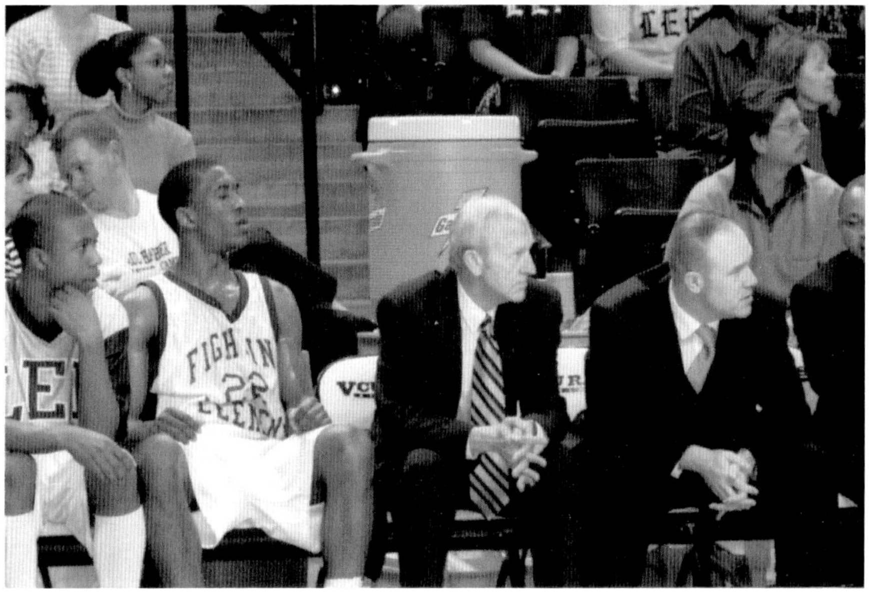

Jarrett Hatcher began coaching with his dad when he took over the Lee High jayvee team while a senior in college. By 2003, he was a varsity assistant. *Jason Jordan's collection.*

He even cut Jarrett from the team. It wasn't just fair but it also gave the coach ammunition if a parent ever complained to him.

Hatcher said, "If anybody said, 'You cut my son,' I'd say, 'Well, hell, I cut mine, too.'"

Jarrett became the jayvee coach for the 1992–93 season, his senior year at Bridgewater. Paul Hatcher knew his son understood the system and could be counted on to get the players ready for the varsity level. That didn't mean he went easy on his new jayvee coach. If Jarrett thought his dad was hard on him as a player, that was nothing.

"He was really, really, really hard on me as a coach, making sure I did things right, making sure I knew what I was doing," said Jarrett. "That's our relationship…I think it paid off down the road."

There was a time when Jarrett Hatcher wasn't sure coaching was in his future. As a freshman at Bridgewater in 1989, Jarrett wondered what life would be like without basketball. He never really considered coaching, and playing in college wasn't an option. At the same time, he couldn't completely give up the game, not yet, so he joined the Bridgewater team as a manager. In the back of his mind, however, he thought his future might include law school and perhaps a career as a sports agent.

There was never one lightning-bolt moment when Jarrett Hatcher went from not wanting to coach to wanting to coach. There was the game Bridgewater, a Division III school, played at Division I Virginia Military Institute. It may not have been a major D-1 school, but the atmosphere was enough to fire up Jarrett's coaching instincts. And that first year in charge of the jayvee team, every game he coached made it less likely that he would end up in law school. But there's no doubt that the 1989–90 high school season made a huge impact on his future job choice.

Jarrett Hatcher always dreamed of being the first person to hug his dad after a state title win. When Paul Hatcher won his first state championship in 1984, Jarrett was in middle school and a manager on the team. By the 1990 title, Paul Hatcher's second, Jarrett had graduated from Lee a year earlier. Unlike the 1984 players, who were Jarrett's idols, the players on the 1990 team were his friends and former teammates. He called them "a bunch of chumps" with whom he used to play pickup ball.

But those chumps were on the bench with his dad during a state championship run. Jarrett Hatcher wasn't.

Best Ever?

In March 2006, the *News Leader* asked its readers to name the best area basketball team ever. They overwhelmingly chose the 1990 Leemen, which finished 28-0 and won the state championship.

Hubert Grim III started watching Lee High basketball in the mid-1960s. His dad was the sports editor of the *News Leader*. Later, Grim became a sports writer then the sports editor for the same newspaper. No one without the name Hatcher saw as many Lee games in the forty-three years that Paul Hatcher coached as Grim.

"I will go to my grave…that was the best team that Paul Hatcher ever had," Grim said of the 1990 squad. "That team would walk on the court for warmups, and you could see the pee running down the legs of the other team because they knew they were going to get their ass kicked."

In the *News Leader*'s story about the 2006 readers' poll, Grim wrote that "the Leemen put their foot on the opposing teams' throats from the opening tip and wouldn't let up until the final horn. If they had a team down 30 points, they wanted to make it 40."

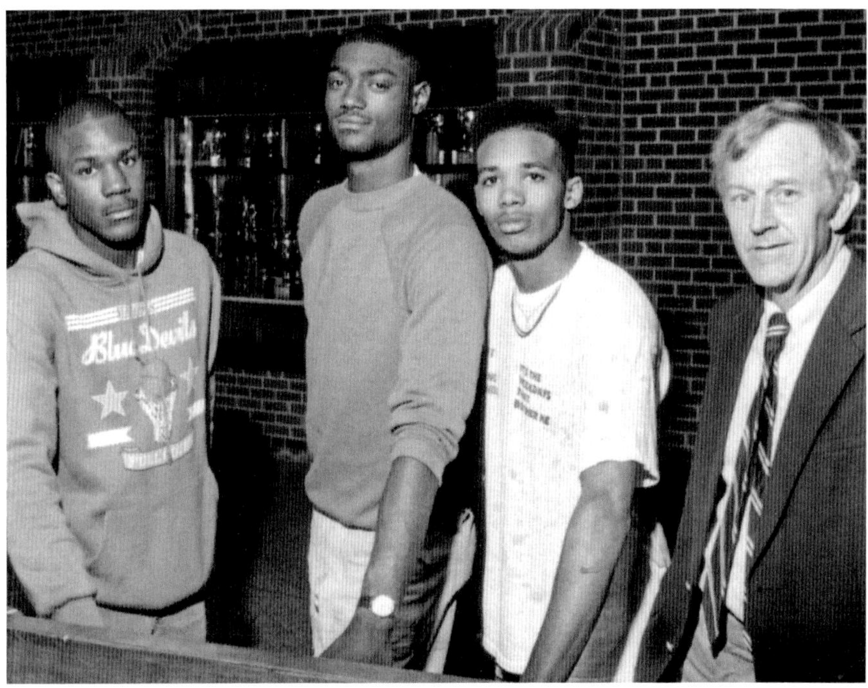

Joe Joe Stuart, Reggie Waddy and Keith Scott helped Paul Hatcher win his second state title. *Paul Hatcher's collection.*

The team trailed once in the fourth quarter all season, and that came in the regional final against Culpeper.

"I don't get into comparing teams," said Hatcher. "I'll tell you one thing, they didn't have any weaknesses."

The two years before, Lee High had failed to make it out of the Valley District tournament after reaching the state tournament five years in a row. The 1987–88 team finished 16-6, and the 1988–89 team was a pedestrian 14-7 and was one-and-done in the district tournament.

"We came in that year really hungry," Adam Huffman told the *News Leader* in a 2006 story about the 1990 state championship team. "I felt we were failures, and we wanted to prove ourselves. By losing the way we did the prior two years, there were no expectations for us."

Huffman was part of the starting five that year, along with Marcus Reed, Keith Scott, point guard Joe Joe Stuart and Reggie Waddy, who was named Group AA player of the year after that season.

"I never expected Reggie Waddy to turn into a player of the year in the state," said Grim. "I saw that kid as a sophomore. That kid couldn't walk and chew gum at the same time. He'd fall over his feet standing still."

But he improved. A lot. Grim said he improved some his junior year, and by his senior year, he was a different player. Paul Hatcher remembered a Christmas tournament in that state title year in 1989. It was just a scrimmage, with Lee playing Altavista for a half and Rustburg for a half. The coach preferred that.

"No winning or losing," he said. "It didn't ruin your holidays."

Against Rustburg, Lee led by forty points, and Waddy had seven or eight dunks. The Rustburg players were telling teammates not to guard Waddy. They wanted to see him dunk more.

"Anybody can get a running start and dunk," said Paul Hatcher. "Catch it and go up and dunk it. Then you're going to impress me. Kevin [Madden] could do that. Reggie [Waddy] could do it. We haven't had a lot that could do that. To me, that's dunking."

Defensively, that leaping ability came in handy also. A Rustburg player attempted a shot from the corner, and with the ball halfway to the basket, Waddy jumped up and blocked it. It was just a scrimmage. It was a quarter century ago. Hatcher is still furious that the official called goaltending on his player. At the time, he was so upset that he picked up the basketball and, for a few moments, refused to give it back to the official. Eventually, he handed it back.

All five Lee starters on the 1989–90 state title team went on to play in college. Stuart went to Anderson Junior College before transferring to Elon, while Reed and Scott both went to Trinity Texas Junior College. Reed then moved on to Virginia Commonwealth. Waddy played at Allegany Community College before signing with James Madison University. And Huffman started at Presbyterian before eventually playing for Longwood.

Scott led the team in scoring, with seventeen points a game, but all five players averaged double-digit points that season. If any of the five had been the central figure on a team, they could have probably averaged twenty-five points a game. But Paul Hatcher didn't need one star. He needed a balanced team, and that's what the players gave him.

"It was just a perfect fit," said Hatcher. "We had it all. They all could score. Joe Joe didn't look to score that much."

In fact, Stuart was probably better known for his defense. He was so good that the *News Leader* named its defensive-player-of-the-year award after him, although the paper has forgotten about it over the years. The team was so good defensively that opposing teams struggled all year to get the ball over halfcourt.

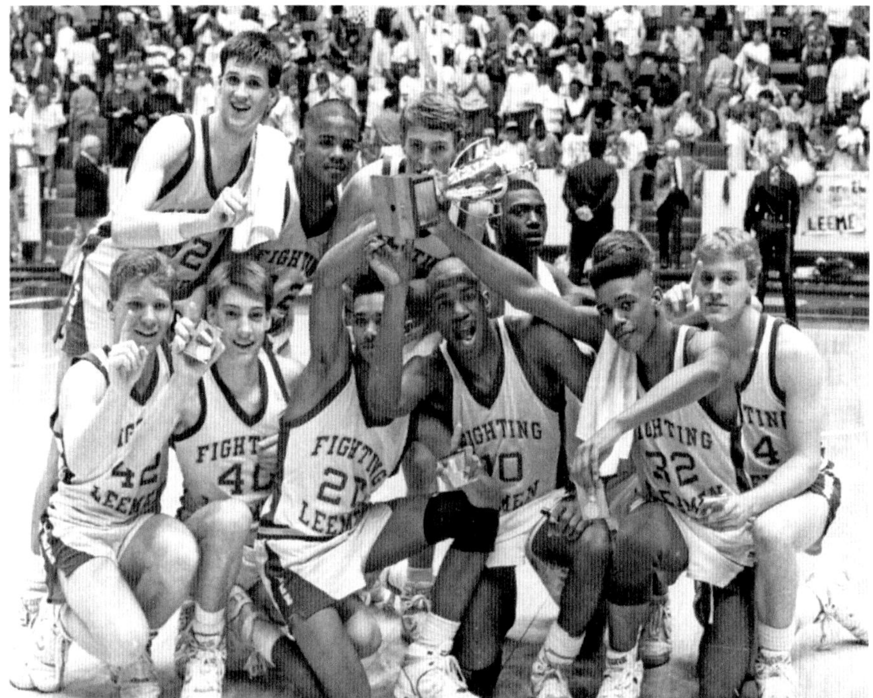

Lee High's 1989–90 team celebrated an undefeated state championship. *Paul Hatcher's collection.*

"He's just a coach's dream," Hatcher said of Stuart. "Just the perfect point guard."

Lee wasn't challenged in the state tournament, beating Laurel Park 69–47 in the semifinals before winning the title with a 70–53 win over Matoaca. The win marked the second state title for his dad, and Jarrett Hatcher hadn't been the first person to hug his dad after either one. Within three years, however, Jarrett would be the jayvee coach and the de facto varsity assistant. That position would allow him to be on the bench right next to his dad, a spot he occupied for the rest of Paul Hatcher's career and one where he could easily hug his dad if the moment called for it.

3
And So It Begins

A sign hung above the locker room door in Paul Hatcher Gymnasium. It read, "102 miles from our front door to the Siegel Center front door."

That was the plan. Finish the season at the Siegel Center, the basketball arena for Virginia Commonwealth University. It was the first year that the Virginia High School League would hold its tournament in the 7,500-seat building. The official name of the basketball arena at the time was the ALLTEL Pavilion at the Stuart C. Siegel Center, but most people shortened the name to Siegel Center. The arena, which opened its doors in May 1999, is located on Broad Street, the main east–west thoroughfare in Richmond.

It wasn't the first time that Virginia's capital city had played host to the state's high school championships—as recently as 1989, the boys' and girls' championships in Group AAA, the classification for the largest schools by enrollment in the state, were played at the University of Richmond's Robins Center—but this would mark the first time that both the boys' and girls' tournaments for all three classifications would be held at the same venue.

Prior to the 2003–04 season, girls' basketball in Virginia, with the exception of Group AAA, was played in the fall. A lawsuit claiming gender discrimination was filed by eleven female student athletes in Suffolk, Virginia, against the VHSL. The students thought it was unfair that certain girls' sports—including basketball, volleyball and tennis—were scheduled during different seasons based on school size. The U.S. District Court in Charlottesville, Virginia, agreed and decided in favor of the plaintiffs in July 2000. The court found the VHSL in violation of the U.S. Constitution's

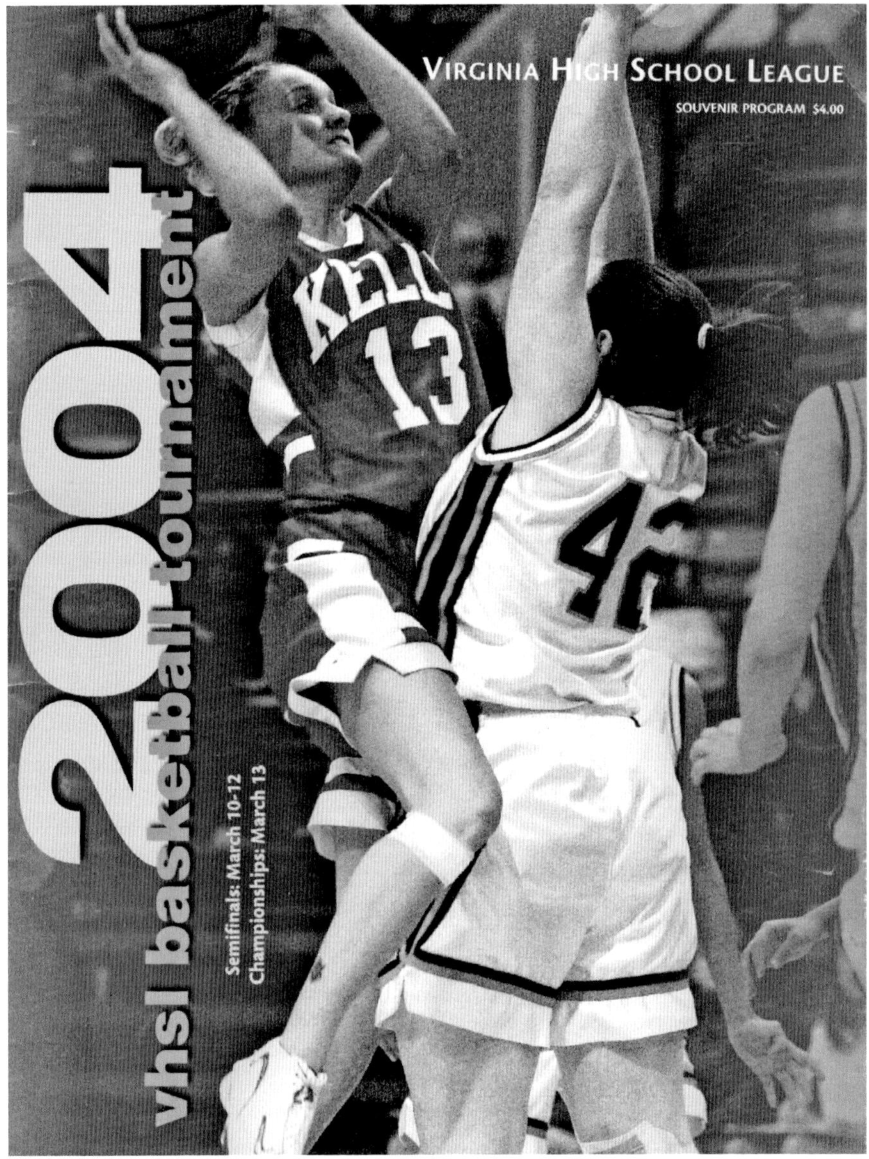

The 2004 VHSL state basketball tournament was the first to feature all the boys' and girls' classifications in the same season. *Jason Jordan's collection.*

equal protection clause and Title IX, a federal law prohibiting discrimination based on sex by federally funded education programs or activities.

Instead of appealing the ruling, which the VHSL did consider, the high school governing body decided to align sports equally across all classifications.

Starting in 2003–04, girls' basketball was a winter sport for all high schools in Virginia. The VHSL decided to hold the state semifinals and finals of both boys' and girls' basketball in all three classifications in one location, eventually choosing the Siegel Center. The first game was scheduled for Wednesday, March 10, at 3:00 p.m., and the last game would tip around 9:00 p.m. on Saturday, March 13. That final game would cap a day being billed as Super Six Saturday, when state champions would be crowned for both boys and girls in all three classifications. The final game would be for the Group AA boys title, and Lee High was planning on playing in that game.

That was down the road, though. After watching his team lose to Culpeper in the holiday tournament, Paul Hatcher was more concerned about getting a win the next time out than he was about playing for a state championship.

As Hatcher had hoped when scheduling the games in the holiday tournament, Lee High did get a chance to play at the University of Virginia's University Hall, even if it was the third-place game instead of the championship. Lee faced Albemarle on Tuesday afternoon, the day before New Year's Eve.

As Andrew Joyner of the *Daily Progress* wrote, "This might have been the case of facing the wrong team at the wrong time for the Albemarle boys' basketball squad." Lee High jumped out to a fifteen-point halftime lead, then hit the Patriots with a 13–3 run to start the third quarter. Albemarle had no chance, eventually losing 86–55. Tyler Crawford, still battling a sprained ankle from the tournament's opening game and a swollen eye resulting from a poke by an opponent's finger in the semifinals, led the way with twenty-seven points. One wonders what he would have done if he had been perfectly healthy that day.

Paul Hatcher liked the idea of coming back to play the next day after losing. It helped get rid of the taste of defeat a little quicker, although as the coach would tell you, that taste is never completely gone.

"Once you win again…the loss never goes away, but still you're in a better mood to move on," he said. Little did he know at the time, but he wouldn't have to worry about getting over another loss for a long time.

Lee High began the new year with a game that would become an annual tradition in Staunton: playing an Australian club team. A tour group from Australia was in the United States, playing games in California before coming east to play in Washington, D.C.; North Carolina; South Carolina; and Virginia. The group contacted Lee's athletic director about arranging a game.

"We agreed," said Jarrett Hatcher. "We had no idea what we were getting into."

Here's one thing you find out quickly about playing a team from another continent: it's tough to scout them. Hatcher hated when he or his staff couldn't see a team in person before playing them. In 1994, Hatcher wanted to scout Louisa but was told the game was postponed. He then found out the game was actually being played and had to scramble to find someone to scout the game, but it wasn't someone on his staff. The scout reported back to Hatcher that Robert Shelton, Louisa's star player, who ended up playing at Ohio State, couldn't go left.

Shelton scored twenty-six points in Louisa's 66–61 win.

"He went left every damn time," said Hatcher, who decided after that game that he or his staff would scout future opponents if at all possible.

Scouting the Australian team proved to be difficult, though, considering they weren't playing in Virginia before arriving in Staunton. So Jarrett Hatcher tried the next best thing: he contacted the Myrtle Beach newspaper to see if it had covered the team when it played in South Carolina. He didn't find out much and was worried his lack of information would doom Lee High.

Turned out, he didn't have to worry. Future Australian teams would be better competition, but this one got crushed by Lee, 89–27. The Australians thought since Lee High was a small school, they probably wouldn't be very good. The team's coach hadn't seen any of his nine players before boarding the airplane, and after flying for a day and a half and driving nine more hours to Charlotte, North Carolina, the team got in a thirty-minute practice before its first game. After two more games, the team finally arrived in Staunton to play Lee High.

"These kids have never seen basketball played at the level Lee played back home," the Australian coach, Scott Balsar, told the *News Leader*.

While the outcome of the game was never in doubt after Lee jumped out to a 13–2 lead, the one historical note that was made came in the second quarter, when Tyler Crawford became the first player in Lee High history to record one thousand rebounds in a high school career.

The other bit of history being made that year was on Lee's coaching staff. For the first time in Paul Hatcher's career, he had an official varsity assistant: Jarrett Hatcher. After eleven years as the jayvee coach—and putting together a forty-game win streak in his final two seasons—Jarrett Hatcher moved up in the program to focus solely on helping his dad with the varsity team.

"I thought it would be good," said Paul Hatcher. "He'd coached those kids. He's rah-rah, and I don't have time for all that nonsense. But that's the way

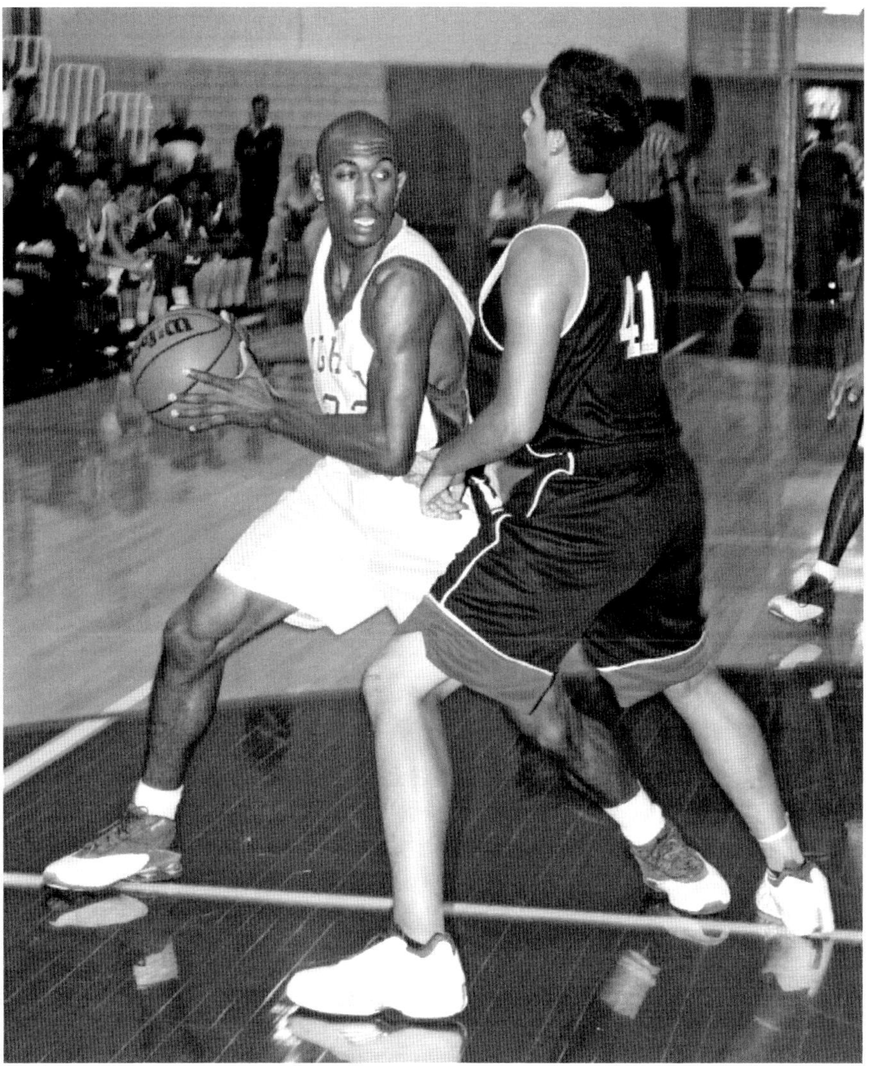

Tyler Crawford became the first player in Lee High history to record one thousand rebounds in a career, reaching the milestone against a touring Australian team during the 2003–04 season. *Vincent Lerz/the* News Leader.

things are today, so I said, 'I'm going to move you up here with me, and you can work with them and you can hoot and holler and carry on with them."

That suited Jarrett Hatcher just fine. He knew how talented some of the players moving up from jayvee to varsity were and also figured he had accomplished pretty much all he could with the jayvee program. He agreed to join his dad on the varsity team.

The season had gotten off to a pretty good start with an 8-1 record in early January, but a big test loomed four days after the win over the Australian team against the team that had provided some big tests for Lee in the past: Harrisonburg.

BATTLING RALPH

Robert E. Lee lost to just one team during the 1977–78 season. Unfortunately for the Leemen, they lost to that team three times and couldn't get out of the regional tournament. Lee High and Harrisonburg played five times that season. Harrisonburg won three of the games, Lee's only losses that season. Lee won two of the games, Harrisonburg's only losses that season.

Ralph Sampson, who grew seven inches between his freshman and senior seasons at Harrisonburg and stood seven-foot-three by the time he graduated, would eventually become the most sought-after college recruit in the country. The 1977–78 season was Sampson's junior year in high school, and he was very much on the national radar.

Lee countered with Mike Madden, who gave up almost a foot to Ralph Sampson but was willing to battle the big man inside. Despite standing just six-foot-four, Madden weighed in at 250 pounds and earned the nickname Big Mike. Paul Hatcher knew he had something special when Madden scored forty points against Turner Ashby as a freshman.

"He was such a good shooter and could come away from the basket," Paul Hatcher said of Mike Madden. "That's what gave Ralph problems."

The games between Lee and Harrisonburg in the late 1970s are still described as "epic" by those who saw them. Wherever they played, the gyms were packed. At Lee's gym, the line would often stretch down the sidewalk and past the school before the jayvee game started.

Mike Madden remembers sneaking his younger brother, Kevin Madden—who would eventually become the biggest star in Lee High basketball history—into the games through the locker room. An administrator caught him once and said Kevin would have to enter like all other fans, but Mike said he wouldn't play if Kevin was forced to stand in line. There was no further discussion of making his younger brother leave. Mike Madden was too important to risk him sitting out a game.

"[Lee] was the rival, for sure," Ralph Sampson said in early 2016 while waiting to watch Harrisonburg and Lee renew the rivalry at Paul Hatcher

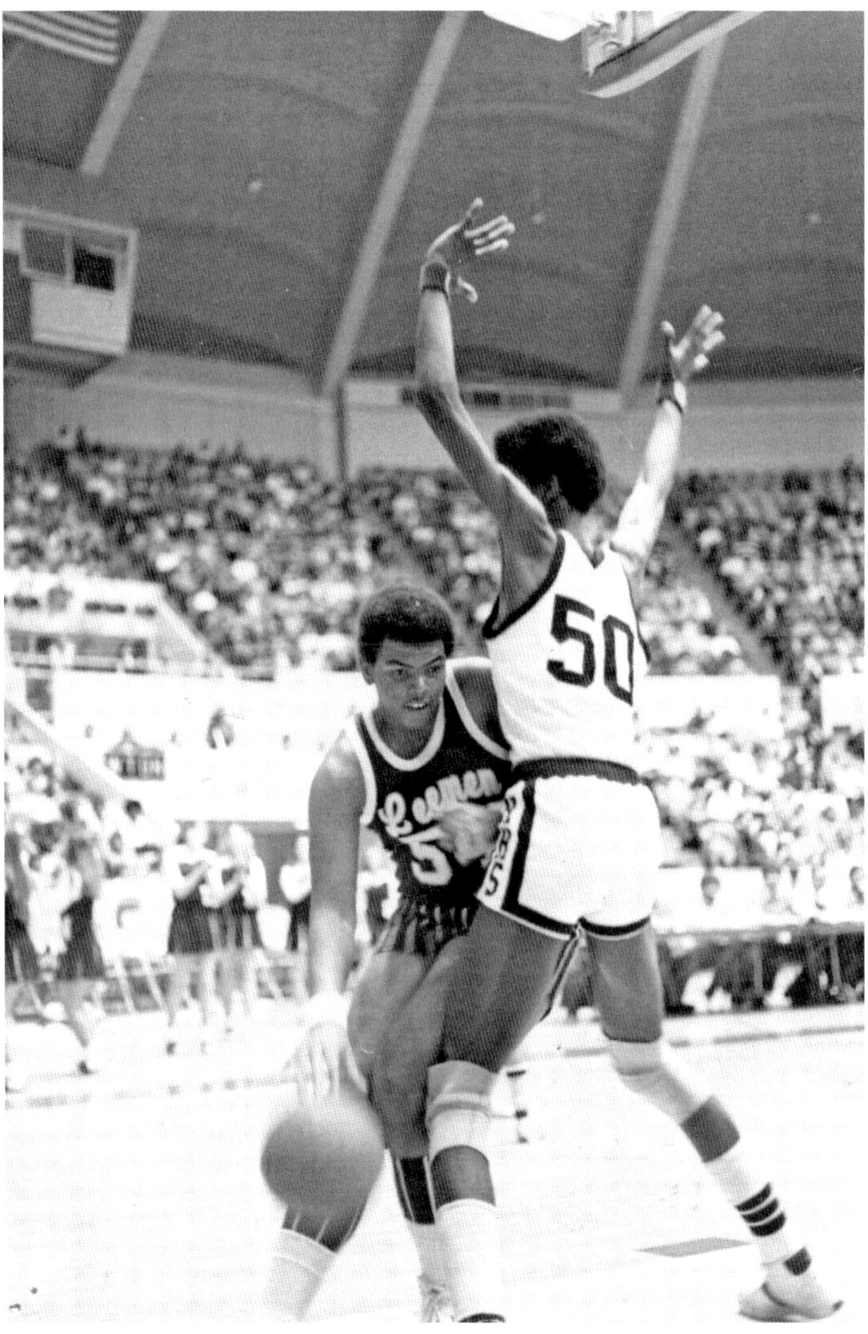

Despite being almost a foot shorter, Lee's Mike Madden held his own in some classic battles against Harrisonburg's Ralph Sampson in the late 1970s. *Paul Hatcher's collection.*

Gym. "The Valley District was pretty tough across the board, but obviously Harrisonburg and Lee had the best two teams. To look back thirty-some years later, it's still a special memory to come back to the same gym and say, "OK, we played here and had a packed house.'"

Sampson said the mentality of the players when he played at Harrisonburg was different than it is today. It started with the coaches. He said his own coach, Harrisonburg's Roger Bergey, and Lee's Paul Hatcher taught the game the right way.

"It was very special to watch and very special to look back on," said Sampson. "I commend Hatcher and Bergey for being innovators, and they stood the test of time. Both of them got great wins and halls of fame and all that kind of stuff as well. You look back at coaches like that and there's none like that these days."

Bergey coached for thirty years at Harrisonburg, starting in 1972, and won 435 games and two state championships, both with Ralph Sampson. He was inducted into the Virginia High School Hall of Fame in 2008.

Madden agreed with his former rival that the game has changed from the time he played.

"Fundamentals are the biggest thing that has changed," said the former Lee star. "A lot of guys want to go out there and shoot three-point shots or dunk, which is fine for the game, but what about the in-between game? We talk about guys [in the 1970s] scoring 1,800, 1,900 points with the two-point shot. …It's not what it used to be."

Madden said the Lee players knew, when they played against Harrisonburg, that they had to hit a high percentage of shots because there weren't going to be too many offensive rebounds with Sampson under the basket.

The two teams split their regular season games in the 1977–78 season, both winning at home. Since neither had lost another game that season, they were tied for first and had to play a third game to determine the regular season champion. Paul Hatcher came up with the idea that Lee and Harrisonburg play that special playoff game at the University of Virginia's University Hall. He knew UVA wouldn't protest because it wanted Sampson to sign with them. He was right. University Hall was almost full for the game, which Harrisonburg won 60–49.

"We probably had ten thousand people watching," said Sampson. "It was unheard of back in those days, still unheard of today as far as high school players playing in front of ten thousand."

The following Saturday night, the teams played for the Valley District Tournament championship at James Madison University's Godwin Hall. Lee won by eighteen.

"We played zone and kind of packed everything in on Ralph," said Hatcher. "We pressed them then went back to our zone."

The two met for a fifth time the next Saturday in the regional finals at Culpeper High School. The winner would advance to the state tournament, while the loser's season would be over. Lee had a shot to win it but missed, and the game went to overtime. Harrisonburg then hit a shot just before the buzzer in the extra period to give the Blue Streaks the win.

Lee's season came to a crushing end with a 24–3 record. It may have been one of Hatcher's better teams, but Harrisonburg was one game better. Harrisonburg went on to win the Group AA state championship, beating Blacksburg by twenty in the semifinals and Bruton in the finals by thirteen. The Streaks were 25-2 that year.

"It was tough," said Mike Madden. "We knew that whichever one of us won the regional championship had a chance to win the state, which it played out. They beat us on a last-second shot in overtime, and they went through the state with no problem. [If it was] like now, you have two teams going [to the state tournament] from the same region, we might have met again for the [state] championship."

Harrisonburg won the state title again the next year, Sampson's final year there. Lee wasn't taking two out of five games from the Blue Streaks that season. Sampson averaged thirty points, nineteen rebounds and seven blocks as a high school senior.

"Nobody beat them his senior year," said Hatcher. "He was in a class by himself."

It may not have mattered, as dominant as Sampson was his senior season, but in the first meeting between the two teams that year, early in the season, Mike Madden hurt his knee. He slipped on someone's jacket that was on the floor along the baseline, but Madden said he hurt his knee before falling. He missed three or four games, and according to Paul Hatcher, "never was the same."

When Madden went into the locker room to have someone look at his injured knee, he joined sophomore teammate Tony Randolph, who tried to block a Sampson dunk and flipped over the Harrisonburg star, landing hard on the floor. Lee didn't stand a chance two players down.

Four years later, Randolph would once again play against a Sampson-led team, but unlike the games between Lee and Harrisonburg, the one on December 23, 1982, made national headlines. Chaminade University, a small NAIA school in Honolulu, pulled off what may still be the biggest upset in college basketball history when it beat number-one-ranked Virginia 77–72.

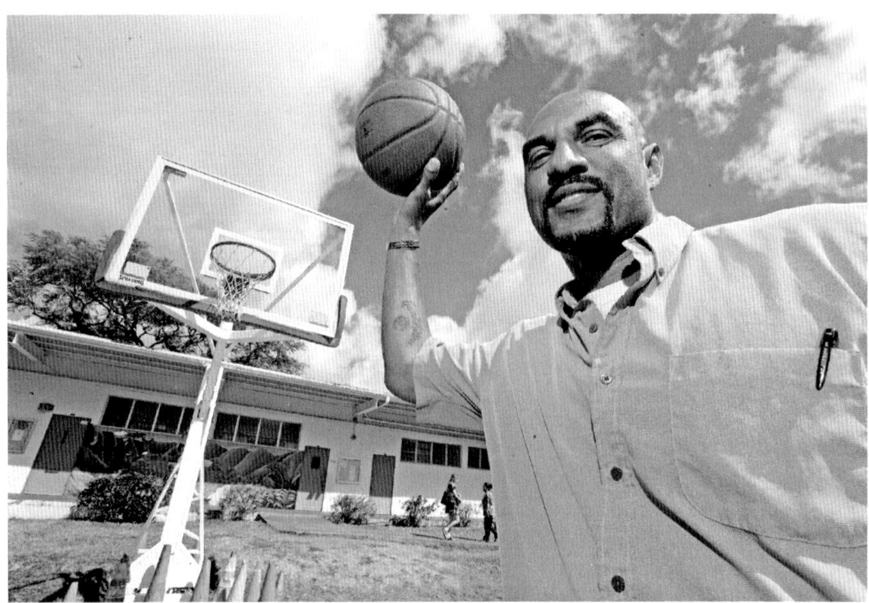

Former Lee High player Tony Randolph remained in Hawaii after college. He was a key figure in Chaminade's upset of the number-one-ranked University of Virginia in 1982. *Photo courtesy of the* Honolulu Star-Advertiser.

Randolph, by then a six-foot-seven center for Chaminade, scored nineteen points and grabbed five rebounds in the win, outplaying Sampson, who was a senior at Virginia that season and, at the time, a two-time college player of the year. Sampson finished with twelve points and seventeen rebounds.

After the game, Randolph told reporters about his connection to Sampson, having played high school and pickup basketball against each other.

Paul Hatcher had stayed up late to listen to the radio broadcast of the game. The Lee coach said, even listening to it, he got the sense that Virginia was going to lose. He could feel Chaminade had the momentum. When Chaminade finally pulled out the win, around 3:00 a.m. on Christmas Eve, Hatcher went to bed, and since his plan was to sleep late, he left a note with the final score on the refrigerator for his sons to see when they woke up.

But Hatcher's idea of sleeping late didn't work out as planned. By seven o'clock that morning, Hatcher's telephone started ringing. He got calls from *Sports Illustrated*, the *Washington Post*, the *New York Times* and the *Chicago Tribune*, among others. He was the high school coach of the player who had been the key reason his college team had shocked the world. Hatcher was in demand.

One of the stories that Randolph had told reporters, prompting the telephone calls to his high school coach, was about Hatcher's practice techniques before games against Sampson. He used a broom, held high over his head, to simulate playing against the seven-footer.

"You can take the shot over there, and he's over here and he's going to block the shot," Hatcher explained of his strategy to attack Sampson. "You've got to get to him and then do something with it because the farther you get away from him, you're in trouble."

Not a lot of attention had been paid to the game before it tipped. Virginia had played a pair of games in Japan and had stopped over in Hawaii on the way back home. Chaminade had just lost to Wayland Baptist, and Virginia was the top-ranked team in the country. No one expected the tiny Hawaiian school to even challenge the Cavaliers. But the *Washington Post* lucked out, somewhat, because one of its reporters, Michael Wilbon, who would later become famous for being one of the co-hosts of ESPN's *Pardon the Interruption*, was in Honolulu covering the University of Maryland's football team, which was playing in the inaugural Aloha Bowl.

"He knows what it's like to be on the bottom and take his knocks," Hatcher was quoted as saying about Randolph in Wilbon's story. "It couldn't happen to a better person to get the recognition he's getting now."

Randolph was raised in Washington, D.C., but his mom died when he was eleven, and less than two years later, his father passed away, so the seventh-grade orphan moved to Staunton to live with his aunt. The adjustment of moving from D.C. to Staunton wasn't easy on Randolph.

"I had a hard time getting centered," Randolph said, remembering back on his days in high school. "I was living day to day, trying to find something to believe in again."

Hatcher said Randolph couldn't conform. His attitude kept him off the Lee varsity as a freshman. He played for Lee as a sophomore, getting his chance to face Sampson, but as a junior his attitude got the best of him again, and he ended up transferring to Augusta Military Academy in Fort Defiance.

Randolph told Wilbon that he acted as if the world owed him something after his parents passed away, but late in his junior year, he had an attitude adjustment.

"I realized it wasn't that way, and if I wanted something, I had to work for it," Randolph was quoted as saying by Wilbon in the *Washington Post*'s game story.

Hatcher remembered Randolph coming to him before his senior season and saying, "Coach, I'm going to do it your way." Randolph said he was interested in playing basketball in college and thought he had a better chance of being seen by a scout at Lee High.

That senior season, 1980–81, Randolph did it his coach's way and helped lead the Leemen to the first unbeaten regular season under Hatcher. Lee finished 18-0 in the regular season, then won the Valley District Tournament before finally losing in the second game of the regionals.

"Paul Hatcher was more of a very firm disciplinarian," said Randolph. "Now, looking back, I know that's what I needed."

Randolph graduated after that season; however, his troubles weren't over. He had decided to join the army, so he signed up at the recruiting office before changing his mind. He called Hatcher, begging his coach to get him out of the commitment.

"Well, I don't know much about the army," Hatcher told Randolph, "but it's my understanding that if you tell those people something, they expect you to do what you tell them you'll do."

Randolph wanted out because he had received a chance to go play college basketball at Panhandle State in Oklahoma. Hatcher talked to the army recruiter, explaining that Randolph had had a troubled childhood and now had a chance to go to college. The coach thought that might be a better situation for him than the army. Eventually, Randolph was allowed out of his commitment, although Hatcher is still not quite sure how because the MPs even got involved when Randolph bolted for Washington, D.C., instead of attending a meeting with the recruiter.

He remained at Panhandle State for a semester, averaging 8.4 points per game in nine of the team's fourteen games before the semester ended. He wasn't happy, though, and on the advice of his brother, who was in the U.S. Air Force and stationed in Honolulu, Randolph transferred to Chaminade.

After Chaminade's win over Virginia, Hatcher called the basketball offices at the small school and congratulated Randolph. Hatcher was happy that his former player finally seemed to be in a good place.

Even now, more than three decades after the upset, Randolph is still asked about it.

"It's like a story that doesn't have an ending," he said.

Randolph remains in touch with his former high school coach. The two talk now and again on the telephone.

"I've gotten to know him over the years," Randolph said. "He's a wonderful person who devoted his whole life to helping develop young men."

The Rivalry Continues

By the first month of 2004, Lee High and Harrisonburg were again battling for Valley District supremacy, although there was no seven-foot-three superstar and no players who would eventually play in one of the greatest upsets in college basketball history. Instead, both teams had one star; Lee's was, of course, Tyler Crawford, who was averaging 14.8 points a game. Justin German was Harrisonburg's top player that year, scoring 11.8 points and pulling down 10.5 rebounds per game. Both teams also had some very good players around their leaders. Lee was 8-1 overall, while Harrisonburg came into the game with a perfect 10-0 record.

"Harrisonburg, to us, was a big game because we knew a lot of those guys," said Jason Jordan, a junior on that Lee team. "To lose to them, it would have been a big deal. It would have been talked about to this day."

Lee's assistant coach was more direct.

"I hate Harrisonburg," said Jarrett Hatcher. "And always have. So that's the game I always want to win."

Harrisonburg had revenge on its mind after blowing a fourteen-point, fourth-quarter lead the previous year and losing by five at Paul Hatcher Gym. Lee winning at home shouldn't have surprised anyone. Since the 2000–01 season, Tyler Crawford's freshman year, Lee was 36-2 at home.

"I think it was the crowd," Harrisonburg's David Diggs told the *Daily News-Record* in a preview story of the team's first meeting in 2004. "They got a nice crowd. Tyler's mom gets the crowd cronking. That's hard to deal with."

In the first meeting between the two teams in the 2003–04 season, Lee didn't need a miracle rally to pull out the win—that would come later in the season. Lee beat Harrisonburg 70–53, and Tyler Crawford's cousin, Eli Crawford, showed some of the talent that would eventually make him a Lee High star, scoring a then career-high thirteen points in the victory, nine of them coming in the fourth quarter.

Three games later, the big news wasn't Lee's opponent but who was in the stands. Georgetown coach Craig Esherick got to see his recruit, Tyler Crawford, for the first time in a high school game. The *News Leader* made sure to have a photo of Esherick on the front page of the sports section and quotes from the Hoyas's coach in the story about the game, which Lee easily won, beating Spotswood 83–58.

Crawford scored twenty-five points and finished with ten rebounds in the win. Esherick talked to Hubert F. Grim III of the *News Leader* about the future Hoya, saying the biggest transition would be moving from playing

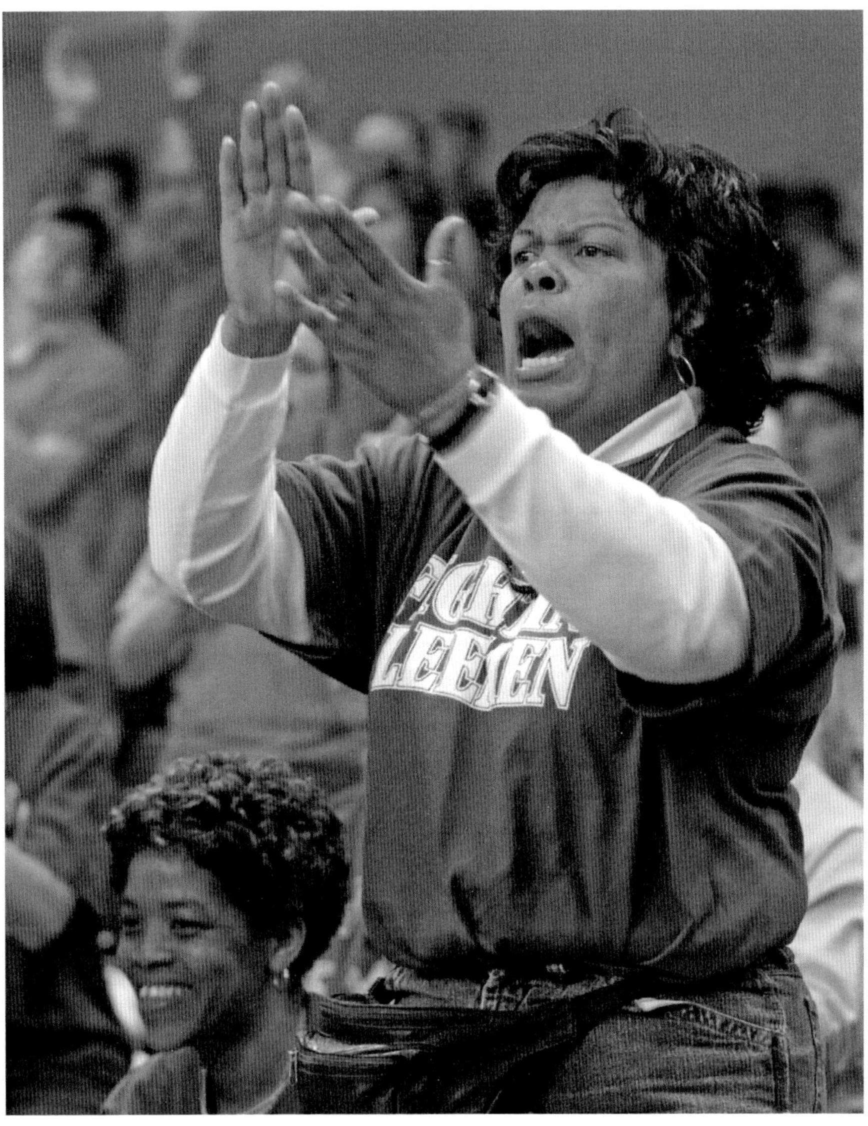

Tyler and Ryan Crawford's mom, Angela Crawford, was one of Lee's most vocal fans when her sons played. *Vincent Lerz/the* News Leader.

inside to on the perimeter. Esherick said he didn't see that being a problem, though, because of the high school program in which he played.

"Paul Hatcher is a coaching legend," Esherick was quoted in the paper as saying. "I heard of Coach Hatcher when I was in high school in Silver Springs [Maryland]. We finally have a player coming to Georgetown from Lee."

That, however, could wait. Crawford had more pressing matters at the moment, like trying to lead Lee High to a state championship. The Leemen were barely being challenged in the district, mowing down one opponent after another. When the first high school basketball rankings were released by the Associated Press in late January, no one was shocked that Lee was the number one team in Group AA. Some coaches don't like rankings, perhaps thinking it puts too much pressure on a team. It doesn't bother Paul Hatcher.

"If you are going to be ranked, it might as well be number one," the coach told the *News Leader*.

As Lee High entered the final Friday of January, it was 15-1 on the season, riding a nine-game winning streak since losing to Culpeper. Waynesboro wasn't going to be the team to end that streak or dethrone the top-ranked Leemen. On January 30, Lee beat its rivals 106–31, the largest margin of victory in Lee basketball history.

"I had all these visions, 'Oh, we're going to turn Waynesboro basketball around,'" said C. Jay DeWitt, who was in his first year of coaching the Little Giants. "I'm sitting over on the bench saying, 'What have I gotten myself into?'"

Jim Sacco was the sports editor of the *News Virginian*, Waynesboro's daily newspaper, at the time. His photographer had taken a picture of the scoreboard when the game ended. Sacco decided to run it on the front page of the sports section, in the upper right-hand corner of the page above the game story.

"My God, the next morning, you would have thought I murdered sixteen people in that town—the phone calls," Sacco said of the community's reaction to him running the photo. "It was just the phones [ringing] and people coming by."

Much like Harrisonburg and Lee High, although maybe just a little less intense, was the Waynesboro–Lee High rivalry. In 1991, the two had done what no other Valley District opponents had pulled off: playing each other for the state championship. Waynesboro won that game by twenty, ending Lee's pursuit of back-to-back state titles.

Over the years, the two schools, separated by less than thirteen miles, played many memorable games. The rivalry was an old one, going back to 1926, when Lee High played its first ever basketball game, a 16–11 win over Waynesboro. During Lee High's eighty-five-game winning streak, however, Waynesboro's basketball program was struggling. So while members of the community were upset at Sacco and his newspaper for running the photo of the scoreboard, the sports editor didn't think the players got too upset.

"Those Waynesboro teams at that time were too bad to even get angry," said Sacco. "It was just like, 'Oh great, we've got to play Lee.' Wasn't that everyone's attitude in the valley at the time, maybe other than Harrisonburg or TA, teams that could hang with them a little bit?"

The seventy-five-point win by Lee broke the previous record, a seventy-two-point win over Broadway in the 1991–92 season.

Paul Hatcher remembers that win over Broadway, mainly because the next day on a Harrisonburg radio station, WSVA, callers to the morning show were accusing Lee High and Hatcher of running up the score. Hatcher said he never tried to run up the score but always wanted his players, whether it was the starters or the backups, executing and trying to improve.

"Because there's a game tomorrow or the next day," he said.

Besides, even the Broadway coach at the time, Gary Leake, maintains to this day that Hatcher didn't run up the score. Broadway gave Lee too many opportunities to score, Leake said, and Lee took advantage. He remembers looking down at Lee's bench in the second half and seeing Hatcher with his head in his hands, not even looking at the basketball court.

"He was staring at the floor," said Leake. "And I believe he was feeling bad for me. If someone would have been trying to figure who was winning and who was losing, you would have decided that Paul was losing by his demeanor."

A lot of times before jayvee games between the two schools, Leake and Hatcher would grab a soda and find a place to talk. Leake said Hatcher was always helpful in teaching him various techniques, including Lee's defense, which Leake wanted to use. The two coaches are good friends, and Leake said he firmly believes Hatcher would never try to embarrass Broadway or any team.

"After the game, Paul said he was sorry for the lopsided score," Leake said. "I told him not to worry at all about it and to ignore our fans. He played everyone on his team, a lot. He may not even remember this, but Paul had his kids play zone in the fourth quarter, something R.E. Lee never did. So how was all of this running up the score? He can't tell his kids to not score. Those kids want to score like all the starters."

The same held true against Waynesboro in 2004. Hatcher used his entire bench, but just because the backup players were in the game wasn't reason for the Leemen to rest. He always preached that his teams play thirty-two minutes and play hard for thirty-two minutes, no matter who is in the game.

"We wouldn't accept it," said Hatcher. "[The starters] have gone in there and shutout the other team for three quarters, and you better not let them score. Don't come out of there 15-15 or something in the fourth quarter. You've wasted my time."

By the end of the first week of February, Lee High had wrapped up the Valley District regular season. Lee did its part in its last big test of the regular season, but it wasn't easy. Harrisonburg hadn't lost since the first meeting with Lee High, climbing to number four in the Group AA rankings. Lee was still in the top spot when the two met on a Friday night, February 6, at Harrisonburg's Claude E. Warren Fieldhouse.

By halftime, Tyler Crawford was in foul trouble, and Lee trailed 37–31. Paul Hatcher walked in the locker room and told his players that very soon the season would be over and they would take their uniforms off for the final time and the seniors' careers would be over. All of their dreams would end because they wouldn't do what they had been taught to do.

Travis Stuart, the team's point guard, said, "I'm taking my jersey off halfcourt at the Siegel Center."

That motivation, if indeed that is what it was meant to be, didn't work immediately. Crawford picked up his fourth foul with less than a minute left in the third quarter, and by the end of that quarter, Harrisonburg led by fifteen. The number one ranking was in serious jeopardy.

"I actually panicked that game," said Jason Jordan. "I don't know about anybody else. I won't say panicked as far as giving up, but I will say panicked as far as being nervous about the situation."

If he was nervous, it didn't show in his play. Without Tyler Crawford on the floor, Lee scored the first sixteen points of the fourth quarter, led by Jordan, who scored fourteen of his game-high twenty-three points in the final quarter. Lee hadn't needed Jordan to be the main scorer much that season with Tyler Crawford on the team. Instead, it needed him to do the little things that make a team a champion.

"Tyler got lots and lots of recognition, and deservedly so," said Paul Hatcher. "But Jason was doing a lot of those things behind the scenes that coaches preach and love when a kid does it."

Jordan was a great screener and rebounder and defender. He ran the floor exceptionally well. And he complemented Crawford. The two worked well together, but against Harrisonburg, Jordan had to do it without Crawford on the floor. He came through with flying colors, helping give Lee a 62–61 lead with 4:40 left in the game and, from there, pull away for a 76–67 win.

The win was the twelfth in a row since losing to Culpeper in December, and it was the only one of those twelve where the margin of victory was less than seventeen points. It also assured Lee of at least a tie for the regular season title, and the next night Spotswood upset Harrisonburg, who was perhaps suffering from the hangover of losing the lead to Lee. That loss gave

Lee the regular season title outright. It was the twenty-eighth regular season district title for Paul Hatcher in his thirty-six years of coaching.

Lee rolled through the rest of the regular season, finishing the season 21-1 before winning the Valley District Tournament. In the third game against Harrisonburg, in the tournament championship, Lee didn't need to rally in the fourth quarter but was leading only by two in the third quarter before a 22–9 run put Lee in command.

The win gave Paul Hatcher his eighteenth district tournament championship. That was great, but Hatcher had more important things on his mind. The regional tournament was the next step in trying to win Hatcher's third state championship. That's the title the veteran coach wanted.

4
A Photo on the Wall

Lee opened the Region II Tournament with a relatively easy win over Western Albemarle before facing Liberty-Bealeton, an overtime winner against Potomac Falls. Tyler Crawford scored the first nine points of the game, significant because it gave him exactly two thousand for his career.

"That wasn't planned," said Crawford. "That wasn't done on purpose. That just happened. Two or three of them were outlets from Eli; one might have been a steal."

Crawford became just the second player in Lee High basketball history to score at least two thousand points, joining Kevin Madden on the list. At the time, Lee was also just the fourth VHSL school to have two players with at least two thousand points.

The next Lee basket was on an assist from Crawford, and with an 11–0 lead, the Leemen coasted the rest of the way. Crawford finished with twenty-three points and thirteen rebounds, while Daryl Taylor added twenty points in the 69–39 regional semifinal win.

"It's a game I go back and watch all the time," said Paul Hatcher. "We just executed so well. We just destroyed that bunch. In fact, I gave it to Jarrett to show to some of his teams. This is how it's supposed to be played."

Lee assumed it would next be facing a very good Orange County team, which had knocked off Harrisonburg by twenty-four points in the quarterfinals. As Lee's players walked off the court at James Madison University's Convocation Center after the win over Liberty, several Orange County players started jawing at the Leemen, yelling, "We got next!"

"I had been working on Orange for weeks," said Jarrett Hatcher. "I had a buddy who was our secret scout. He was on that side of the mountain watching all those teams. He had seen Orange. I had seen Orange. Had not seen Loudoun Valley at all."

Well, Jarrett Hatcher got to see Loudoun Valley up close and personal the following night in the regional championship because they upset Orange County 62–54. The Loudoun Valley coach, Chad Dawson, told the *Washington Post* that his team was starting to like the whole underdog thing after they upset Fauquier and Orange to advance to the Region II championship game.

The string of upsets stopped, though, in the second half against Lee. Eli Crawford scored twenty-five points and helped lead Lee to a 71–49 win, a victory margin that was a bit shocking because Lee trailed by six at halftime. Paul Hatcher made a halftime adjustment that may have saved the game, moving Tyler Crawford to the wing and putting Eli Crawford on the baseline.

"[Eli] was versatile," said Hatcher. "He wasn't real tall, but he moved well enough, and he was strong enough that he could play inside. So you think, 'I don't believe they can guard him so let's put him down in there.'"

The move worked, as Loudoun Valley's players came out to guard Tyler Crawford, leaving his younger cousin alone under the basket. Eli Crawford scored the first bucket of the third quarter, sparking an 11–0 run. After that, Lee ran away with the regional title.

Lee opened state play at Spotswood High School on a Saturday night, March 6, 2004. The opponent in the Group AA quarterfinals was Spotsylvania, which entered the game 21-6. The play of the game came at the end of the first half, when Tyler Crawford got the ball on the left wing with ten seconds left and drove the baseline for a ferocious dunk over two Spotsylvania players. The basket gave Lee an eleven-point halftime lead.

According to the game story in the *Daily News-Record*, the Spotsylvania coach, Alan Dunn, thought the officials should have given Crawford a technical foul for the scream he let out after the dunk. Crawford admits that he screamed, saying he actually turned toward one of the players guarding him and screamed in his face.

But there's a reason. If you look at the photo of the dunk published in the *News Leader*, the Spotsylvania defender has his left hand squarely on Crawford's right bicep. No foul was called on the defender.

"When I dunked the ball, it was kind of like he wanted to go for a ride," Crawford said of the play almost twelve years after it happened. "I'm not a big screamer or yeller after dunks and stuff like that…it just came out. My

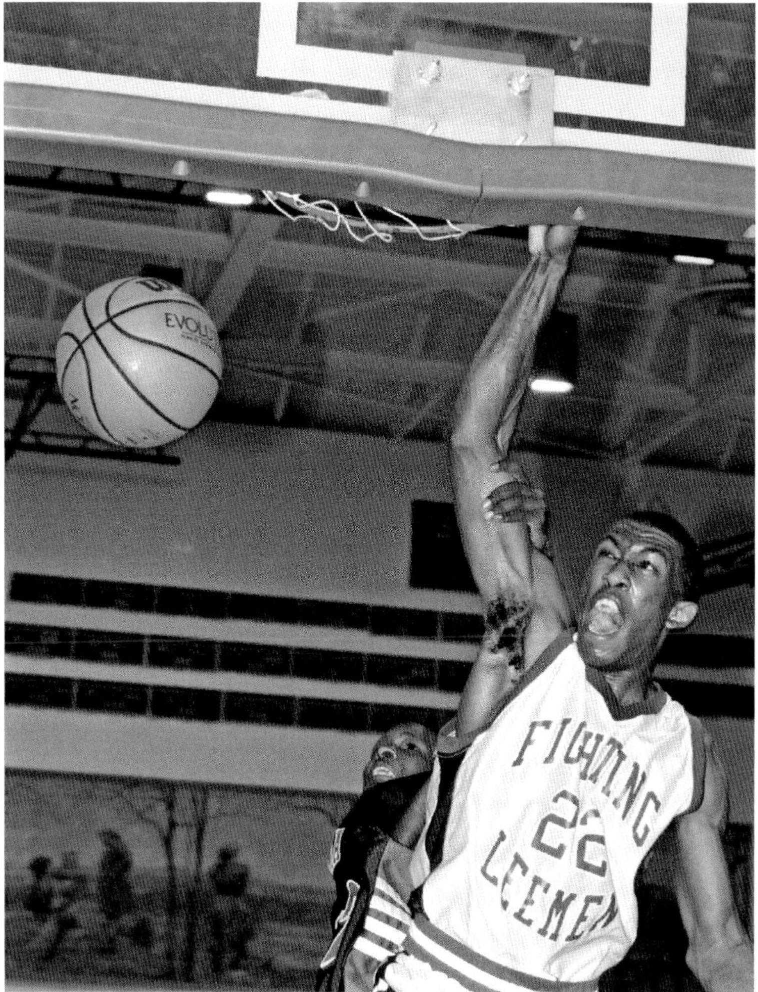

Tyler Crawford's dunk against Spotsylvania in the Group AA state quarterfinals almost caused Crawford to get a technical foul after he let out a scream following the play. *Vincent Lerz/the* News Leader.

mom's always said if someone was going to hold on to you, you're supposed to wear them like a London Fog."

The dunk, described by the *News Leader* as "LeBronesque," got both the Lee fans and players pumped as the teams headed for the locker room. Spotsylvania never got closer than seven in the second half, as Lee won 78–68, advancing to the state semifinals.

It's About Ws

Jarrett Hatcher had a friend in the Roanoke area leave him tapes of the other three semifinalists: Greensville, Heritage and Salem. The tapes were left for him at a Roanoke Dunkin' Donuts.

"I asked to order a thing of coffee and asked for a satchel of tapes that a guy had left for me there," said Jarrett Hatcher. "I looked like a drug courier. The kid's all pimply faced looking, and he's like, 'What do you mean?' and I guess the manager was a little older, and he's like, 'It's in the walk-in.'"

The first tape that the Hatchers watched was the next opponent, Salem, which got to the semifinals after beating Paul Hatcher's old nemesis, Martinsville. In the week leading up to the game, Paul Hatcher talked a lot to his players about close games, something the Leemen hadn't been involved in often that season. But the veteran coach had a feeling that Lee's semifinal game might just be a nail-biter, so during practice he worked on last-second plays. It would stand to reason that if Lee needed a last-second bucket, Tyler Crawford would be the go-to player. Hatcher had a suspicion, though, that it would be another player taking the shot.

So Hatcher ran a last-second play with Eli Crawford during Monday's practice. Then he ran one with Daryl Taylor. And Tyler Crawford just stood on the floor next to Paul Hatcher saying, "Coach, I'm ready."

Hatcher was blunt. He told Tyler Crawford that he probably wouldn't be in the game in the final seconds because he'd probably foul out. That had been an issue with Crawford throughout his high school career.

Tuesday, it was the same thing. Wednesday, more of the same.

"I finally had enough," said Jarrett Hatcher. "I went over and said, 'Would you stop it? Stop talking about close games. We've been winning by fifty. You're freaking them out."

Then he told his dad to put Tyler in to run a last-second play. The head coach refused. He had lost a state tournament game six times in the final seconds, and he wasn't going to let it happen again.

Looking back, Crawford said that was just one of the many ways Hatcher used to think outside the bubble. At the time, sure, he wanted to be involved, but now what the coach was doing makes perfect sense.

"It's never been about points," said Crawford. "It's about Ws."

Hatcher's hunch was right. With 6:17 left in the third quarter against Salem, Crawford picked up his fourth foul. Lee trailed 28–24 at the time, but the Leemen had seen this before just a few weeks earlier, when Crawford was on the bench as Lee rallied to beat Harrisonburg. Crawford always said it wasn't just about him. The Leemen had a chance to prove it against Salem.

"Just punch and punch on me if you want to," said Crawford. "But we've got [other] guys who are going to bust your ass."

Neither team could gain control, and the game went back and forth throughout, but with 37.5 seconds left, Tyler Crawford, back in the game, hit two free throws to put Lee in front, 50–49. Nineteen seconds later, Crawford's night came to an end when he fouled Salem freshman Kenny Belton.

"I thought they were going to call a technical," said Paul Hatcher. "He just clobbered him."

During the radio broadcast of the game on Harrisonburg's WSVA, play-by-play announcer Jim Britt asked on air, "Is this the last time we'll see Tyler Crawford in an R.E. Lee uniform?"

Crawford certainly didn't want that to be the case. After the foul was called, Crawford remained on the floor long enough for Britt to wonder out loud if the foul was actually called on him. Crawford knew it was called on him, he just didn't believe it.

"Tyler was the only person in the Siegel Center that didn't think it was a foul," remembered Jarrett Hatcher.

Even now, Crawford refuses to believe it.

"You still can't tell me that was a foul," he said during a 2015 interview.

With the Lee star on the bench, Belton hit his first free throw to tie the game at fifty. Paul Hatcher tried to call a timeout, but the official handed the ball to Belton before he saw the coach's signal. Belton's shot circled the rim and fell out. Jason Jordan grabbed the rebound, and Lee called a timeout to discuss the final seventeen seconds.

Paul Hatcher decided to let Daryl Taylor take the shot in the final seconds, just like he had worked on during practice. Jason Jordan inbounded the ball to Eli Crawford, who then passed to Taylor.

Taylor dribbled for a few seconds, almost lost control of the ball but regained it, drove to the left of the foul line and fired up a fifteen-foot jump shot. Swish. Taylor finished with fourteen points, but none bigger than the final two with two seconds left.

"Everybody was jumping up and down," said Jordan. "You look over at Paul, and he's just standing there, like, shaking his head."

Salem threw the ball away on its final play as time expired, and Lee claimed the victory. Tyler Crawford was watching it all from the bench, but he had no doubt his teammate would make the basket.

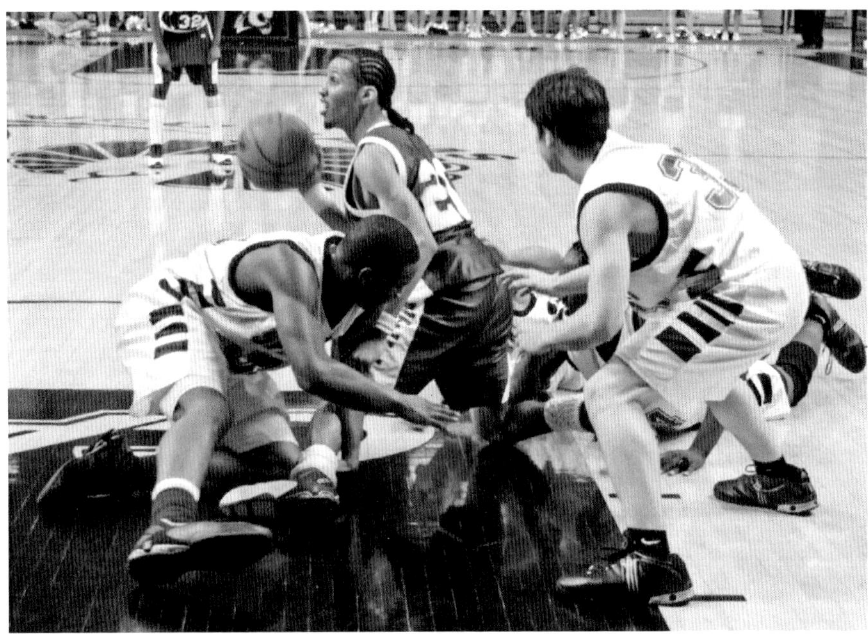

Lee's Daryl Taylor needed some help against Salem in the 2004 Group state semifinals. So did his team. Eventually, Taylor provided it with a game-winning shot. *Vincent Lerz/ the* News Leader.

"Daryl is one of those guys, even in practice, I was like, 'This guy is really hard to guard,'" said Crawford. "He's long, lanky. His moves are just...he makes you be indecisive on defense. Daryl having the ball, I'm confident it's going down."

In the locker room, the coaches and players were celebrating, but they couldn't find Taylor. Then he walked in and said, "I am so glad I made that shot. My grandma has had reservations in a hotel for this whole weekend through Sunday since October."

It may be one of the biggest shots in Lee High history, but it was only good enough to get Lee to the state championship game. The 52–50 win earned the Leemen a date with unbeaten Greensville County the very next night. The Eagles had survived Heritage-Lynchburg when Deon Bullock hit a shot just before the buzzer to end the second overtime. Fans from both teams rushed the floor, believing their school had won, but after the officials discussed it, they ruled the basket was good, and Greensville hung on for the 67–66 win.

After that game, the Group AA girls' semifinal game was played and also went to overtime. Lee was supposed to tip at 9:00 p.m., but it was 10:10 p.m. before the game started. By the time Taylor's shot went through the net and the players finished celebrating and got dressed, it was after 12:30 a.m. on

Saturday morning. No restaurants were open except Taco Bell, which closed at 1:30 a.m. The Leemen ordered every taco they had made and ate in the lobby of the hotel.

Jarrett Hatcher couldn't sleep. His rollaway bed smelled, although he thought it was his roommate and freshman coach Ron Herr's shoes. Didn't matter. The real reason he couldn't sleep was because he was so close to his dream of being the first person to hug his dad after a state championship win. He finally fell asleep at 4:00 a.m., and two hours later his dad was knocking on the door, ready to watch tapes of Greensville. Later that day, Paul Hatcher talked to his players about the opponent.

"Dad just said that they're big and they're quick and they're athletic and they're explosive and they score and they shut people down," said Jarrett Hatcher. "He said it's the exact type of team you've been playing against every day in practice since November."

Before the game, Jarrett Hatcher walked in the locker room and saw several of the players in tears. He asked what was wrong. Travis Stuart looked at him and said, "Tonight's the last night I'm a Leeman."

Win or lose, this was it for the seniors. They wanted it to be win.

If the Leemen had to wait until less than two seconds were left in the game against Salem before knowing the outcome, they had a good idea after the first quarter against Greensville that it would be win. After a 10–10 tie, Lee went on an 11–0 run and never looked back, winning 96–57.

"The big surprise was Greensville," said Paul Hatcher. "It wasn't even close."

The coach wasn't the only person who was surprised at the outcome. Lee junior Keary Bonner, who came off the bench to score two points against Greensville, assumed the game would end dramatically, perhaps with Tyler Crawford hitting a last-second shot.

"But we just ran away with it," he said.

Lee continuously pounded the ball inside because Hatcher had a feeling Greensville would foul them by trying to block every shot. Then when the Eagles had the ball, they just shot threes, not many of which were falling. Lee grabbed the rebounds and ran. They continuously got it inside and either made the bucket or shot foul shots. Lee made forty of forty-nine from the line.

Hatcher thought his team's defense, and Greensville's lack of it, was the big difference. He always told his players that if they weren't willing to play defense, they could pay for a ticket to watch the Leemen because they wouldn't be on the team.

"A lot of high school guys don't want to play defense," said Hatcher. "They're going to play for a few seconds, you know, so you reverse the offense, you reverse it a couple of times, and there'll be somebody down there looking around and all of a sudden you're going to get a layup. But the kids have to be patient."

Lee outscored Greensville 32–12 in the fourth quarter, but Paul Hatcher wasn't finished coaching. Lawrence Lightfoot made a mistake right in front of the Lee bench with forty-five seconds remaining and caught the wrath of his coach, something the younger Hatcher couldn't understand. The state title would be Lee's in less than a minute. Why was his dad still coaching so hard?

"Because he's going to have to know how to do it next year," was his dad's response.

MISSION ACCOMPLISHED

As the fans spilled onto the court to celebrate with the players, Travis Stuart took off his jersey. It's what he said he wanted to do at halftime of the second Harrisonburg game.

"On the *News Leader* the next morning they had [a photo of] him on somebody's shoulders with his hands up," said Tyler Crawford. "That made me feel good."

Crawford met Stuart in eighth grade, shortly after he transferred from Augusta County. They immediately became best friends. Crawford still says other than his college teammate Jonathan Wallace, Stuart is the best point guard he's ever played with.

"Travis is the biggest reason we went as far as we did," said Crawford. "Everybody talks about Tyler Crawford, Tyler Crawford…no, no, no, no."

Stuart was named the defensive player of the year by the *News Leader*. He took to heart his coach's emphasis on defense. Perhaps it was on display most during Lee's semifinal win over Salem. Stuart's assignment was A.J. Dowell, the Salem senior guard who averaged 17.5 points a game that season and was both his district's and region's player of the year. Against Lee, Dowell finished with just one field goal, a three-pointer, and four total points.

"Other than Daryl's shot, Travis was one of the biggest reasons we beat Salem," said Crawford. "He guarded A.J. Dowell ninety-four feet for thirty-two minutes. A.J. Dowell scored the first bucket, and he didn't score again after that."

Against Greensville in the state championship game, everyone played defense. The Eagles shot just 33 percent in losing their first game of the

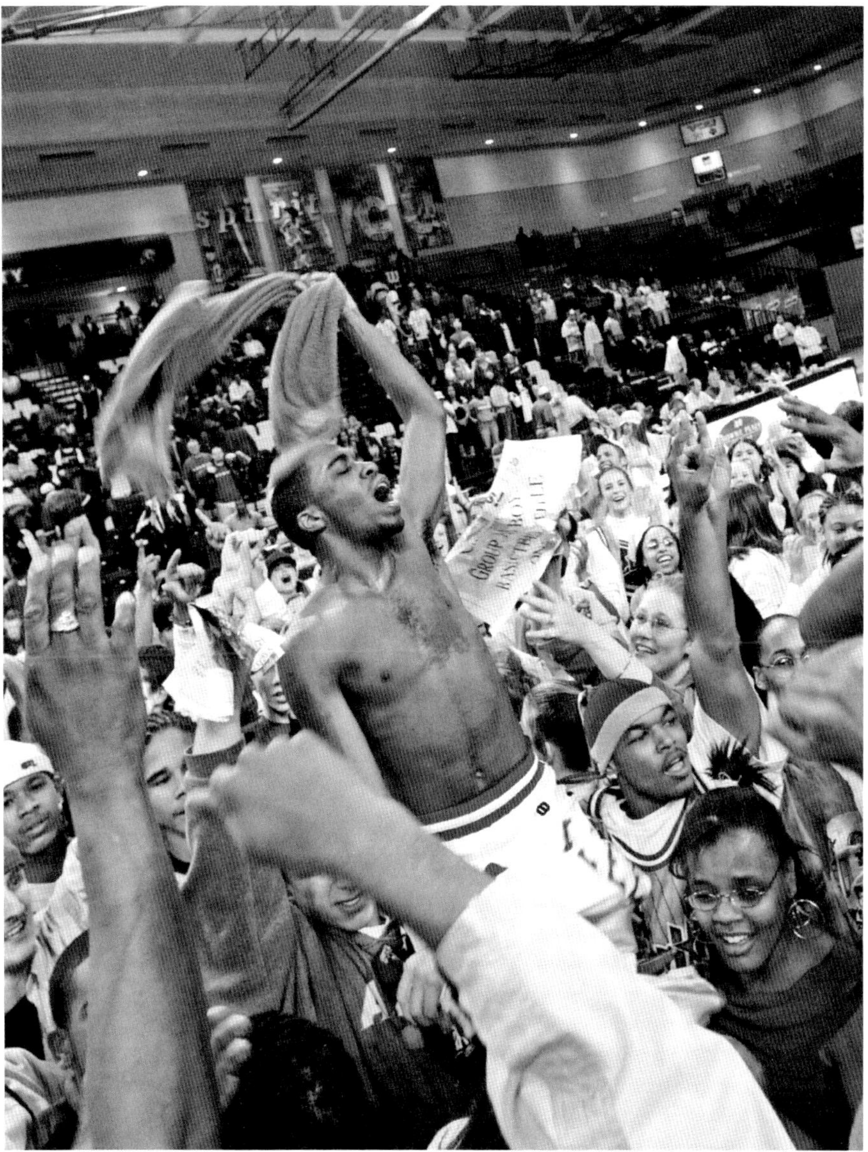

Travis Stuart said he would take his jersey off at the Siegel Center. He did just that when Lee beat Greensville for the 2004 state championship. *Mark Miller/the* News Leader.

season. In the locker room after the game, senior Johnny Fowler said to his coach, "I thought you said there weren't going to be any more easy games."

From day one of practice, the Leemen had been focused on getting to the Siegel Center and winning a state championship. Now they had done

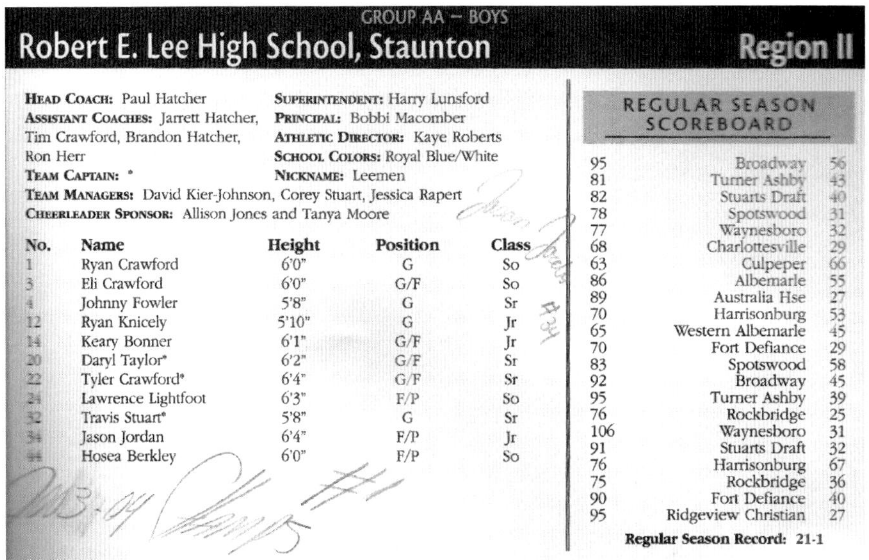

GROUP AA – BOYS

Robert E. Lee High School, Staunton — **Region II**

HEAD COACH: Paul Hatcher
ASSISTANT COACHES: Jarrett Hatcher, Tim Crawford, Brandon Hatcher, Ron Herr
TEAM CAPTAIN: *
TEAM MANAGERS: David Kier-Johnson, Corey Stuart, Jessica Rapert
CHEERLEADER SPONSOR: Allison Jones and Tanya Moore

SUPERINTENDENT: Harry Lunsford
PRINCIPAL: Bobbi Macomber
ATHLETIC DIRECTOR: Kaye Roberts
SCHOOL COLORS: Royal Blue/White
NICKNAME: Leemen

No.	Name	Height	Position	Class
1	Ryan Crawford	6'0"	G	So
3	Eli Crawford	6'0"	G/F	So
4	Johnny Fowler	5'8"	G	Sr
12	Ryan Knicely	5'10"	G	Jr
14	Keary Bonner	6'1"	G/F	Jr
20	Daryl Taylor*	6'2"	G/F	Sr
22	Tyler Crawford*	6'4"	G/F	Sr
24	Lawrence Lightfoot	6'3"	F/P	So
32	Travis Stuart*	5'8"	G	Sr
34	Jason Jordan	6'4"	F/P	Jr
44	Hosea Berkley	6'0"	F/P	So

REGULAR SEASON SCOREBOARD

95	Broadway	56
81	Turner Ashby	43
82	Stuarts Draft	40
78	Spotswood	31
77	Waynesboro	32
68	Charlottesville	29
63	Culpeper	66
86	Albemarle	55
89	Australia Hse	27
70	Harrisonburg	53
65	Western Albemarle	45
70	Fort Defiance	29
83	Spotswood	58
92	Broadway	45
95	Turner Ashby	39
76	Rockbridge	25
106	Waynesboro	31
91	Stuarts Draft	32
76	Harrisonburg	67
75	Rockbridge	36
90	Fort Defiance	40
95	Ridgeview Christian	27

Regular Season Record: 21-1

Robert E. Lee's roster in Jason Jordan's copy of the 2004 VHSL state basketball tournament program. The then Lee junior even signed it. *Jason Jordan's collection.*

that. Comparing teams was never Paul Hatcher's thing, but that focus to win the title may be one difference between this state championship team and Hatcher's first two.

"It was special because of the way they approached it," said Hatcher. "This was their goal. The others, we weren't…being state champion wasn't something that [the other teams] talked about every day. Of course, everybody wants to be, but still, this group, this was it. It's all they talked about."

Another difference was that the first two titles under Hatcher, in 1984 and 1990, Lee High went undefeated. The 2004 championship team had one blemish on the record. Jarrett Hatcher actually worried about that following the loss, but after winning the title, it didn't matter if there was a zero or a one in the loss column. He got to hug his dad following a state championship. That's what mattered.

It didn't take long for reporters to ask Paul Hatcher if he was going to retire. Even Jarrett told him as they walked off the court that this was the perfect time to quit, with thirty-six years and 740 wins under his belt. The coach wasn't having any of it, though.

"Why do you retire?" he said. "If somebody is out here making a big business deal and makes a ton of money, they're going to keep on doing it, wouldn't they? It's when they're losing money and things are going bad, that's the time to quit. We're on top. Why would I want to stop now?"

Yes, three of Lee's starters were graduating, but Hatcher knew there was a lot of talent returning. He wanted to stick around to make another run. After all, one thing he had yet to accomplish was back-to-back titles. After winning it in 1984, the 1985 Leemen lost to Martinsville 62–61 in the state semifinals. And after Lee took home the championship in 1990, the team got all the way back to the state championship game the following year, only to lose to Waynesboro by twenty. Maybe the 2005 team could finally take the final step and give Hatcher back-to-back championships.

As for Tyler Crawford, he was just happy to have one championship. After the title eluded him his first three years, he finally had one. He said anything less just wouldn't have been right.

"The whole Tyler Crawford and his legacy," said Crawford. "This was it. You can either go out on top or you'll always be a second-place…he almost made it."

However, he might have still been second place in his home. Tyler met his wife, Meredith Cox, when both were basketball players at Georgetown. Cox was a high school star at Delone Catholic in Pennsylvania, where she won three state titles in a row and was player of the year two years in a row.

"We don't ever compare stats," said Crawford. "Because I lose."

That bugs Crawford.

"He doesn't like to lose," said Cox. "Whatever he does, he wants to be the best at, whether it be fishing, going to the gym…it's always be the best at whatever you're doing."

At Lee, Crawford accomplished just that. He was named the Associated Press Group AA player of the year, and he helped lead his team to a state championship. He was the best, and the proof was on the wall.

It was early in the morning one day in August after Crawford graduated from Lee. Jarrett Hatcher, who was also the Lee High golf coach, was at the school getting ready for a golf tournament. He noticed some maintenance workers putting the team photo of Lee High's state championship team on the gym wall.

He left a voicemail message for Crawford, who was at Georgetown, telling him the picture was on the wall. When Jarrett Hatcher returned to the school later that day, he noticed the lights were on in the gym. He walked in to turn them off and heard the sound of a bouncing basketball. There was Tyler Crawford, shooting jump shots.

The two walked to the elbow on the floor at Paul Hatcher Gym, the exact spot where, one year earlier, Crawford had promised his assistant coach that

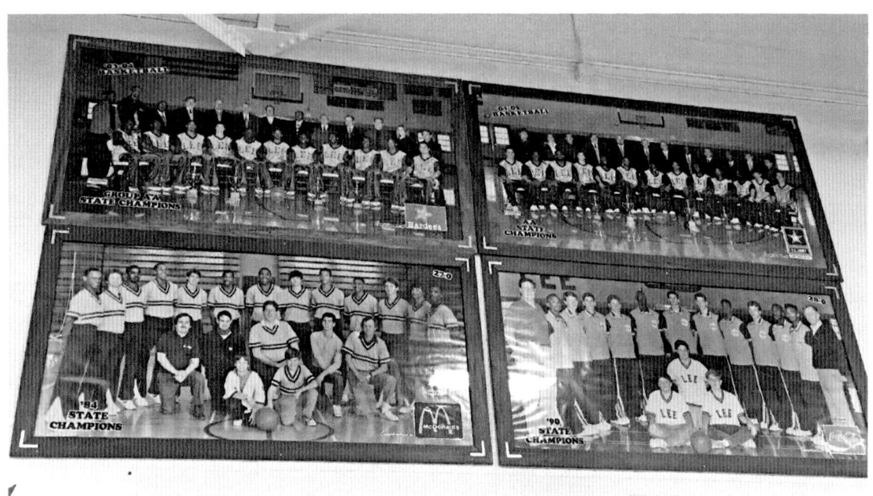

Four team photos—representing Lee's four basketball state champions under Paul Hatcher—hang in the Paul Hatcher Gymnasium. *Photo by Mike Tripp.*

the team would win a title, that they would put a picture on the wall. Now, that picture was on the wall, and the two stood next to each other, looking at it.

Jarrett Hatcher turned toward Crawford and said, "We accomplished our mission."

5
Highs and Lows

Basketball was Paul Hatcher's passion. He remembers nailing a coat hanger to a pine tree behind his house in Bassett Forks, Virginia, when he was five years old. That was his basketball goal. He jokes now that he probably invented the first breakaway rim, but for hours as a kid, he would shoot a ball through that coat hanger.

"I just played ball all the time," said Hatcher. "There really wasn't much going on in Bassett Forks."

He played through high school and college before coaching the boys' team at Robert E. Lee High School for forty-three years.

But the sport also became his escape.

Paul and Judy Hatcher met when both were students at Bridgewater College. Judy was sixteen at the time, an exceptionally intelligent young woman who had skipped two grades in elementary school. She was a cheerleader for the Eagles. He was a basketball star.

Judy's maiden name was Hayslett, so at orientation when students sat alphabetically, she was seated next to a freshman named Paul Hatcher. The two became best friends that first year of college and, by sophomore year, were dating. Three days a week, Bridgewater students had to attend chapel, where Paul and Judy again sat next to each other. The two said they may have been the only ones who looked forward to going to chapel.

"We could talk about basketball in chapel instead of listening," said Judy.

Judy graduated a year before Paul and returned home to Alleghany County to teach elementary school for a year. The next year, after Paul

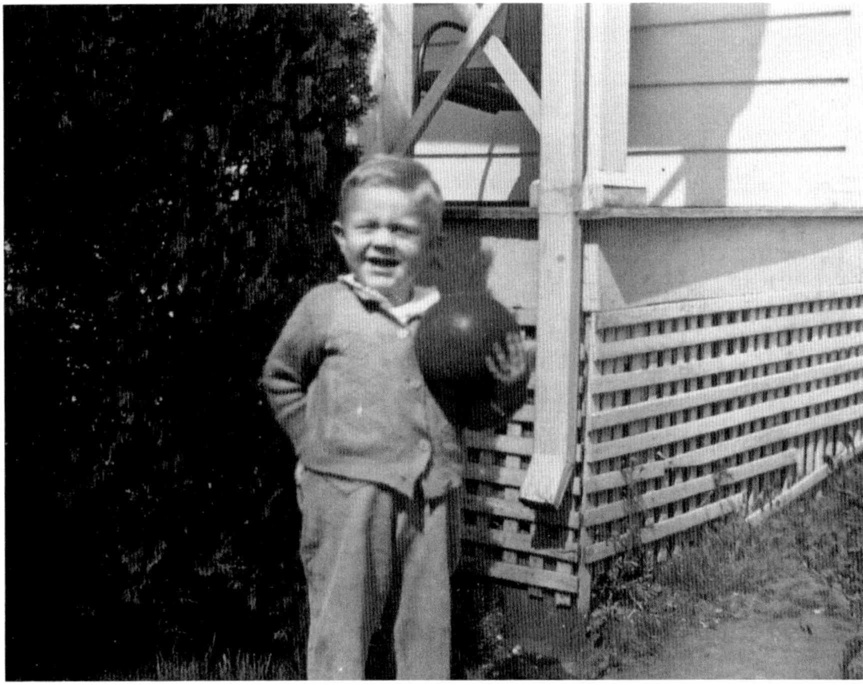

Even a young Paul Hatcher was a basketball fan. *Paul Hatcher's collection.*

graduated from Bridgewater, they were married on June 18, 1966, and both landed teaching jobs in Staunton, Paul at Shelburne Junior High and Judy at Westside Elementary. Paul became head coach at Lee High in 1968, and from that point until he retired, basketball was king in the Hatcher family.

Brandon Hatcher said, when he was older, he would pack two bags for vacation—one for his clothes and one with a VCR and cable cords so the Hatchers could watch game film.

"I would have four or five different cables just in case the hotel had a different television, so I was prepared," said Brandon.

Everything revolved around basketball, said Judy. She didn't live her life but Paul's life. Still, she wouldn't have changed anything.

"It was a hard life, but it was a very rewarding life because of all the people—kids, the parents, the reporters, the coaches, the college coaches—all these people that we met that became like family, really."

What a lot of those people—and, for that matter, most people who followed Lee High basketball—didn't know was just how hard a life it was off the court for the Hatchers.

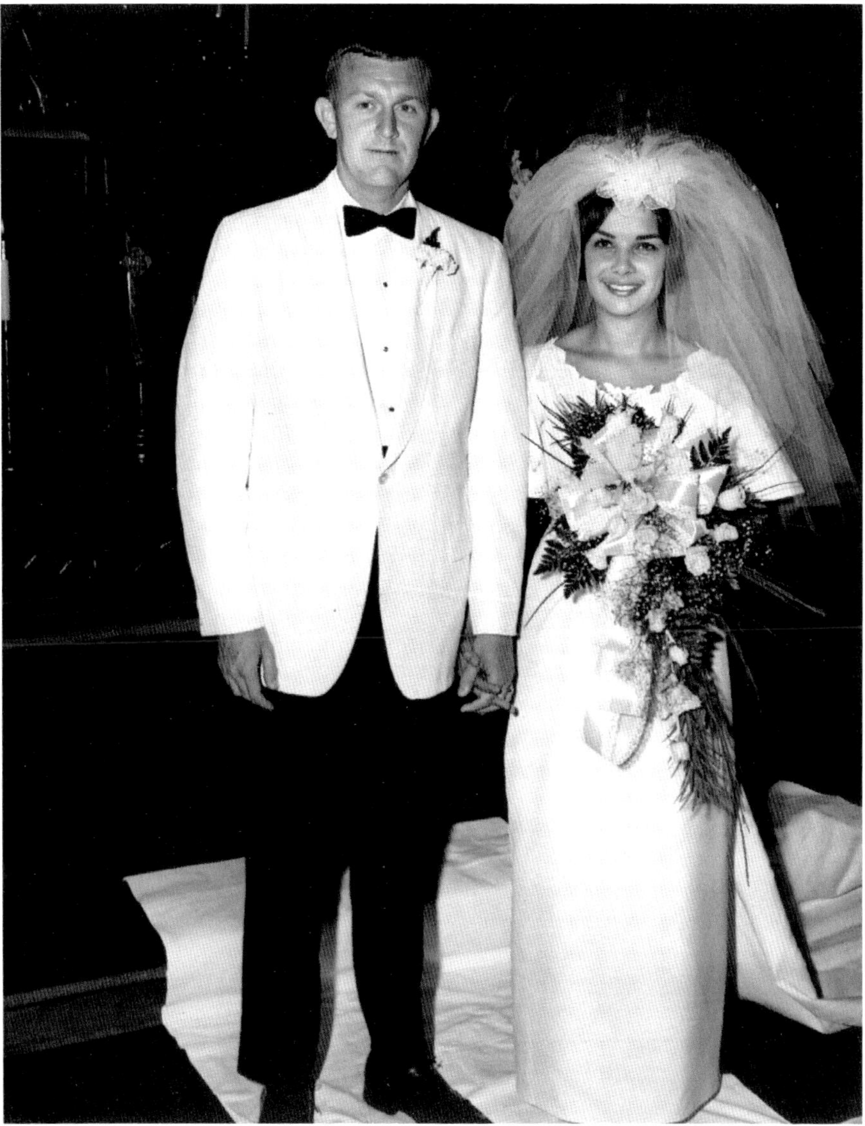

After dating in college, Paul and Judy Hatcher were married on June 18, 1966. *Paul Hatcher's collection.*

In August 1988, the first symptoms appeared. For years, Judy Hatcher had suffered from migraines and was on several prescription drugs, including Valium. She became addicted, although not many people realized it.

"I covered it up pretty well," Judy said.

In the spring of 1988, Judy had been reading how dangerous Valium was and decided to take herself off the drug. However, she remained on Fiorinal, a barbiturate used to treat headaches. That summer, her doctor wouldn't refill her prescription for that drug. She quit cold turkey and started suffering from panic attacks.

"Everything you would think of somebody coming off an addiction, we kind of dealt with that all summer," said Jarrett Hatcher, who was getting ready to start his senior year of high school.

The week before school started in late August, things got worse.

"I flipped totally out of reality," said Judy. "I was so crazy. Just mind gone."

She was hospitalized until October for what everyone, including her family, thought was rehabilitation for drug addiction. She hadn't been home for long when, on the Tuesday before Thanksgiving, Judy went back to the hospital for gallbladder surgery. She developed an infection and was prescribed pain medication, which caused a bad reaction.

When she returned home, she refused to come out of her room, prompting another stay in a drug treatment center in Charlottesville. There, the Hatchers were told Judy wasn't a drug addict but was depressed. She was admitted to a clinic in Culpeper in December, right at the start of the 1988–89 high school basketball season.

"My senior year, on nights that we practiced, we'd finish practice at five and drive to Culpeper," said Jarrett. "One of Dad's toughest years."

The only days they didn't visit Judy were game days. Otherwise, they were there every night and weekend. The Hatchers even spent Christmas together in the hospital. After the season, Paul visited Judy, who had moved to a facility in Charlottesville, for forty-five straight days, sometimes twice a day. After running out of other treatment options, the doctors used electroconvulsive therapy (ECT), a treatment sometimes used for depression when drugs aren't working. It worked, and by Easter, Judy was finally back home, better, but as time would tell, not well.

Judy relapsed in September 1989 and was hospitalized for a month in Harrisonburg. She managed to stay out of the hospital during that entire basketball season, one in which Paul Hatcher won his second state championship.

"That was a big deal, thinking about where we had been the year before and how basketball had been a struggle," said Jarrett.

For the time being, things were improved. They wouldn't stay that way. Judy Hatcher was diagnosed with manic depression. Judy said the doctors explained that her "brain was broken."

The next few years were difficult, with Judy in and out of hospitals. And when she wasn't hospitalized, there was always a fear of what might happen.

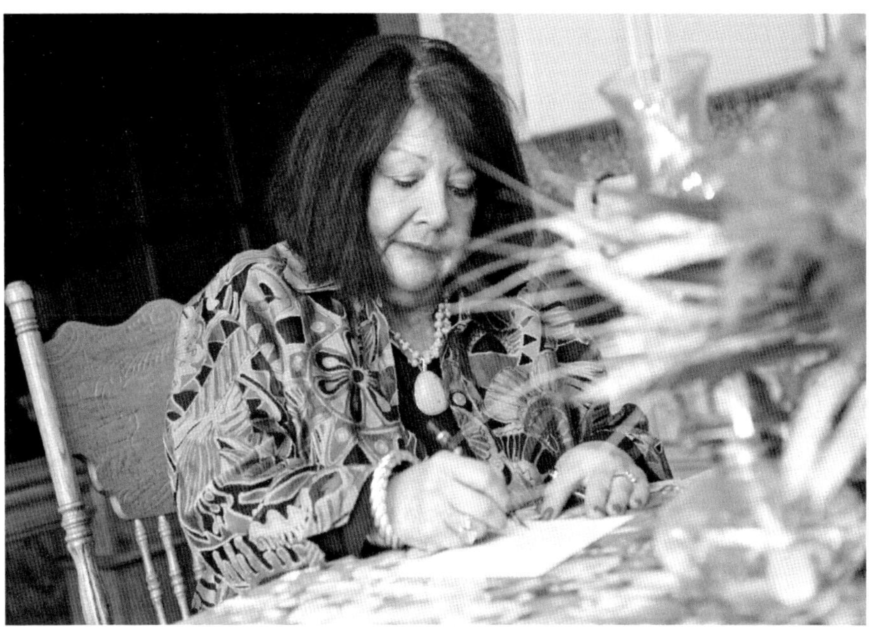

One of the activities Judy Hatcher uses to help her cope with her manic depression is writing cards and letters to various people in the community. *Mike Tripp/the* News Leader.

"That manic stuff is about as bad as it comes," said Paul Hatcher. "When they're manic, you don't know what they're going to do."

Once, during a manic period, she bought a car with cash and then decided, a week later, that she no longer liked the color. One night, she just walked out of the house, and after a search, Jarrett found her walking back from the 7-11 a mile or so from their house.

And there was the night following a Lee win at Jefferson Forest. Paul Hatcher remembers two things about that night. The first was that the gym was so cold that his players had their coats and hats on while sitting the bench. The second was that, after making the two-hour trip home after the game, Judy was missing. She had gone to a nursing home in Alleghany County in western Virginia, where her mom was a patient. Someone from the nursing home called and said Judy was causing problems.

"That was a long day," said Paul Hatcher, who drove to the nursing home to get her. Judy ended up back in the hospital.

Both Paul and Jarrett said the low periods, when Judy's depression was at its worst, were so sad to watch, but at least she was in her room, and there wasn't a fear of where she might go or what she might do.

"The classic depression of Mom sitting in the room and not coming out and not eating was so much easier," said Jarrett.

Sometimes Judy would go to the hospital willingly. Other times, she wouldn't, and there was a need to get the police involved. It wasn't always pretty, but for Judy's safety, it was a necessity.

"That's one of the worst things you ever do," said Paul. "They come in here and handcuff them and take them out, but it had to be done."

Paul became a self-taught expert on his wife's illness. He read everything he could about it and talked to Judy's doctors. He wanted to understand the illness as best he could so he could help his wife with her battle. He still had a job to do at school and on the basketball court, but he had the extra pressure of what was happening at home. The support of others helped.

"We didn't hide it," said Paul. "It's an illness, and you've got to deal with it."

In March 2003, with Judy at Western State, a state psychiatric hospital in Staunton, the Hatchers knew Judy's mom wouldn't live much longer. Paul made the trip alone to the nursing home to see his mother-in-law one last time. Then, when she passed away, they broke the news to Judy. She skipped her group therapy to write her mom's eulogy and, on the day of the funeral, got an eight-hour pass.

"She went up and gave the eulogy," said Paul. "And it was fantastic."

That also happened to be Tyler Crawford's junior season, when Lee lost in the regional tournament to Turner Ashby. Jarrett Hatcher said losing to TA was tough, but maybe God had it figured out that the family had more important issues than a state tournament game to deal with the following week.

By the following winter, the first year of the streak, Judy Hatcher was again in the hospital, spending about six weeks that winter at Western State.

"She liked Western State better than any other place," said Jarrett. "We always tried to get her a bed there."

She was out, however, when March rolled around and Lee was pursuing a state title. She even got to ride the bus with the team to Richmond and the Siegel Center for the state semifinals and finals.

"I was just overcome with emotion remembering how terrible it had been going through all of this with basketball and her and Dad and the stress," said Jarrett. "And here we are, I've always wanted to be with my dad in the state championship game. I cried. I had puddles under my seat. I was just so happy that Mom was going to be with us."

TRYING FOR A REPEAT

On the homefront in late 2004, the state title defense began with some temporary good news. Judy Hatcher was home from the hospital, but that wouldn't remain the case throughout the basketball season.

On the basketball court, the streak wasn't really a thing yet, with Lee having finished the previous season with twenty-four wins in a row. Tyler Crawford was gone. So were Daryl Taylor, Travis Stuart and Johnny Fowler. Those were no small pieces of the championship puzzle from the year before.

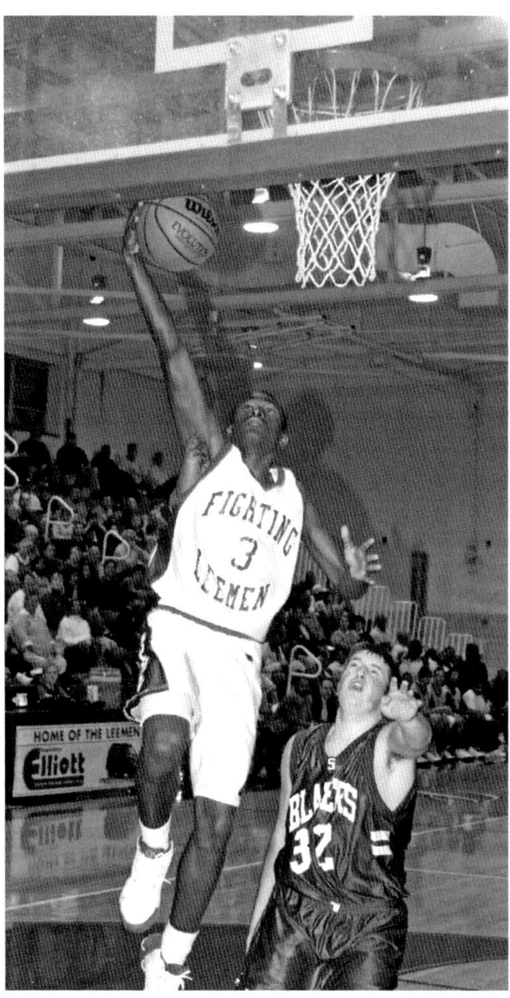

Eli Crawford was counted on in 2004–05 to help his team overcome the graduation of his cousin, Tyler Crawford. *Vincent Lerz/the* News Leader.

"I thought losing Daryl was going to hurt a little more," said Eli Crawford. "Daryl was a key part. If Daryl wouldn't have hit that shot [against Salem], there is no Lee streak, no Lee state championship. Tyler was a huge part in Lee history and for the program and stuff, but I thought losing Daryl and even Travis would hurt even more."

But after his breakout sophomore year, Eli Crawford was back. He averaged 11.2 points per game but had really peaked during the postseason. Jason Jordan also returned, giving Lee two starters back from the previous season.

Tyler Crawford's brother, Ryan, would take on a starting role in Lee's backcourt after coming off the bench as a sophomore. Keary Bonner, Hosea Berkley, Lawrence Lightfoot and Ryan Knicely also returned after coming off the bench the season before, while four new players joined the team from the Lee jayvees, and two players who didn't play for Lee in 2003–04 rounded out the varsity squad.

"The kids wanted to prove something—that they could do it without Tyler," said Jarrett Hatcher, in his second year as the team's varsity assistant under his dad.

Ryan Crawford felt that a lot of fans thought, without Tyler Crawford on the team, Lee would not be the same dominating team it was the year before. But Ryan Crawford had grown a lot the previous season, especially getting to work against Travis Stuart in every practice. The other young players also got that experience of going up against some of the best players in the state day after day.

Ryan Crawford said the team was eager and hungry to show everyone that Lee High basketball was still a dominant force. He knew how good his older brother was, but he also knew about the talent returning that season.

"Everybody knew how good Eli was just because of his late emergence [the season before]," said Ryan Crawford. "People saw snippets of Hosea. Hosea was a freak athlete. There [were] some things that he did at practice that were just absurd. And Lawrence was somebody who, I think, was the biggest sleeper on the team for the next two years. Lawrence was really, really good. And Jason, being in the position that he was, I think Jason was ready to have a big year, and Keary was ready to have a big year. We kept working at it, and I think Coach Paul knew that he had a special team."

Talent is one thing Lee basketball always seemed to have, but so was pressure. There was pressure involved in putting on that Lee High jersey and playing for Paul Hatcher. Keary Bonner felt it. He called it positive pressure that forced him to play hard all the time, whether that was in open gym, practice or a game. It didn't matter who was starting for the Leemen. It didn't matter if Tyler Crawford was there or at Georgetown. It didn't matter what names were on the roster. Year in and year out, Lee High had talented players. The most talented players in the area. Bonner knew, even if he was starting early in the season, there were other guys ready and willing to take his place.

"I'm pretty sure those years the eighth guy, the ninth guy off our bench, would have started at Fort Defiance or Stuarts Draft," said Bonner. "That was the pressure I felt. I better take care of my business because there are guys who would take my spot in a heartbeat."

The players proved it, at least through the first seven games. Lee was barely tested, beating teams by an average of thirty-eight points a game. A twenty-point win over Turner Ashby was as close as any of the first seven opponents came to beating Lee. In that game, TA actually led 10–2, perhaps the result of a week off for the Leemen, but Lee scored the next seventeen points and ran away from there.

If there was any doubt about how good that year's team would be, it was erased after those first seven games.

"That's when our confidence kept going [up]," said Ryan Crawford. "We pretty much got the ball rolling and picked up where we left off."

The tests would get more difficult after the Christmas break, however, with a much-improved Australian team and an unbeaten Harrisonburg squad up next.

After the Australians underestimated Lee High the year before, the tour group in charge of sending teams from Down Under to the United States sent a much better team the second year: the Melbourne Tigers. The previous year's team didn't have a player taller than six-foot-three. The Tigers, the eighteen-and-under national champions in Australia, had four players taller than that, including one who stood six-foot-eleven.

Lack of size was an issue for Lee. J.R. Ware, who came off the bench, was listed at six-foot-five, the tallest player on Lee's roster. Jason Jordan and Lawrence Lightfoot were both listed at six-foot-four. It was never much of a problem during the regular season because there weren't many opponents who had much size. But getting to play the Aussies would be good preparation for down the road.

"That's always a concern when you move on into state play and into regional play," said Paul Hatcher. "Usually those teams, somebody's got a big guy and he carries them and then all of a sudden you're running against a big guy and you haven't played one all year."

Lee always countered their size by running their offense and forcing other teams to guard them but also by playing tenacious defense and forcing turnovers that turned into transition points.

"A lot of times you get those easy buckets and you're not going against those big guys every possession," Paul Hatcher said. "That was always my philosophy. We pressed a lot. Our defense was good. Turnovers, easy buckets, get fouled."

Keary Bonner doesn't recall the streak being talked about often among the players. Honestly, it wasn't very important, or at least a lot less important than winning a state championship. But that night, watching those taller Australians on the court dunking in warmups, Bonner remembers hearing someone from the stands yell out that the streak would be over after that night. The fans weren't the only ones who thought that might be the case.

"I was actually nervous that game," said Jason Jordan.

And with good reason. A year to the day of Lee's last loss to Culpeper, the Melbourne Tigers almost snapped the Leemen's thirty-one-game winning streak. Melbourne—playing the first game of its thirteen-game tour through Virginia, Maryland, North Carolina and South Carolina—led 29–26 at halftime. But in the third quarter, Hosea Berkley came up with a steal and a basket to start a 16–4 Lee High run as the home team went on to win 56–50.

"To be quite honest, if that had not been their first game of the tour, they would have beaten us," said Jarrett Hatcher. "I think they were jet-lagged. I think they were a little overwhelmed with the crowd."

Just like the previous season, the best regular season battle was between Lee High and Harrisonburg. Unlike the previous season, both teams entered the first meeting undefeated. Lee was 8-0. Harrisonburg 9-0. Plus, it was the final game the two would play at Harrisonburg's Claude E. Warren Fieldhouse. The high school would be in a new building for the start of the 2005–06 school year.

Lee had beaten Harrisonburg three times the previous season, and Justin German, Harrisonburg's leading scorer, told the *Daily News-Record* before the first meeting of the 2004–05 season that Lee had been on their minds all summer.

Lee would remain on Harrisonburg's mind a little longer. Keary Bonner hit two free throws with 12.1 seconds left as Lee held on for a 57–54 win. There was just one tie in the game, but otherwise Lee led the entire game. Still, that lead never got larger than ten points.

"All in all, we got the win," Eli Crawford was quoted as saying in the *Daily News-Record*. "It doesn't matter how we did it, as long as we did it."

The win got January off to a good start for Lee High. Unfortunately, the month also brought around another hospitalization for Judy Hatcher. Lee had put together thirty-three wins in a row, but there were other things for the Hatchers to worry about.

"All this great stuff that's going on and everybody knows about," said Jarrett Hatcher. "We're dealing with all this other stuff. I think it helped… both distractions helped each other. Basketball was two and a half hours during the day—before practice, practice and after practice—that we didn't have to deal with it. Then it was the time with Mom afterward that we're not talking about basketball."

Over the next four years, Judy Hatcher was in and out of the hospital multiple times, but by 2016, she had not been hospitalized for more than six

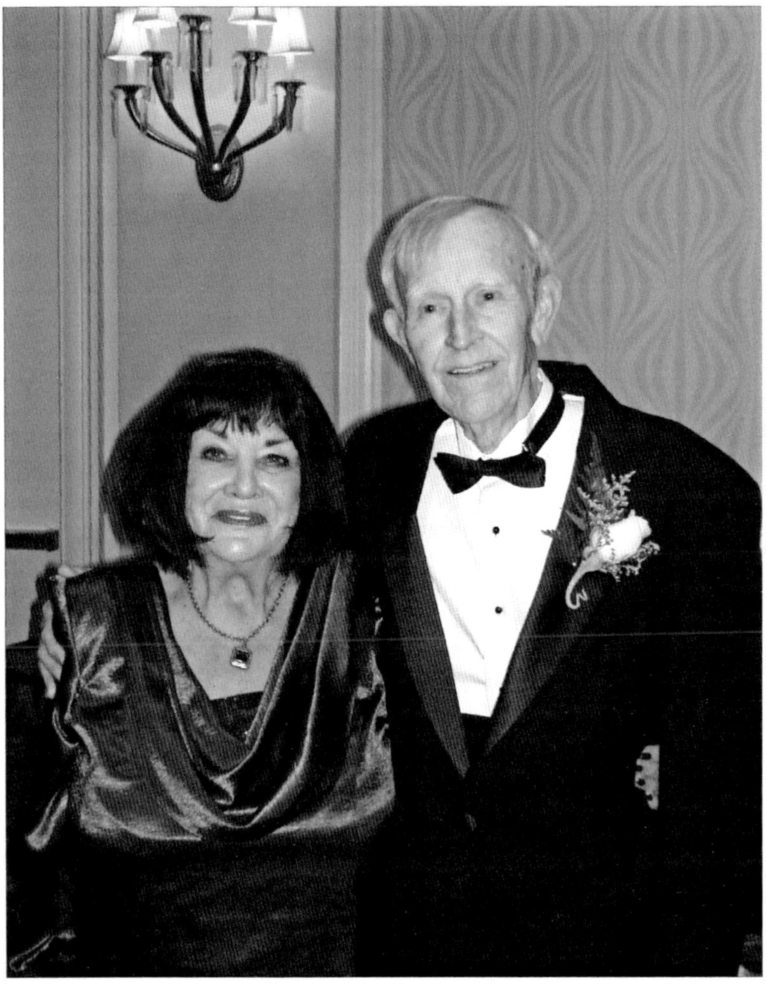

Judy and Paul Hatcher at the 2015 Virginia Sports Hall of Fame and Museum induction ceremony in Portsmouth, Virginia. *Paul Hatcher's collection.*

years. Paul Hatcher makes sure she takes her medication and looks after her as much as he can. Mental illness, like any long-term illness, can sometimes drive a wedge in a marriage. That wasn't the case with the Hatchers.

"She's been through a hard time," said Paul. "It just hurts me when we talk about it sometimes. It was so bad, but I think now how well she's doing and all that she does for people, and she's just a remarkable person. To go through all that…it sure wasn't easy, but I'm still here."

Laughing, Judy added, "I can't get rid of him."

6

THE FIRST STAUNTON STREAK

Three nights after his team beat Harrisonburg for the ninth win of the season and 33rd in a row, Paul Hatcher had what the *News Leader* called in its headline, "Another Milestone Victory." Hatcher coached his 900th game, a 69–22 win over Rockbridge County. It was the second-lowest point total by a Lee opponent since Hatcher took over, with only Spotswood scoring less, with twenty-one points in 1984. It was the lowest point total by an opponent since the three-point shot came into existence.

Nine hundred games into his career, Hatcher was still the master motivator. Walking out to the floor, Hatcher stopped Keary Bonner, Lee's senior guard and defensive whiz, and asked if he was up to the challenge of guarding Rockbridge's leading scorer, Marcus Mayo.

Following Keary Bonner's junior season, his dad, Dan Bonner, suggested his son build up his strength and conditioning and become a better defensive player.

"Dad would say, 'Keary, what are you going to be able to do on nights when you aren't shooting well, how are you going to help?' That was kind of our answer, the defensive stuff," said Bonner. "Looking back, lots of guys can kind of shoot it well, but [playing defense] kind of gave me...dug out a niche for me personally."

The advice wasn't just friendly fatherly advice. Dan Bonner knows his basketball. He played for the University of Virginia in the early 1970s with Wally Walker and Marc Iavaroni and, after graduating, took over as head coach of the UVA women's team, which had been varsity status for only a couple of years.

After two seasons in that position, Bonner resigned, and Debbie Ryan, who had been his assistant, replaced him. Bonner moved into broadcasting, first working Virginia games and eventually calling ACC basketball and even serving as a television analyst in the early rounds of the NCAA Tournament for CBS. It's a job he still holds.

In 1999, with the coaching itch evidently not quite scratched, Dan Bonner became the girls' basketball coach at Lee High, coaching games in the fall for four years while still broadcasting college basketball in the winter. As a coach, Dan Bonner had a key to the Paul Hatcher Gym. He would often accompany his son to the gym to run through drills. That's where Keary Bonner developed the skills that made him Lee's defensive stopper.

So when Paul Hatcher asked Bonner if he was up to the challenge of guarding Mayo, it set off something in the Lee senior.

"That made me so mad that he would say that to me," said Bonner. "I wanted to say, like, 'What do you mean? We've been crushing everybody. You put me on the other team's best guy every game and I always try my best, and now you're going to challenge me?'"

It worked, though. An angry Bonner, along with his teammates, didn't let Rockbridge get across halfcourt the first three possessions of the game. Bonner drew a charge the first time down against Mayo and then stole the ball from him on trip number two down the floor. Mayo didn't score until late in the third quarter and ended up with just seven points in the game.

"They never had a chance," said Bonner. "Looking back now, that's what Hatcher had to do. The only way we were going to lose to a team like Rockbridge was if we went out there and we weren't particularly motivated. I don't know if he thought maybe I was the weak link that game, but he lit a fire under me unlike…I don't know if I ever started [another] game and not let the guy I was guarding get back halfcourt three times in a row."

The numbers Hatcher had accumulated by that time, in his thirty-seventh year, were staggering. Through 900 games, the Lee coach had won 750. He had led his teams to twenty-eight regular season district titles, eighteen district tournament titles, eleven regional tournament titles, three state championships and four second-place finishes in the state.

Over the next sixteen games, including three Valley District Tournament contests, just two teams really challenged Lee High. The first one came a night after the win over Rockbridge when Lee played at Western Albemarle. Lee opened the season at home against the Warriors and won by thirty, but on the road, things were a little hairier. In fact, Lee trailed 44–40 late in the third quarter before putting together a 15–4 blitz and eventually winning 61–53.

The game gained attention more because of one play than the final score. Keary Bonner was on the wrong end of an opponent's elbow in the third quarter and got his nose broken. Lee High's athletic trainer gave Bonner a standard mask with pads across the cheekbones and forehead. The mask didn't help his peripheral vision. When he reentered the Western game, wearing the mask, he missed a wide-open layup, hitting the other side of the backboard.

Before Bonner's next game, he had a clear, plastic protective mask for his nose courtesy of North Carolina State. The night his son's nose was broken, Dan Bonner happened to be in Miami to call a game between the Hurricanes and North Carolina State. He mentioned the incident to the NC State athletic trainer, who let Bonner borrow a mask that Wolfpack player Engin Atsur had used when his nose was broken.

"Of course, it didn't fit at all," said Keary Bonner. "But it was clear, and it served the purpose of protecting my nose. It didn't have those big pads. I remember, though, that the lower strap would just dangle."

It took him a game to get used to wearing it, but by the second game after the injury, the shooting guard was on fire. He scored what was at that time a career-high eighteen points, including four three-pointers, in Lee's thirty-four-point win over Spotswood. He joked after the game that he hoped Atsur wouldn't need the mask back anytime soon because it might be a good-luck charm.

Two games later, Lee High played the closest game it would play the rest of the season when it beat Turner Ashby 63–60. It matched the three-point win over Harrisonburg in early January as the tightest game Lee played all season.

TA entered the game second in the Valley District standings, tied with Harrisonburg, two games behind Lee High. The Leemen actually led 20–8 early in the game and were up eight points at halftime. The Knights battled back, however, and got their deficit to one point early in the fourth quarter but could never tie the game. In the final seconds, TA's Andrew Armstrong missed a short jumper with his team down two, and Jason Jordan grabbed the rebound. Jordan hit a free throw with three seconds left, and Lee held on for the win.

The following Monday, to no one's surprise, Lee High was the top-ranked Group AA team in the Associated Press's debut poll for the season. Lee then went out and destroyed Stuarts Draft 79–32. Eli Crawford had twenty-one points, while Jordan finished with fourteen points and ten rebounds.

Over the final eight games of the regular season, Jordan stepped up his production. After averaging 11.4 points a game through the season's first fourteen games, Jordan averaged 15.6 points a game the rest of the regular season. In that eight-game stretch before the start of the playoffs, the two performances that stood out for Jordan were his 21 points and ten rebounds against Broadway and 25 points and eleven rebounds against Fort Defiance. He also stepped up defensively. In a win over Harrisonburg, in which Jordan scored 16 points, the Lee senior kept the Blue Streaks' star Justin German scoreless in the second half. After being a complement to Tyler Crawford the previous season, Jordan was becoming a star just at the time Lee was getting ready for another postseason run.

"We just liked the way he played," said Paul Hatcher. "He was just a tough kid, and he just played hard. He got better each year in his role and in what he could do. [He] rebounded, he could score, but he wasn't a flashy type of kid. He wasn't going to make some spectacular type of dunk. I mean, he did from time to time, but he just did those things—toughness, defensively, rebound. The kind of guy you've got to have on the team."

After the TA scare, no team came any closer than fifteen points against the Leemen to finish out the regular season. Harrisonburg, of course, was the team that got within fifteen, but even that game wasn't as close as the score indicated. Harrisonburg's Courtland Whitelow made a fatal flaw the day before the game by telling the *Daily News-Record* in Harrisonburg that "Lee don't stand a chance."

Whitelow gave his team a 3–0 lead, but Bonner answered with a three, and Lee went on a 10–0 run. The Leemen never trailed again. After the game, Ryan Crawford told the *News Leader* that Whitelow's comment "got us pumped." He also said that if someone makes those comments, they better be ready to back them up. Whitelow scored twenty-one points, but his team didn't do enough to help him back up his words.

Paul Hatcher didn't remember if he did so in that particular incident, but he did say from time to time he would put opponents' comments on the wall in the locker room for his players to read. Whether or not they were all comments actually said by opponents is up for debate.

"Let's be honest," said Jarrett. "We used to make up stuff. We'd do whatever we could to try to motivate them."

Paul Hatcher had five unbeaten regular seasons prior to the 2004–05 season, the last one coming in 1989–90. If Lee could beat the Miller School on February 11, Hatcher would have his sixth undefeated regular season; however, this one would be a step up from the other five. In 1980–81, Lee finished 18-0, and the next four times Lee was 20-0. In '04–'05, Lee played twenty-two regular season games and had won the first twenty-one as it got ready for Miller.

Miller is a private school in Crozet, a small community just west of Charlottesville. While Lee was the top-ranked Group AA team, Miller was number one in the Virginia Independent Schools Division II state poll. The game would help prepare Lee for the postseason. Paul Hatcher knew one issue his team had was size—or lack thereof. Just like the Australian team, Miller had some tall players. Plus, Lee was looking for games, and Hatcher heard Miller needed games, so he approached them about playing in Staunton.

"We weren't going over there in that little cracker box," said Hatcher. "But if they want to come to Staunton, we'll be glad to play them."

Lee jumped on the Devils right away, forcing nine first-quarter turnovers and jumping to a 22–8 lead. Eli Crawford led the way with twenty points, six assists and four steals in a 69–53 win. The win sent Lee into the postseason on a forty-six-game winning streak with the Valley District Tournament up next.

Lee won the Valley District Tournament with three easy victories, including a twenty-one-point win over Harrisonburg for the championship. Then the Leemen beat Handley by thirty-three points to open up the regional tournament. By that time, the streak was a very real thing, although more because Lee was closing in on its own record and less because of the state record, which was still sixteen games away. The Handley win gave Lee fifty wins in a row, two shy of Lee High's fifty-two consecutive wins from 1983 to 1985.

VALLEY TALENT POOL

Ralph Sampson ushered in a decade that many consider to be the best ever for high school basketball in the Shenandoah Valley of Virginia.

Sampson led Harrisonburg to back-to-back state championships in 1978 and 1979 and in the process became the most sought-after college recruit in the country. Because Lee was one of the few teams that could give Harrisonburg competitive games—beating the Blue Streaks twice in Sampson's junior year—recruiters tended to show up when those two teams played. Paul Hatcher remembers coaches from UCLA, Kansas, Kentucky and, of course, Virginia at games between the two teams.

"It was just exciting for everybody," said Hatcher.

The excitement kept on coming in the Shenandoah Valley.

Dell Curry led Fort Defiance to a state championship in 1980 as a sophomore and as a senior was named to the 1982 McDonald's All-American team, along with future University of North Carolina star Brad Daugherty and future Duke Blue Devil Johnny Dawkins. Curry also won a baseball state championship as a pitcher for Fort Defiance in his senior year and was drafted in the thirty-seventh round of the Major League Baseball draft by the Texas Rangers. Instead of signing with the Rangers, Curry took a scholarship offer from Virginia Tech, where he was named Metro Conference basketball player of the year in 1986. Then he spent sixteen years in the NBA, where he is still the Charlotte Hornets' all-time leading scorer.

About fifty miles north of Fort Defiance, the Lambiotte brothers—Kenny and Walker—were stars at Central High School in Woodstock. Kenny's team lost to Curry and Fort Defiance in the 1980 state title game. Kenny then signed with the University of Virginia and played on the Cavaliers team that was upset by Chaminade. He eventually transferred to William & Mary to play football.

His younger brother, Walker, played for Jimmy Valvano at North Carolina State before transferring to Northwestern. He was a McDonald's All-American in 1985, along with future college stars Sean Elliott (Arizona), Danny Ferry (Duke) and Pervis Ellison (Louisville).

"For basketball fans during that period of time, it couldn't get any better than that," said Paul Hatcher.

Harrisonburg even produced another star, Pee Wee Barber, who played at Florida State and, in 1987, was drafted by the Portland Trailblazers. Hatcher maintains that Barber was more difficult for his defense to contain than Sampson.

"Ralph's going to be underneath the basket," said Hatcher. "We can put five guys around him if we want to so he can't move a whole lot. But Pee Wee…we went down there late in the year [1982–83], we were like 13-0 or something like that, and [Pee Wee] got forty. We were only giving up like forty-two points a game and Pee Wee got forty by himself."

Hatcher had his own star during that span. His wife was actually the first to spot him. Judy Hatcher was a long-term substitute teacher at Thomas Jefferson Elementary School when she saw a fifth grader playing basketball. She came home and told her husband that she had seen the best player he would ever coach at Lee High. She was right.

Kevin Madden finished his career at Lee High as the school's all-time leading scorer—and, as of 2015, is eighteenth in the Virginia High School League—with 2,236 points. He also started his career with an impressive

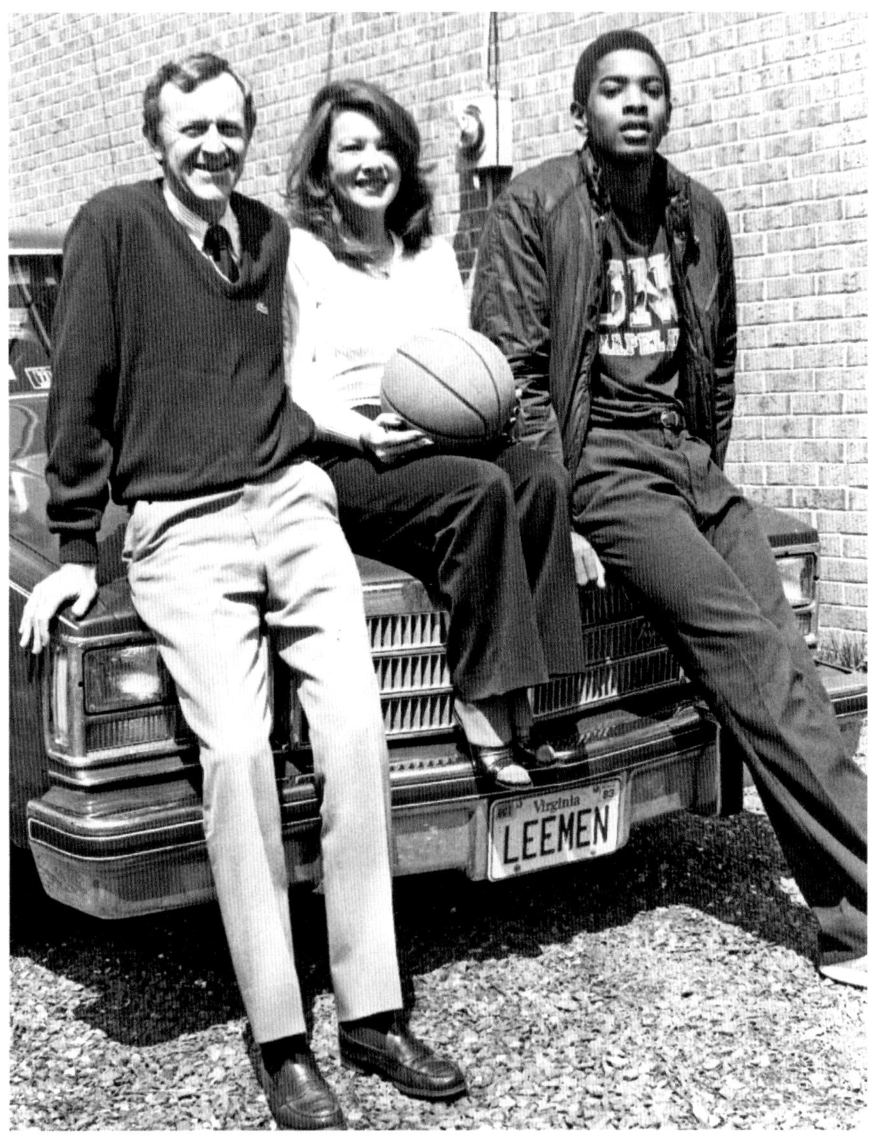

Paul and Judy Hatcher and Kevin Madden take a break on the hood of the Hatchers' 1970 Buick Regal. *Paul Hatcher's collection.*

effort, scoring 26 points and pulling down thirteen rebounds in his first varsity game as a freshman in 1981. In between, Madden led the Leemen to a 93-8 record, three state tournament berths and the 1984 state championship.

"Watching my brother Mike play, I was always intrigued with wanting to play for Coach Hatcher and wanting to be as good as Mike," said Madden.

Hatcher admits there was extra pressure coaching a player the magnitude of Madden. Not only are you expected to win, but there's also the recruiting aspect. Madden was rated the top recruit in the country by the Blue Ribbon College Basketball Yearbook and, according to Hatcher, received hundreds of recruiting letters. Hatcher offered to handle the letters and phone calls for Madden, shielding his player from the recruiting process as much as possible so he could focus on playing.

Sports Illustrated even sent a writer working on a story about college recruiting to Hatcher's home in Staunton to discuss the pursuit of Madden. The writer asked to see some of the recruiting letters, but the Lee coach refused, saying that if a coach wrote something personal to Madden, he didn't want it splashed across the pages of a magazine.

In Madden's sophomore year, Hatcher attended a basketball game at the University of Virginia when the Cavaliers played Duke. Mike Krzyzewski had just become the Duke head coach in 1980, so he was still in the process of building the powerhouse program that Duke eventually became. Duke was no match for Ralph Sampson and Virginia that particular evening in Charlottesville, with the Cavaliers winning 105–84.

After the game, Hatcher decided to pay one of his high school friends a visit. The friend had moved to Charlottesville and bought several Mister Donuts franchises. As the two old friends were sitting in one of the stores and catching up with each other, a charter bus pulled up between the store and the Arby's restaurant next door. The Duke players got off the bus and went to Arby's, but Krzyzewski came into the doughnut shop.

"I was thinking, 'He's in bad shape. He doesn't look good.' And I know how he feels," said Hatcher. "He wanted to get away from everybody. I would have done the same thing."

Krzyzewski had already inquired about Madden, so Hatcher thought he should introduce himself to the Duke coach. Hatcher had talked to members of the Duke staff on the telephone but had never spoken with or met Krzyzewski in person. Hatcher doesn't remember what the two talked about that night, but he did get a nice letter from Krzyzewski referencing the conversation the following week.

"Every time I see them anymore, they're at the top," said Hatcher. "They've been there, and he's won gold medals and everything else and championships. But I think back to that day. That was probably one of his lowest points. Sitting at a Mister Donuts after he just got killed by Virginia."

When Hatcher talks to his young athletes, he often emphasizes that no matter how bad things are or how low they feel, they can work to change things. He uses Krzyzewski as an example. The coach went from that point in his career to winning more games than any Division I men's college basketball coach in history and guiding his teams to five national championships.

That same year, then Virginia assistant coach Jim Larranaga, who is now the head coach at Miami, attended a Lee High game against Wilson Memorial and, afterward, invited Madden, his coach and a few other members of the Lee High family to Charlottesville the next night to see Virginia play.

Madden was excited, but not about seeing the Cavaliers. He wanted to see their opponent, the University of North Carolina. Madden was a Tar Heel fan. He had been since seeing a photo of Dudley Bradley dunking the ball on the cover of *Sports Illustrated* in March 1979, following North Carolina's win over Duke in the ACC Tournament.

Madden's mom liked North Carolina's coach, Dean Smith, after seeing him coach against Georgetown in the 1982 NCAA National Championship game. She told her son that if he ever had a chance to play for Smith, he should do it. Madden agreed. Unfortunately for Madden, at that point in his career, Carolina was one of the few schools that hadn't offered him a scholarship.

After the game, which North Carolina won 101–95, Madden visited the Virginia locker room, but then he and Jarrett Hatcher, along with a few others, found the North Carolina locker room. Carolina assistant coach Eddie Fogler met them at the door and said everyone could come in but Madden. He was there as Virginia's guest, and it wouldn't be right, he explained. Jarrett was in sixth grade at the time and remembers telling Madden, "See you later," as he went in the locker room and got autographs, including one from Dean Smith.

"You know how hard it is when you're [that young] and somebody tells you, 'no,'" said Madden

Fogler called Paul Hatcher the next day, a Sunday, and explained that they didn't want to upset Madden, and they were planning on recruiting him, but told the coach it wouldn't have been right to let a guest of Virginia in the Carolina locker room. To this day, that impresses Hatcher. He said Carolina was above board in everything they did while recruiting Madden.

Madden committed to Carolina after his sophomore year but couldn't sign until he was a senior. Hatcher made it clear to his player that, if he committed early, he couldn't back out. Madden promised he wouldn't and eventually carried through with his pledge, signing with the Tar Heels. That's one of the reasons the recruiting battle over Madden never got too intense, although some schools, like Virginia, did keep pursuing the Lee player even after he committed.

Growing up, Paul Hatcher was a fan of both North Carolina and Virginia Tech, listening to games on radio stations out of Greensboro, North Carolina, and Roanoke, Virginia, both cities about forty-five minutes from his home in Bassett Forks.

"I didn't even know Charlottesville existed," Hatcher said of the home of the University of Virginia.

So when Carolina became interested in Madden, it pleased Hatcher. He was more than happy to accompany his star player on an unofficial visit to Chapel Hill, going to a football game against Clemson and the basketball team's intra-squad scrimmage—the Blue-White game—in the fall of Madden's junior season.

Hatcher remembers sitting in North Carolina coach Dean Smith's office that day and seeing former Carolina coach Frank McGuire. By that time, Smith had already won his first of two national championships two years earlier. McGuire led North Carolina to a 32-0 season and the national championship in 1957. Carolina beat Wilt Chamberlain and Kansas that year 54–53 in a triple-overtime final.

"I regret to this day not getting a picture with those guys," said Hatcher. "I would have never asked, but I wish there was some way…we didn't even think. I was in awe really. That's one of the highlights of my whole career."

Things just kept getting better, though. North Carolina junior Michael Jordan was the next player to walk in the office. Smith asked Jordan to take Jarrett and Brandon Hatcher to meet the team. Jarrett remembers Jordan bought two bags of Peanut M&Ms for the Hatcher boys. Jarrett ate one and kept one, which he still has to this day.

Madden said it wasn't that big of a deal for him. The previous summer, he had attended the North Carolina basketball camp and got a chance to play with Jordan, Sam Perkins, Al Wood, Kenny Smith and other Tar Heel greats.

"I knew them, and they were real nice to be around and fun to talk to and things like that," said Madden. "It felt like family. It felt like being at Lee High."

Before the football game with Clemson, the Hatchers and Madden all went to a tailgate with some boosters whom Smith introduced them to, but there was one stipulation: the visitors from Staunton had to pay for the food. Carolina couldn't give a recruit anything for free because it wasn't an official visit.

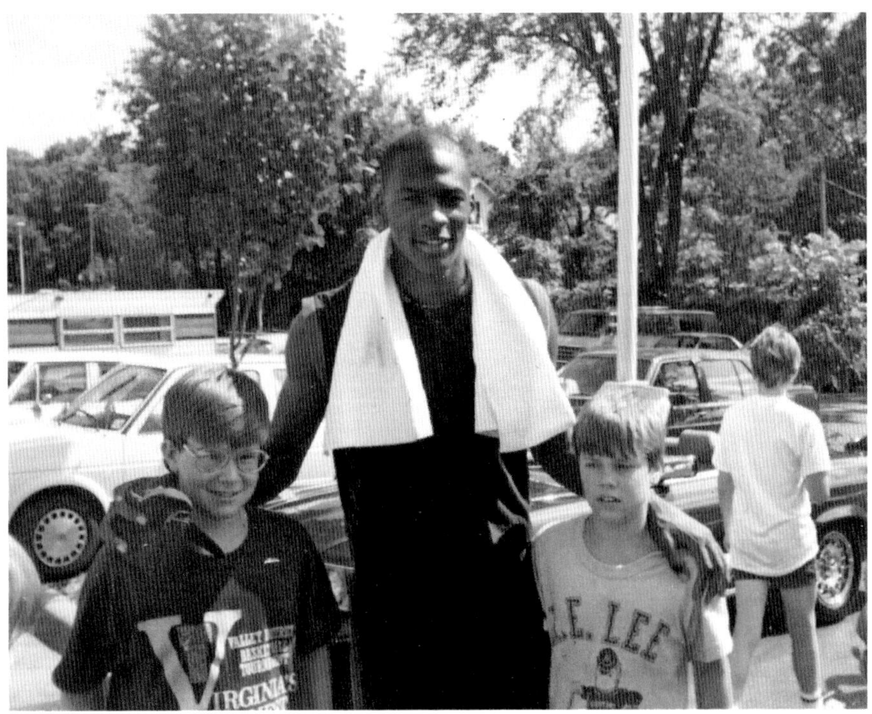

Jarrett and Brandon Hatcher got a chance to catch up with NBA Rookie of the Year Michael Jordan at the Carolina Basketball School in the summer of 1985. *Paul Hatcher's collection.*

"That just impressed the heck out of me," said Paul Hatcher. "They didn't have to do that. Nobody was going to know if the Hatchers and Kevin were at a tailgate out there in the parking lot of the football stadium."

After football and basketball, the Hatchers and Madden all went to a postgame meal at Granville Towers, off-campus apartments for North Carolina students. Jarrett and Brandon sat with Michael Jordan and his parents. Both were so nervous that they remember Jordan's mom cutting Jarrett's steak and Jordan's dad cutting Brandon's.

Paul Hatcher remembers fans of the University of North Carolina driving in from the Tar Heel State just to see Madden play. The *News & Record* in Greensboro, North Carolina, sent a reporter to cover the Lee High–Central Woodstock game because Madden was going to Carolina and Walker Lambiotte was headed to North Carolina State. Every game that Lee played with Madden, especially his final two seasons, seemed like a big game.

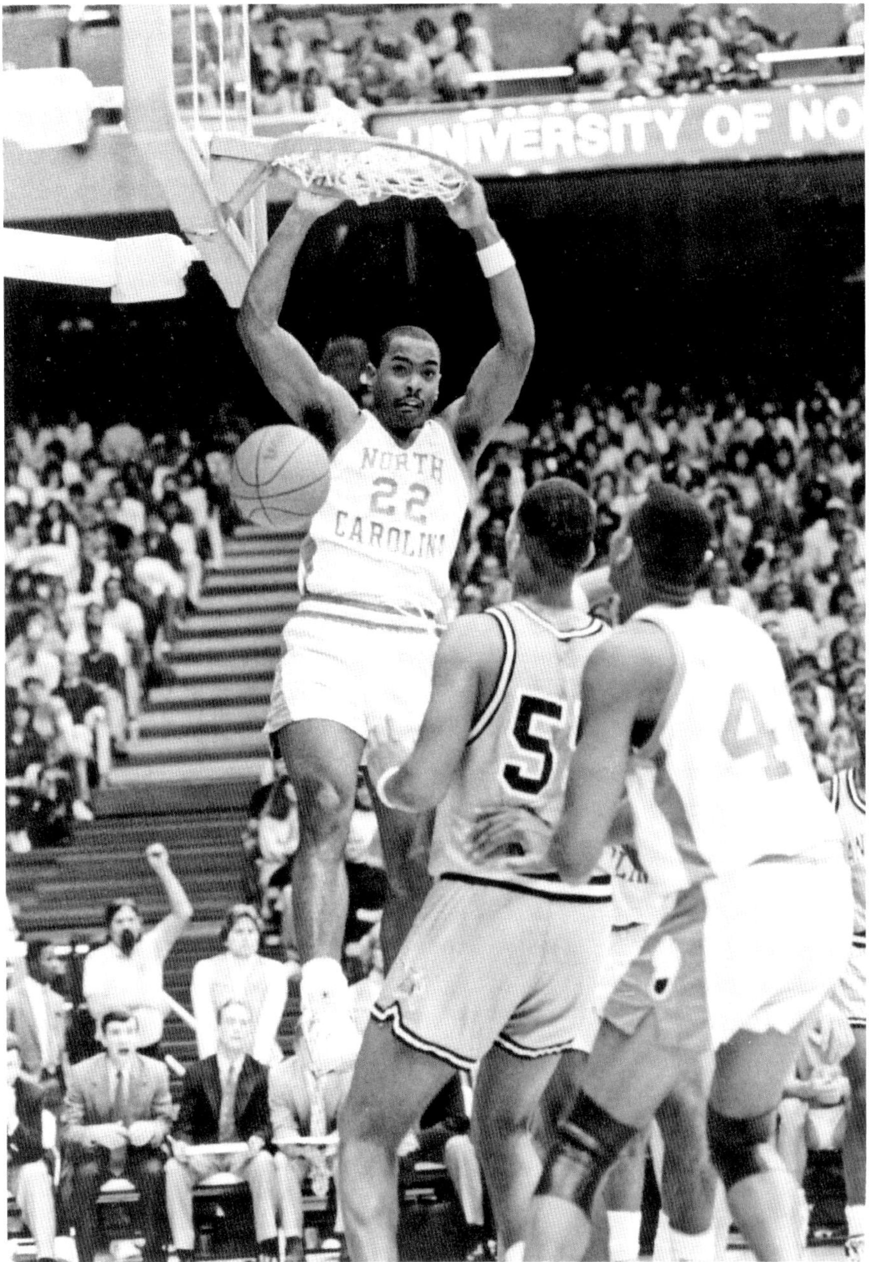

Kevin Madden finished his career at the University of North Carolina with 1,296 points, fortieth on the school's all-time scoring list as of the 2014–15 season. *Photo courtesy of UNC Athletic Communications.*

"As a coach, just like the players and the fans, you get excited about that," said Hatcher. "That's what you like to be. You don't like to be playing games that don't mean anything."

Kevin Madden finally signed his letter of intent at the bar in Paul Hatcher's house. He was officially a Tar Heel. "There was a backlash against Kevin for going to Carolina," said Jarrett Hatcher, who remembered how upset Virginia fans were at what they perceived to be Madden turning his back on the local school. None of that bothered Madden.

"I didn't worry about that," he said. "I did what was best for me and not worry about if somebody else likes Virginia or JMU or Virginia Tech. I didn't have

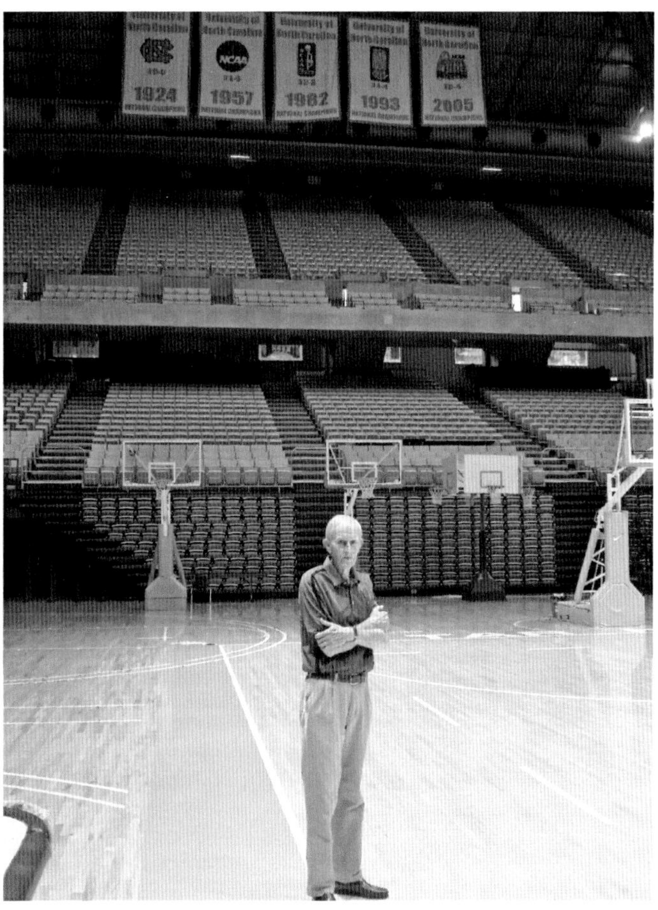

Paul Hatcher has not only been on the floor at the Dean E. Smith Center but also, over the years, has developed a relationship with the building's late namesake. *Photo by Brandon Hatcher.*

anything against those schools, but you've got to make a decision what's best for you and where you feel comfortable. For me, I made the best decision."

With Madden signing at Carolina, Hatcher developed a relationship with Dean Smith. One of the Lee coach's favorite stories is about a basketball clinic in Chapel Hill that Paul and Judy Hatcher attended. It happened to be Judy's fortieth birthday, and Carolina assistant Eddie Fogler found out and told Dean Smith. The Carolina coach called and invited the Hatchers out for dinner. The Hatchers remember that it was a French restaurant and that they didn't have to wait in line. Dean Smith was a legend in Chapel Hill. He, his wife and the Hatchers walked right in and sat down.

"It wasn't a real comfortable feeling," said Paul Hatcher. "You know, all of a sudden, to be sitting there and everybody's staring at you. 'There's Coach Smith and who's that idiot with him?'"

Hatcher doesn't remember much of the conversation. He was too nervous. "I was just trying to figure out which fork to use," said Hatcher, who, over the coming years, received Christmas cards and letters from Smith. The Carolina coach even sent Hatcher an autographed copy of his book.

That connection between the Hatchers and North Carolina also continued. Brandon Hatcher's college roommate had played high school basketball with Dante Calabria, who went on to play at North Carolina from 1992 to 1996. Brandon remembers his roommate saying he could get them tickets for a Tar Heels' game whenever he needed, but when he tried for a game once, he was unsuccessful. Brandon called his dad and said they wanted tickets for the North Carolina–North Carolina State game. The next day, someone in the ticket office called and said they had four tickets for the game.

"Dad won't tell you this," said Brandon. "But they loved Dad. Coach Smith [and his assistants] were after him every year to come down and play golf with them, hang out with them, and he never would do it because he felt like he was imposing on them."

The Madden Years

Before he went off to Chapel Hill, Madden accomplished plenty in Staunton, although for some maybe it wasn't enough.

"Everybody expects you to win," said Paul Hatcher. "Maybe you should. We got there three times, and we only won once, so maybe we didn't do a very good job with Kevin."

Lee lost a one-point game in the state semifinals of Madden's sophomore year, falling in overtime to John F. Kennedy 53–52. Kennedy couldn't guard Madden, fouling him time after time as he went to the basket. The downfall for Lee was Madden finished ten of twenty-two at the foul line.

Hatcher admits that Kennedy was probably a better team, but he also feels that Lee should have won. Lee went up one in overtime with twelve seconds remaining. Kennedy took a timeout to set up the final play.

"They take the worst shot that you could possibly take," said Hatcher. "The guy comes across halfcourt, and there are still a few seconds left and he throws up a jumper from halfcourt almost. Worst shot in the world."

The "worst shot in the world" hit the back of the rim and bounced toward another Kennedy player, who grabbed the rebound at the top of key and hit the shot at the buzzer for the win. Kennedy beat Martinsville for the state title by twenty.

"With Lee basketball, you always—at least with me—you always expected something bad to happen in the state tournament," said the *News Leader*'s former sports editor Hubert Grim III. "That was their MO. When you got to the state tournament, the bad juju was going to come out somewhere, somehow, at the most inopportune time."

It's losses like the one to Kennedy and the other close ones in state tournament play that make Paul Hatcher sometimes think that life would be much better if everything just stopped at the district tournament. That way, according to Hatcher, you'd have a lot of champions.

"You win the district, you win the region and then you get beat by somebody throwing something in at the buzzer," said Hatcher. "You go home, and it just spoiled the whole season. Hey, just stop at the district. 'I'm sorry. We don't want to go. We're not going any further.' Just think how many people would go home happy."

The next season, though, made Hatcher realize why ending the season at the district level would be a bad idea. Having committed to North Carolina, Madden led Lee High to a 27-0 record and the state championship, Paul Hatcher's first, in 1984.

Madden said the loss to Kennedy motivated the returning players.

"We said, 'We're going to come back, we're going to mean business next year,'" said Madden. "The thing that helped us so much is that, in the offseason, most of the guys played together in pickup, AAU we played together. The more time you spend with your team that you're going to play with the next year, you become a better team."

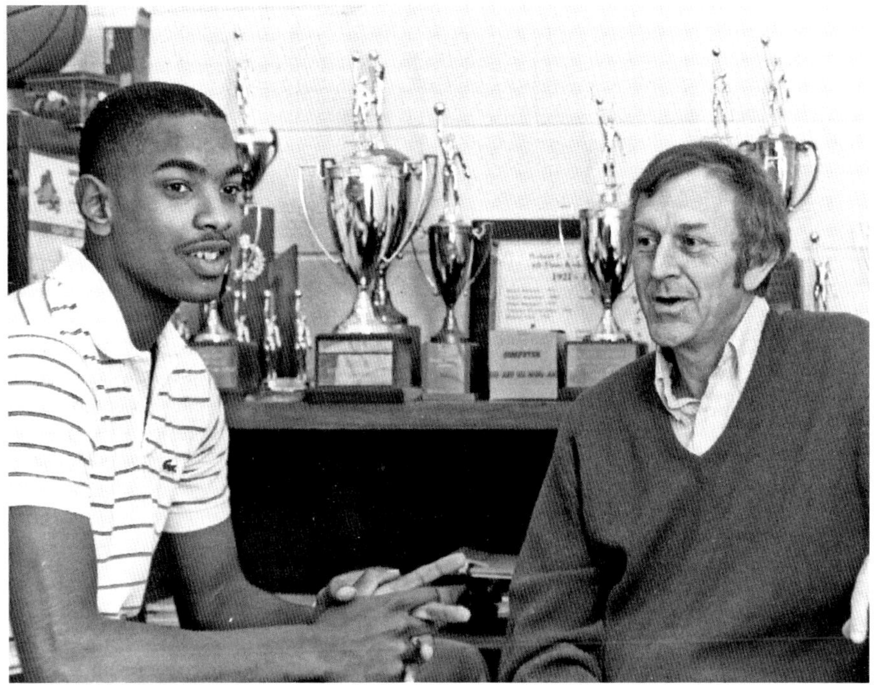

Kevin Madden helped Paul Hatcher win his first state championship in 1984. *Paul Hatcher's collection.*

There were a few close games, but not many during Madden's junior season. Jamie Taylor, Michael Toye, Kirk Gray and Henry Ritchie were the other starters.

"We had a really good group of complementary guys," said Hatcher. "They didn't have a lot of hangups or whatever. They knew Kevin was the man, but they knew the other people were going to be trying to stop him, and they had to pick up the slack. It was just a really good group."

Paul Hatcher told his other players before the season that more would be written about Madden and more photos would be taken of Madden. He told them to be glad he was on their team and to do what they could to help him. They did.

Lee beat George Wythe from Wytheville, Virginia, 62–51 in the Group AA state semifinals and won the championship with an 81–70 win over Martinsville. *USA Today* ranked the Leemen number twelve in the newspaper's listing of the top high school programs in the nation that season.

The next season, Lee lost four of five starters off that state championship team, but the one starter who was back was Madden. Lee won twenty-five

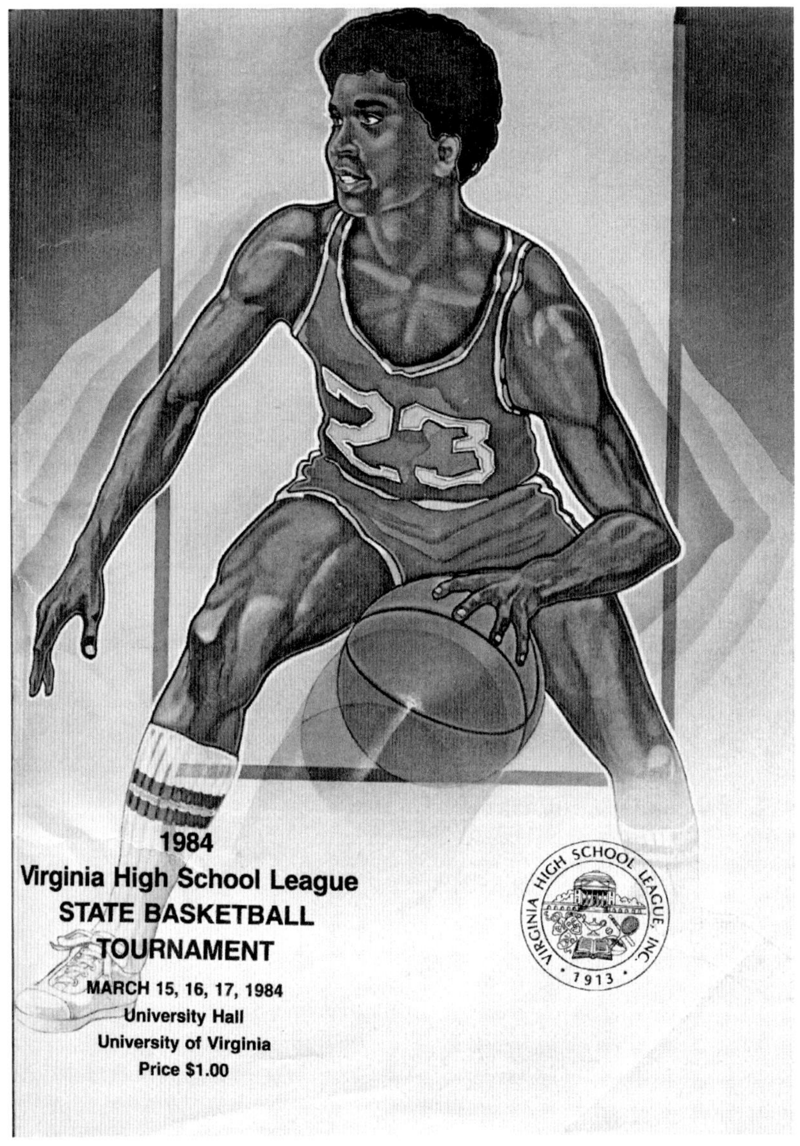

Lee High won the 1984 VHSL state tournament, the school's third and Paul Hatcher's first title. *Paul Hatcher's collection.*

games in a row to start the next season, setting a school record with fifty-two wins in a row.

Two of the more interesting games Lee played during Madden's senior year came against Long Island Lutheran from New York, a team coached by Bob McKillop, who is now the head coach at Davidson. The team was headed to Greensboro, North Carolina, to play Danny Manning and Page High School. The team stopped in Staunton both on the way to and from North Carolina, losing both times to Lee High.

"They were supposedly the champs of something up in New York," said Paul Hatcher, prompting laughter from his son.

"That sounds so Mayberryish," said Jarrett, who then turned on his best southern accent. "Supposedly the champs of something up there in New York."

Marco Baldi was the star of Long Island Lutheran. The six-foot-eleven center eventually signed with St. John's, choosing his hometown school over Southern California and Maryland. Hatcher said the games against Baldi and Long Island Lutheran were reminiscent of Harrisonburg games when Ralph Sampson was playing.

The fifty-two-game winning streak came to an end with a 62–61 loss to Martinsville in the 1985 Group AA state semifinals. People still tell Hatcher it's the best high school basketball game they've ever seen. It wouldn't be the last time Martinsville ended a Lee High winning streak.

7
Back-to-Back

Win number fifty-one wasn't an easy one to get for the 2004–05 squad. Jarrett Hatcher says the barrier games are always the most difficult. Those are the games that, if you win, you earn a berth in the next stage of the postseason. If you lose those games, your season is done.

The Region II semifinal between Lee High and Potomac Falls was just such a game. The winner not only would play for the regional championship but would also earn an automatic berth in the state tournament since both teams in the regional championship would advance. The losing players would turn their gear in for the season.

Before the game, Chris Lassiter, a sports writer with the *News Leader* and a former point guard for Lee High, wrote a column comparing the two programs. He started by listing the biggest basketball wins in Lee High's history, and it was a long list. He included, of course, the state championships under Paul Hatcher in 1984, 1990 and 2004. He also listed the two wins in 1985 over Long Island Lutheran. He mentioned the first basketball win in school history in 1926 and the state titles that came before Hatcher took over as coach, when Lee won it all in 1931 and 1967. There was also a win in 1970 over defending state champion Jefferson Senior to claim a regional championship.

Then he listed the most significant win for Potomac Falls. Lassiter didn't have to search through a long history—the school opened in 1997. And he didn't have to list all the big wins; instead, he just used the words of Jeff Hawes, Potomac Falls coach. Hawes told a *Loudoun Times-Mirror* reporter that the 68–63 win over Charlottesville—the win that advanced Potomac Falls to the game against Lee High—was the biggest in school history.

Of course, when the two teams played at James Madison University's Convocation Center on Friday night, February 25, 2005, it didn't matter that one program had too many significant wins to choose just one as the biggest and the other program had just one win that qualified as biggest. Potomac Falls gave Lee everything it could handle, leading for a lot of the game and trailing by just three, 71–68, with the ball in the final minute.

With 27.9 seconds left, though, Lee forced a turnover, and Ryan Crawford scored his first two points of the night from the foul line. Lee held on for a 74–68 win. Years later, Jarrett Hatcher asked his dad what he thought was the play of the game.

"When the buzzer went off and we were up six," Paul Hatcher answered.

Eli Crawford matched his career high with twenty-seven points in the win. The Lee junior had clearly stepped out of the large shadow cast by his cousin Tyler Crawford the year before. The season may have started with fans wondering if this team had a star player, but by this point in the postseason, Eli Crawford had emerged as the leader of the team.

Paul Hatcher said the Potomac Falls game was really the first big pressure situation his team had faced without Tyler Crawford, but Lee was never about stars. It was about playing basketball the Paul Hatcher way. If they did that, wins would come more often than not. That didn't mean stars didn't help. Hatcher said the years he did have a true superstar—Kevin Madden, Reggie Waddy, Tyler Crawford—he certainly wanted to make the most of their talents.

"They had to do more in critical situations," Hatcher said of his stars. "We wanted the ball in their hands. But other than that, we just run the offense. We don't know who's going to get the shot."

Next up was Millbrook in the regional championship game. Lee had earned a berth in the state tournament already, but there were two important reasons to beat Millbrook. First, the loser would have to go on the road for the state quarterfinal game, while the winner would get to play a game close to home, although the Virginia High School League didn't allow that game to be played on the winner's home court. Hatcher knew the hazards of traveling and told the *News Leader* after the win over Potomac Falls that his team needed to take care of business in the regional championship.

The second reason, and one less important to Hatcher and the players but still of significance, was a win would mark the fifty-second in a row, tying the Lee High school record. Throughout the three-year run, the streak always seemed more important to the media than the team. The players and coaches wanted something else.

"It was a bunch of typical goofy high schoolers who won [eighty-five straight games] and just having a blast while doing it," said Jim Sacco, who was then the sports editor of the *News Virginian*, Waynesboro's daily newspaper. "They weren't even worried about, and they may tell you differently, but I never got the impression they were worried one bit about that streak. They were just worried about a state championship."

Keary Bonner agreed.

"I don't ever remember anyone saying this is number thirty-six or anything like that," said Bonner. "Obviously when you got into the postseason, it was always so important to win, it didn't matter how many games we had won. We had to get to the regional championship and win in the first round of the states and that kind of thing."

Lee matched the school winning streak with an easy 72–48 win over Millbrook in the Region II championship game at JMU's Convocation Center. A 23–4 second-quarter run by Lee ended any doubt about how Lee would respond after struggling to win the game before. Paul Hatcher and his team could now turn their full attention to the state tournament.

As it turned out, the road to another state championship was, as Jarrett Hatcher described it, "murderers' row." Lee's path would end up going through Brunswick, Martinsville and Greensville County. Combined, the three had played in thirty-eight final fours and had won fifteen state championships coming into that season. Lee High, however, had been in its share of final fours and state championships as well. It would be a highly entertaining state tournament for the fans, no doubt. Entertaining probably isn't the way Paul Hatcher viewed his path, but another state championship was within his grasp. Three more wins, and he'd have that fourth title.

GIVING HIM A CHANCE

As a high school freshman, Paul Hatcher made the Bassett jayvee team, but then again, almost everyone did. He was on the fifth string and got to dress for home games only. Since the team had just fifteen home uniforms, the last ten players, including Hatcher, had to wear away uniforms.

"If you're sitting on the bench with the wrong color jersey on, you know you're probably not going to get in the game," said Hatcher.

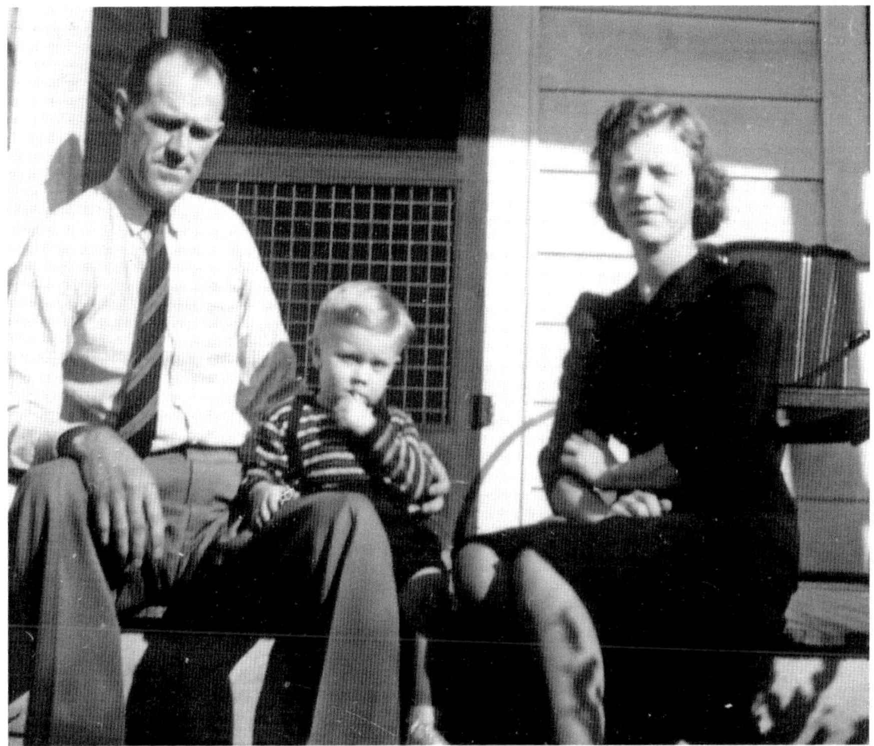

Paul Hatcher remembers a happy childhood in Bassett Forks with his parents, W.T. and Vilma Hatcher. *Paul Hatcher's collection.*

He worked hard at his game, though, and had moved up to second-string jayvee by his sophomore season, allowing him to wear a home uniform at home and travel to away games. By his junior year, he became a starter on the varsity in the third game of the season. His hard work was paying off.

"If I wanted to do something about it, I had to do something about it," said Hatcher. "My parents didn't go complain to the principal that they needed more uniforms and all that nonsense that someone would do today."

In fact, Hatcher's parents, W.T. and Vilma, seldom went to their son's basketball games, and they never pushed him into playing sports. W.T. worked for DuPont before quitting—a move Paul Hatcher thinks his dad regretted for the rest of his life. W.T. always advised his son to get a job and keep it, and Paul must have listened, teaching and coaching at Lee High for forty-three years.

What W.T. spent most of his adult life doing was gambling and running moonshine, although he did own three car lots and a restaurant in Martinsville.

W.T.'s brother, who was known as Peg, ended up serving two years in federal prison as part of the Franklin County Moonshine Conspiracy Trials. When the grandkids asked W.T. what he did for a living, he'd tell them he worked in corn.

"The Hatchers were very heavily involved in the Franklin County moonshine business," said Jarrett.

Even Paul Hatcher's aunt Lilly, his mom's sister, whom Jarrett always thought was a pious woman, was involved. After she passed away, Jarrett remembers hearing what others said about her.

"They all talked about Lilly, 'Lilly's so good, Lilly's so wonderful, it's a shame about Lilly,'" said Jarrett. "Then you start hearing, 'Well, she made the best moonshine in Franklin County.'"

Paul Hatcher's dad died on February 19, 1983. It was a Saturday, and the funeral was two days later. The Valley District tournament was supposed to start on that Tuesday, so after the funeral, there was Paul Hatcher, on Monday night, leading his team in practice.

"[Their grandfather's death] hit the children really hard, but…[Paul] had to go on," said Judy Hatcher. "There are certain responsibilities that he had to meet, and he didn't want to turn it over to anybody else."

Paul Hatcher never missed a practice or game in his coaching career, although he came close a few times. During the 1984–85 season, Hatcher had an abscessed tooth before a game. He arranged with a dentist, Dr. James R. Cooke Jr., to take the tooth out after the game. The dentist told him not to move on the bench, so Paul sat in his chair throughout. He had another abscessed tooth in 2002 before a game with Broad Run. Paul Hatcher sat on the bench, again not moving, while Jarrett did most of the coaching.

Perhaps the closest the coach came to missing a practice was in 1994. He had suffered chest pains during the day at school. He refused to call the rescue squad, instead asking Judy to take him to the emergency room. Paul called Jarrett and asked him to go run the practice.

Jarrett got the players in a circle and started telling them that his dad was in the hospital, and he didn't know what was happening. Jarrett was worried, but his dad had asked him to do a job, and he was going to do it. Then, in walks Paul. He had checked himself out of the hospital and made his way to the gym. He doesn't remember what he told the doctors that made them release him.

"I guess I told them, 'I've got practice,'" said Hatcher.

Turned out, the chest pains were indigestion. Hatcher thinks it was because he ate a Hershey's Whatchamacallit candy bar earlier that day. He hasn't eaten one since.

Paul Hatcher regrets that his dad didn't live long enough to see him win a state championship. That would come a little over a year after W.T. passed away. Hatcher still remembers his dad wearing a "Leemen No. 1" baseball cap.

"He was just the best person in the world," Judy said of her father-in-law.

Hatcher's love of sports came from his sister. Joyce Hatcher Greenwood, who was seven and a half years older than Paul, was the leading scorer in every basketball game she played except one at Bassett High School. Her love of the game led Paul to feel the same way about basketball.

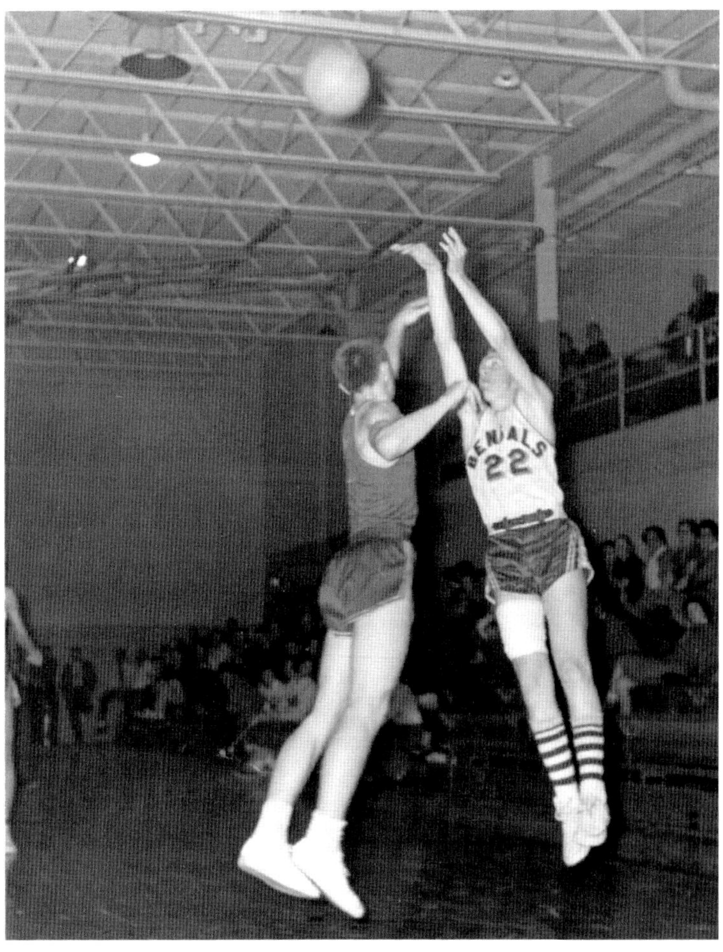

Paul Hatcher played high school basketball for the Bassett Bengals. *Paul Hatcher's collection.*

Between Hatcher's junior and senior years, a community center was built in Bassett, complete with a swimming pool, bowling alley and, of course, a basketball gym.

"I never went to the swimming pool one time," said Hatcher. "I never went to the bowling alley. I went to that gym every day. All those people I passed along the way from being fifth string, you know—they were up in the stands or sitting on the bench or whatever."

Hatcher took a lot of his coaching style from his high school coach, Jim Akers, who was very much a disciplinarian. Hatcher said you didn't want to screw up around Akers. He feared his coach but also respected him.

"Fear was okay," said Hatcher. "That's what's wrong today. There's no fear. There's no fear. I think you have to have a little bit of that."

Lee's players felt that fear. Jason Jordan said it was a privilege playing for Paul Hatcher, but that didn't mean there were a lot of warm fuzzies flowing through the gym. He called it both scary and exciting to play for the legendary coach.

"There were times he would just look at you, stare at you, and you kind of choke up," said Jordan.

Hatcher was good enough as a senior that he made honorable mention all-state. He even got a look from Wake Forest when the school's coach, Bones McKinney, came and watched him play, but Hatcher said he had a poor game and never really had a shot at playing for Wake.

Instead, Hatcher ended up at Bridgewater College, where he had a very successful basketball career. He was a two-time All-Virginia Little Eight and All-Mason-Dixon Conference selection and finished with 1,358 points, averaging just over 16 points a game. He finished third in the state of Virginia in scoring his senior year.

When Jarrett Hatcher went to Bridgewater, he remembers several people telling him how good of a player his dad was. An assistant chaplain told him that, when he was a little boy, his parents would bring him to Bridgewater to watch Paul Hatcher play. And a woman who worked in the cafeteria at Bridgewater told Jarrett that his dad was the best basketball player she had ever seen.

Judy Hatcher compared Paul to Andrew Rowsey, who starred at Rockbridge County High School before signing at North Carolina–Asheville and transferring to Marquette. Jarrett said he always assumed his dad played like Brian Bocock, a Turner Ashby star who caused the Hatchers and Lee High lots of headaches in the early 2000s.

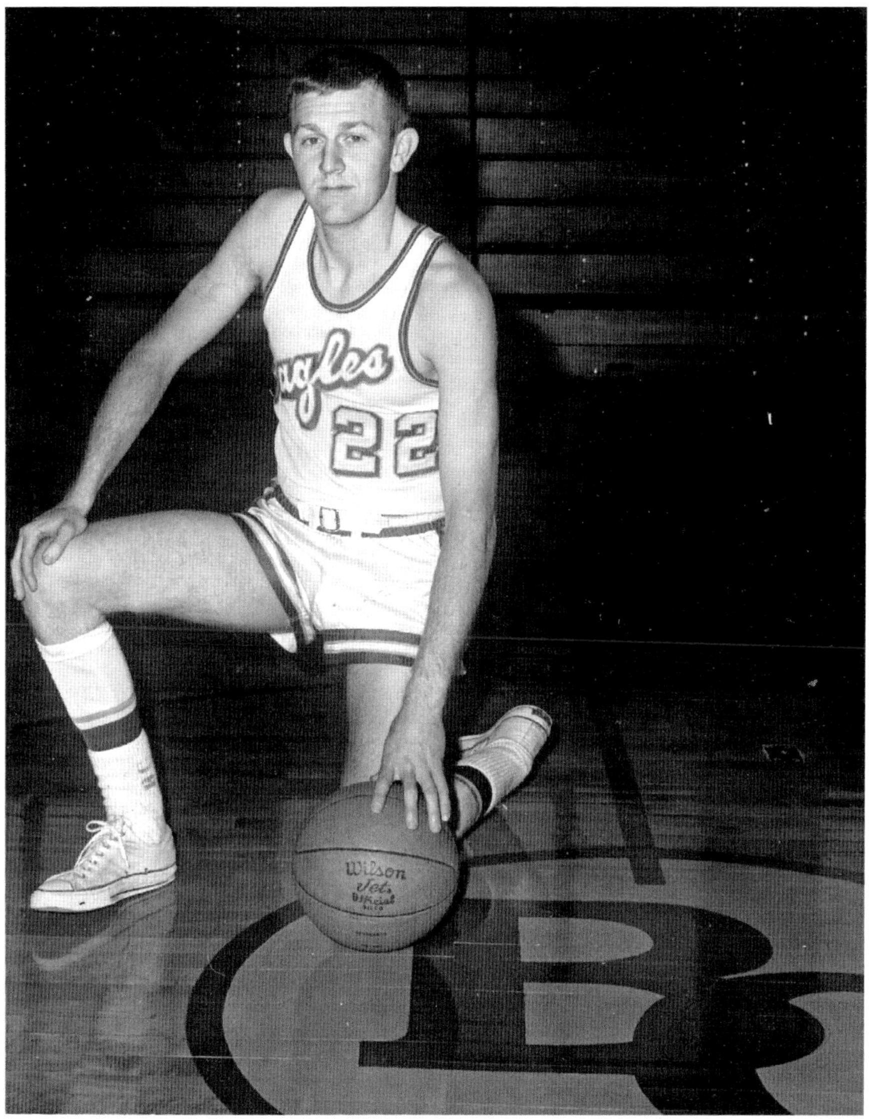

Paul scored 1,358 points in his playing career at Bridgewater College. *Paul Hatcher's collection.*

"I liked the way they played," said Paul Hatcher. "They were probably more athletic than I was. The herky-jerky kind of thing because you're not going to out-quick anybody."

Perhaps the most amusing story to come out of Hatcher's college career was a game against Guilford. Dave Odom, who later served as an assistant at Virginia and then head coach at Wake Forest and South Carolina, played for Guilford.

Hatcher and Odom had been involved in a physical game throughout. Odom even stood on Hatcher's foot at the foul line so Hatcher couldn't jump. Hatcher retaliated by grabbing Odom's jersey. Odom started swinging his fists as he took off after Hatcher, and the two ran behind the scorer's table. Odom was ejected.

Almost twenty years later, Odom showed up at Lee High recruiting Kevin Madden for Virginia. That night, when the Hatchers got home from the game, Judy turned to her sons and said, "Oh my God, that guy who was there today, he tried to punch your father."

Hatcher managed to avoid fisticuffs the rest of his college career, graduating in 1966, marrying Judy in June of that year and getting a job teaching in Staunton. He started a junior high team that first year and scheduled two games, but the team played just one before the school board cancelled the second one and disbanded the team.

After that first year teaching and having his team disbanded, Hatcher had his doubts he would ever be a head coach in Staunton. He calculated that he was fourth in line to coach and looked into a job in Southampton, even going as far as visiting the school to inquire about an opening. Hatcher doesn't remember if he ever actually applied, but he remained in Staunton. For that, Lee High fans can be grateful.

The following year, 1966–67, Lee High basketball won a state championship, beating Northside 88–58 for the Class 1B title. Coach Milnes Austin left after that season to coach football at Waynesboro High School. The jayvee coach, Al Hamilton, also left to take an administrative job at Lee High. Austin's assistant, Delmer Botkin, was named varsity coach at Lee but wanted the job for only a year. Paul Hatcher got the jayvee job for the 1967–68 year

Tom "Mouse" Patterson was on Hatcher's junior high team and, by the next year, had moved up to jayvee, once again playing for Hatcher.

"In those younger days, he was what you'd call a mentor on how to play basketball," Patterson recalled more than forty years after playing for Hatcher. "If you did something wrong, he'd say, 'Well, maybe but maybe not.' That was my impression of him. Not so much you do it his way but how to do it. He taught it that way."

Hatcher taught his players well enough that they finished the season 16-2. When Jarrett Hatcher finished his first year as Lee's jayvee coach in February 1992, getting a big win to finish 15-3, he walked in the locker room and was greeted by his dad, who said, "I went 16-2."

Botkin became assistant principal and athletic director at Lee the next year, and Paul Hatcher was named varsity coach for the 1968–69 season. He was surprised that he got the job with his lack of experience but was happy to get an opportunity to prove himself.

"That's why I thanked him forever," Hatcher said of Botkin. "For giving me a chance. A lot of people wouldn't."

ANOTHER TITLE

Jarrett Hatcher was excited about the chance to play Brunswick, the team that had beaten Lee 54–52 when he was a high school sophomore. He wanted payback.

Revenge would have to wait a day, though. The 2004–05 Group AA state quarterfinal game at Spotswood High School was scheduled for Saturday, March 5, but a snowstorm forced the game to be postponed until Sunday. It was the first time Paul Hatcher coached a game on a Sunday.

"Two disadvantages to that," said Jarrett. "One, we missed the Marvin Williams's Duke-Carolina game because we were on the bus going to Spotswood. As we were waiting to play, kids were hollering at me, 'Carolina's losing! Carolina's losing! Carolina sucks!'"

The Hatchers were Carolina fans. Lee's rescheduled game was set for the same day as the North Carolina–Duke game that ended the regular season. Carolina finished the game on an 11–0 run, including a three-point play by Tar Heel freshman Marvin Williams with seventeen seconds left, to beat Duke 75–73. The win earned the Tar Heels their first regular season title since 1993.

"The other disadvantage to us," said Jarrett, "and Dad and I didn't think of this, was Martinsville and Greensville [and Heritage] are going to come watch us because they're already guaranteed."

The other three teams that got through to the semifinals all played Saturday. Greensville beat Millbrook 83-66, Heritage-Lynchburg beat Abingdon 65–41 and Martinsville beat William Fleming 74–63. Now, the coaches from all three were free to scout Lee and Brunswick on Sunday.

Jarrett Hatcher had scouted Brunswick when the Bulldogs lost to Greensville in the regional tournament. A minute and a half into the game, Lee was trailing 7–0. Paul Hatcher started yelling at Jarrett, asking why he even went to the Greensville-Brunswick game. He said the scouting report was horrible.

Things improved after that early panic situation, though. Jason Jordan scored on a reverse layup with 6:21 left in the first quarter, and Eli Crawford followed with a three-pointer. Those buckets sparked a 23–2 run by Lee.

By the time Lawrence Lightfoot scored on a layup to put Lee up 27–11 with fifty-three seconds left in the opening quarter, WSVA play-by-play announcer Jim Britt said what every Brunswick fan must have been thinking at the time: "It can't end soon enough for Brunswick."

His broadcast partner, Karl Magenhofer, simply added, "Jeez."

Really, what more was there to say? By the time the quarter ended, Lee High was in front 32–13. At the time, the thirty-two points in a quarter was a Group AA record. Things didn't improve for Brunswick the next three quarters, as Lee went on to win 86–55, the fifty-third win in a row for Lee High, a new school record.

Asked if he felt better about the loss to Brunswick in his sophomore year, Jarrett said, "No, because, God, now we have to play Martinsville."

Judy Hatcher had been back in the hospital for part of that season but was given a weekend pass to go watch her husband try to win his fourth state title. Jarrett worried that her presence would be a huge distraction, that his dad would be worried about her instead of the game.

"It's tough," said Paul Hatcher. "But it's kind of an out, too. You're focused on [basketball], and I kind of tend to block everything out."

Judy Hatcher wasn't on the initial pass list to get into the Siegel Center. Her youngest son, Brandon, argued with the person in charge of the list for a minute or two before taking his clipboard and writing his mom's name on it. He said, "Now it's on the list." She got into the arena without any further problems. Two nights later, she would have to return to the hospital, but for now, the Hatcher family was together in a place that only seemed fitting: a basketball arena.

Lee and Martinsville had split four games since Paul Hatcher arrived at Lee. The most recent two had gone to Martinsville, in the 1985 and 2002 state semifinals. The 1985 game ended Kevin Madden's high school career and Lee's bid for a repeat state championship. Eli Crawford had always looked up to Madden, considered him a mentor. Before the game, Jarrett Hatcher told Crawford that Madden lost going for back-to-back titles.

"You want to be as good as Kevin," Jarrett told Crawford, "Here's your chance to do something he can never do."

Crawford must have been inspired by those words, scoring twenty-nine points to lead Lee to the 72–62 win. Lee led by only two with 1:38 to go in the game but finished on a 9–1 run. Crawford ended the game with a dunk just before the buzzer.

Two down, one to go in the state tournament. And that one was a rematch with the team Lee had destroyed a year ago for the state title: Greensville.

"If I'm still upset about [losing to] Brunswick twenty years later, it's the same bunch of kids from Greensville [that Lee beat]," said Jarrett Hatcher. "They can do something about it."

Waiting for the 9:00 p.m. tip on Saturday, March 12, 2005, the Lee players were sitting on one end of the Siegel Center in Richmond. Jarrett Hatcher remembers that the Greensville kids started running their mouths at his players. Jason Jordan asked Jarrett for his state championship ring from the year before, put it on his finger next to his own championship ring and turned around to the Greensville players.

"Are you talking to me and my teammates," Jordan said, flashing the rings. "I got this last year thanks to y'all. After tonight, I'm going to have the matching one."

Before the game, Jarrett Hatcher was talking with Keary Bonner about what a remarkable year it had been when the two heard, over the Siegel Center speaker system, "Danger Zone," the theme song from the 1986 U.S. Navy aviator movie *Top Gun*.

Bonner, who had wanted to be a navy pilot for years, loved that song and that movie. He told Hatcher it was a sign from God. No way Lee was losing that night.

"Like most people, you want the state championship game to go well, so you're looking for omens," Bonner recalled almost eleven years after the game. "When they played that song, it was definitely a good omen."

Everyone expected a tougher game from Greensville this time. The Eagles lost to Lee by thirty-nine the year before, but the coaching staff was so focused on repeating that they didn't savor the state championship. Waiting for the 2005 championship game in the same building, against the same opponent, with a lot of the same players, wearing the same uniforms, Paul Hatcher turned to Jarrett and said, "Where's the last year gone? If we win tonight, let's make sure we enjoy this."

Standing in the tunnel before the game, the Lee High players had no doubt about what the outcome would be. Bonner loved that part of his experience at Lee—waiting with his teammates before running out on the court. That night, just looking around at his teammates, at the Crawford cousins and Jason Jordan and Hosea Berkley and Lawrence Lightfoot—guys who had been dominating their opponents all season—Bonner knew the Leemen were ready.

"That was one of my favorite parts," said Bonner. "To just stand there and go like the Lakers better be out there because we were going to smoke some people unless these dudes know what they're doing."

Greensville was not the Lakers, but it did have a better idea of what it was doing than a year prior, giving Lee a tougher contest than the beat-down the previous March. Lee led by only four late in the third quarter and ran into foul trouble late, forcing Paul Hatcher to put Ryan Knicely in the game.

"Ryan is the king of mop-up time," said Jarrett Hatcher. "Ryan is the king of turn out the lights, the party's over, the Red Auerbach cigar…except now, it's not. He makes a move into the paint and does this move, and the whole bench stands up and yells, 'No!' And he scores and sparks the run that wins the game."

It was Knicely's only basket in the game—Knicely was a much better baseball player —but his shot combined with six-straight free throws by Eli Crawford helped Lee pull away in the fourth quarter to win 74–55. Eli hit all twelve of his free throw attempts in the game, tying what was then a Group AA state tournament record that wasn't surpassed until Brunswick's DeVonne Lewis made thirteen of thirteen free throws in 2008.

When Crawford went to the free throw line with 48.9 seconds left in the game, WSVA analyst Karl Magenhofer said, "What a swagger Eli has as he steps to the line."

Magenhofer's partner, Jim Britt, the radio station's play-by-play announcer, added, "You know what? He's earned every step."

He did just that. Crawford finished with twenty-eight points, five rebounds, two assists and two steals, capping a season in which he would eventually be honored as the Associated Press's Group AA state player of the year.

"Eli had a certain charisma and way in how he carried himself," said Jarrett Hatcher. "He was confident without being cocky or a jerk. He beat your team, and you did not hate him. He outplayed you, and you were in awe of him."

Jarrett described Eli Crawford as just as intense as, but more loose than, his older cousin Tyler Crawford, whom the assistant coach called "all business."

Meanwhile, following the season, Paul Hatcher would be named the Associated Press's Group AA coach of the year for the second year in a row. After the Greensville game, Jarrett remembers the fans chanting his dad's name and described it as movie-like.

"It was rich, it was poor, it was black, it was white, it was old-school Lee fans who had watched Dad in the '70s, it was my teammates. ...It was just this giant thing," said Jarrett.

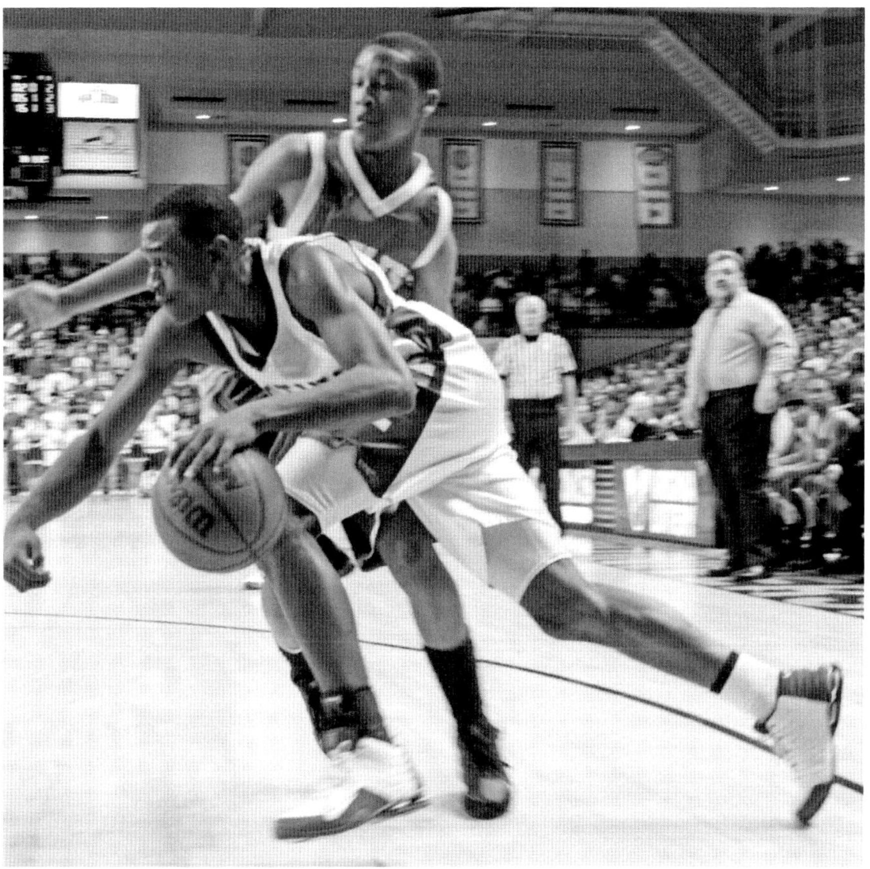

Eli Crawford finished with twenty-eight points, five rebounds, two assists and two steals in Lee High's state championship victory over Greensville County in 2005. *Vincent Lerz/the* News Leader.

Lee's 31-0 record was a state record. No other team had won that many games without losing a game in a season. The win also gave Lee High, and Paul Hatcher, back-to-back titles for the first time.

"Daryl Taylor, Tyler Crawford and the rest of the 30-1 team passed us the torch, and we kept the flame," Keon Scott said of repeating as champions.

As the Lee players and coaches walked off the court, Jarrett asked his dad if he was going to retire. Paul said he had no plans to do so. His plan was to return and win yet another championship.

8
"Let's Do It Again, Do It Again."

Seven schools managed to win a record three-straight VHSL state championships in boys' basketball through the 2004–05 season. Christopher Gist High School in Pound, Virginia, did it twice, from 1934 to 1936 and 1940 to 1942. Robert E. Lee High School began the 2005–06 season with hopes of becoming the eighth school to pull off the feat.

Lee was the favorite to do just that. Riding a fifty-five-game winning streak and returning three starters, including Group AA player of the year Eli Crawford plus Group AA coach of the year Paul Hatcher, the Leemen were in good shape to continue their winning ways. Crawford had finished the previous season averaging 17.4 points and 4.6 rebounds a game. He also set a school record with ninety-two steals.

Two key parts of the team, however, were gone after graduating the season before. Keary Bonner and Jason Jordan had both earned first team honors on the *News Leader*'s All-City/County team and wouldn't be easy to replace. Keary Bonner was the team's best perimeter defender, and Jason Jordan was the best interior defender. Lee was built on defense, so the absence of the two would hurt.

Ryan Crawford described Bonner as a "white Bruce Bowen," a lockdown defender who could knock down the three. Bowen is best known for his eight years with the San Antonio Spurs. Crawford also said Jordan's defense was a huge loss, but the team would miss his rebounding and his play in the post as well.

In March 2004, leading up to the state tournament, the *News Leader* ran a feature with photos of all the players and managers for the Lee High

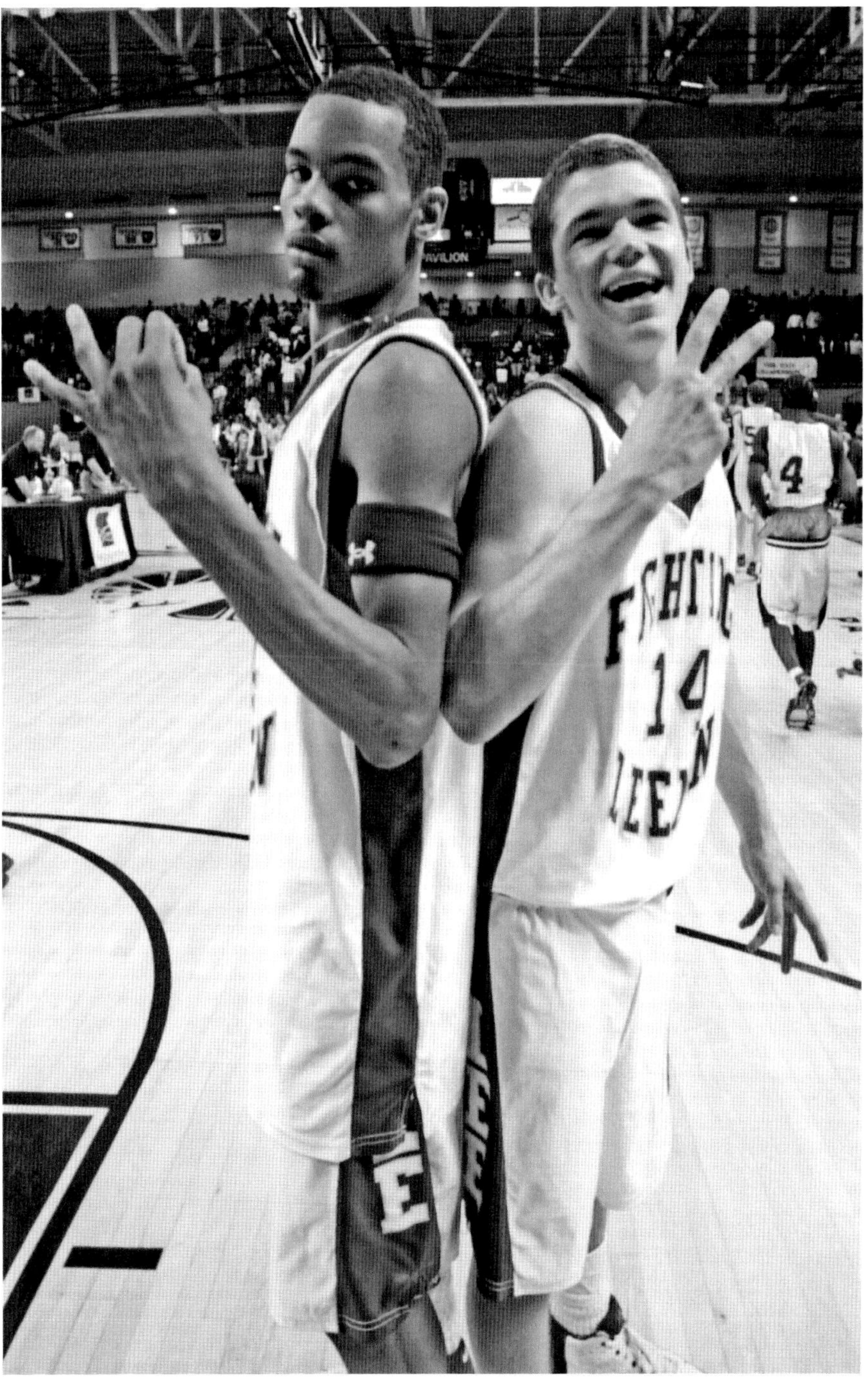

Lee's Jason Jordan and Keary Bonner celebrated back-to-back VHSL state championships. *Vincent Lerz/the* News Leader.

team. Along with each photo, the newspaper ran answers the players provided for various questions. One question was: "What do you want to be doing in ten years?"

Keary Bonner said he wanted to be a naval aviator. Jason Jordan said he wanted to be "Chillin'. Laid back in an office making money."

One lived his dream. The other lived a nightmare.

STRENGTH FROM THE SEA

Keary Bonner's fourth-grade teacher had a daughter who was at the U.S. Air Force Academy in Colorado Springs, Colorado. Bonner remembers seeing a calendar with jets on it that the daughter had sent to the class. That set in motion the nine-year-old's desire to, one day, fly military aircraft. A few years later, someone told Bonner that he'd have a better chance at flying fighter jets in the navy, so his dream changed slightly, from wanting to attend the U.S. Air Force Academy to wanting to go to the U.S. Naval Academy in Annapolis, Maryland.

In high school, Bonner got a chance to attend the Shenandoah Valley Governor's School, a regional school offering advanced classes for juniors and seniors in the three local school districts. Students attended the school in the morning and returned to their home high schools for afternoon classes. At Governor's School, Bonner discovered he enjoyed engineering. About the same time, he was finding out more about how both his grandfathers had served in World War II.

"I became interested in kind of repaying a debt and serving our country, and it all went together," said Bonner.

The week of Lee High's state championship win in March 2005, Bonner found out he had received an appointment to the U.S. Naval Academy. "It was one of the best weeks ever," he said.

He finished high enough in his class at Navy that he was given the opportunity to get his master's degree in engineering at Georgia Tech, an opportunity of which he took advantage.

Beth Weller was from Staunton, a student at Grace Christian High School when Bonner was at Lee, but the two were only acquaintances. However, that changed during winter break of his freshman year at the Naval Academy. Bonner was back home and decided to go check out his old high school basketball team. He and Ryan Knicely, who also graduated from Lee in

2005, went to a game, and as was always the case in those years, the Paul Hatcher Gym was packed.

"There were no seats except for the one up in the corner there next to the pretty girl," said Bonner. "So I took that one."

Weller and Bonner started dating soon after. When she graduated from Virginia Tech and he graduated from Navy, the two got married and moved to Atlanta.

After Georgia Tech, it was off to Pensacola, Florida, for flight training and then to Milton, Florida, for more training, this time in the T-6 Texan for a year. Bonner then started flying T-45 Goshawk jet flight trainers in Meridian, Mississippi. After he finished in Mississippi, there were several places the navy could send him, but Bonner knew where he wanted to go.

"I prayed to every god I knew of and sacrificed like seven chickens to get sent to Virginia Beach," said Bonner. "It worked out."

Throughout every stop, Bonner was an exemplary aviator. He said he owed a lot of that to Paul Hatcher. The coach made Bonner and every Lee player earn their spots on the team. It didn't matter that Bonner's dad had coached the girls' basketball team at Lee or was a college basketball announcer. It didn't matter that Bonner was an amazing student or a good person. What mattered to Hatcher when deciding playing time was who played the best. It was Bonner's first experience in a result-based system.

"Hatcher, in my personal experience, was the response to when people say that my generation is all participation trophies and everybody wins and everybody's nice," said Bonner. "My experience with the real world has been, with the flight training and stuff in the navy, so result based. It doesn't matter how good of a guy you are or how much you studied the night before; if you mess up, you can kill yourself or make a mistake where they just won't permit you back in the plane. They will find another job for you if you can't perform. And I thought I did better in that situation because of my time with Hatcher. He cared a lot about us and about the well-being of his players, but after the ball was tipped, it was results. He was going to win."

The standards Hatcher set for his team helped put Bonner, as well as many other Lee High players, on the track to doing great things.

Bonner ended up getting stationed at NAS Oceana in Virginia Beach. Once there, he started training in the F-18E Super Hornet and was eventually assigned to Strike Fighter Squadron 81.

Three weeks before his first deployment, the Bonners' daughter was born. The couple already had a two-year-old son, but Bonner had to leave both

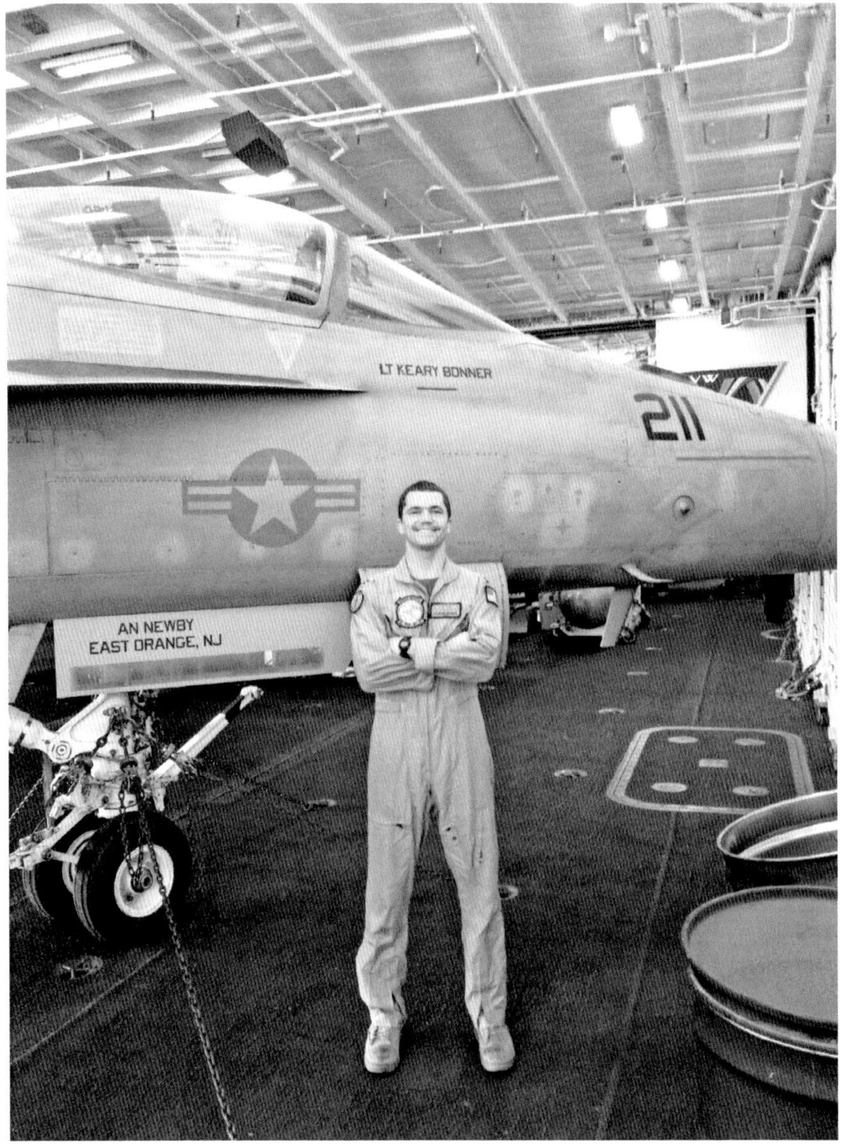

Keary Bonner is living his dream as a navy pilot stationed in Virginia Beach. *Photo submitted by Keary Bonner.*

children and his wife behind for a ten-month deployment in August 2014 to the Persian Gulf on the USS *Carl Vinson*.

"It was probably the greatest challenge I had to deal with, to leave my wife with a two-year-old and a three-week-old," said Bonner. "But it was done for all the right reasons, and it was an opportunity I had worked very hard for, and I married the single most impressive person I've ever met in my life, so she took care of it. Yeah, it was very difficult, but I feel much better off for it now. I couldn't have done it, obviously, without Beth. It was a challenge, but it has been worthwhile."

Bonner and the rest of the crew of the USS *Carl Vinson*, a Nimitz-class aircraft carrier, were part of Operation Inherent Resolve, a U.S. military campaign against ISIS. Bonner flew airstrikes over Iraq and Syria. He often tells people that the missions were the biggest contradiction he's ever experienced.

"I described to you how long we trained, and now I get to go do the real thing, and there are very real threats and I get to have a role in doing something about that," said Bonner. "That was incredibly satisfying, and then just the experience of coming back—missions can be up to eight hours long, and then you'll come back and land on the boat in the middle of the night. To have a day like that, it's hard for any other days to compare in terms of the amount of adrenaline you dealt with and the feeling of satisfaction when you land, the feeling that you've reached a point in your career that you can handle an experience like that. That part of it was amazing."

The part that wasn't so amazing was knowing that his family was back home and his kids were growing up without him seeing it firsthand. He missed holidays and had to keep up with his family through e-mail. Still, he knew what he was doing was the right thing.

"It was part of the equation that works out to where I am sitting right now, which I'm extremely happy about," said Bonner. "You always want…I've seen all kinds of definitions of success, but maybe one of them is you have a very full and fulfilling professional life and you have a very full and fulfilling personal life, and I'm definitely blessed with that."

Bonner returned home in June 2015, and his squadron isn't scheduled to deploy again for another year or so, although Bonner knows things can change rapidly in the military. Still, for now, he's with his family and still busy training for the next mission.

"Now we're back in Virginia Beach," he said, "just living the good life."

A Wrong Choice

About the same time Bonner was getting ready to start his third year at the Naval Academy, his former Lee High teammate Jason Jordan was finding out where he would be spending a big chunk of the rest of his life.

Jordan had the talent to play basketball after high school, but he admits he didn't have the grades for college. Paul Hatcher tried to get Jordan enrolled in a postgraduate program at Massanutten Military Academy in Woodstock, Virginia, about an hour north of Staunton. The school had commitments from other students, though, so it didn't work out. Then Hatcher turned his attention toward Potomac State, a junior college in West Virginia, which accepted Jordan.

But Jordan ended up arriving a few days late, and there was an issue with his meal tickets. Jordan also didn't like the living arrangements, and he wasn't happy that the Potomac State coach wanted to use him—at six-foot-four and 170 pounds—as a power forward. Jordan thought he was undersized for that role. The coach called Hatcher and said they would get it all straightened out, but Jordan didn't have the patience to wait, calling his mom and telling her he wanted to come home. She came and picked him up, bringing Jordan back to Staunton.

Jordan transferred to Hagerstown Community College in Maryland, a school that former Lee players Derrick Fields and Daryl Taylor attended. There was a problem with the financial aid, however, and because he enrolled late, he had to sit out the first basketball season. Without basketball, Jordan wasn't interested in sticking around.

"I based my life around basketball so much," said Jordan. "I didn't think of the academic side. I could do the work, but it was basketball first."

Hagerstown was a little less than two hours from Staunton, so Jordan found himself making the drive more and more, spending more time in Staunton and less time at school. That's when the problems started.

"I always felt like maybe this other wouldn't have happened if he had stayed [at Potomac State]," said Paul Hatcher.

The other was drugs. More specifically, drug dealing.

"I started dealing and dabbling," said Jordan. "I said, 'Maybe I can get a little extra money to do this, to do that.'"

He ended up leaving school but talked to the coach and said he planned on returning at the start of the following year. Unfortunately for Jordan, he was in serious trouble before that next year arrived.

"I was affiliated with the wrong crowd," said Jordan. "I was like, 'I'm not out here shooting people. I'm not out here beating people up, nothing like that.' But if you're around those people who are doing it, you're just as bad."

In July 2006, a little over a year after graduating from Lee High, Jordan was arrested for selling crack cocaine. That, however, turned out to be the least of his problems. He was also caught with two illegal handguns, one that

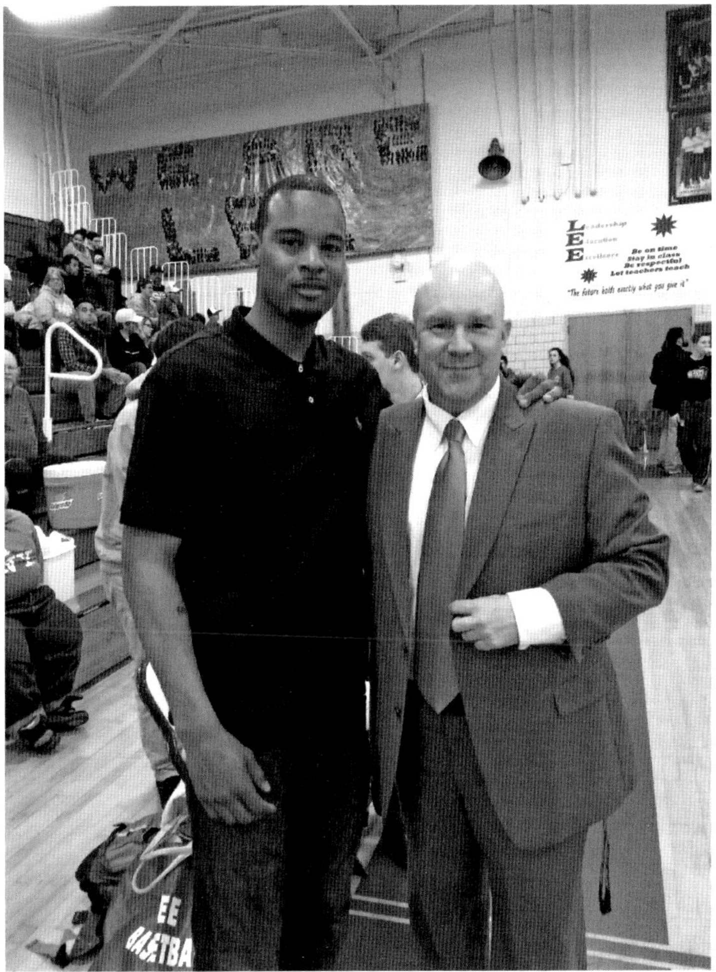

Jason Jordan and Jarrett Hatcher before a Lee High basketball game on January 30, 2016. *Author's collection.*

turned out to be stolen but that he maintains was given to him by a friend. He also said he never used the drugs, just sold them.

Jarrett Hatcher was in Myrtle Beach when Jordan called him with the news. Jarrett helped him get an attorney and served as a character witness at his trial. The following March, Jordan pleaded guilty to one count of distributing cocaine base and two counts of possessing a firearm in furtherance of a drug trafficking crime.

"It was the wrong choice," Jordan said. "I tell everybody that now. I don't dwell on the situation. I learned from it."

He was sentenced to just 37 months in prison for the drugs, but because of mandatory minimum sentences, Jordan received 360 months for the guns for a total of just over thirty-three years. At nineteen years old, Jordan started serving his time in a Beckley, West Virginia prison before being transferred to Lompoc, California, after a few years.

"I let nine months of letting an illegal activity go on with my life, and it took away my family and friends," said Jordan. "I let a lot of people down. The people I let down the most were my family—my mother, of course—but I also feel like I let down Paul Hatcher and Jarrett and my teachers at Lee High because they never saw that side of me."

He stayed in contact with Paul, Judy and Jarrett Hatcher throughout his stay in prison, eventually moving from writing letters with pen and paper to using e-mail once he was given the privilege.

"I really watched him grow just like anybody would grow once they get out of college," said Jarrett. "He's in a terrible situation, and his letters were just so positive and so mature. He just began to show this wonderful kid. I kept thinking, 'My gosh, it's terrible.'"

Meanwhile, his attorney kept fighting to reduce his sentence until, almost seven years into his prison stay, Jordan received a letter notifying him that his sentence had been reduced. It scared him. He wondered if he could adapt to being out of prison.

"I just went back in my cell and just kept reading [the letter] over," said Jordan. "I was like, 'Man, I'm about to go home.'"

Eventually, Jordan was sent to a halfway house in August 2013 before getting his release to go home on January 3, 2014. Since his release, he's worked in both construction and manufacturing and recently obtained his Class A CDL license.

"He really seems to be really mature and has his head squared away," said Paul Hatcher. "I remind him all the time you've got to keep on what you're doing. Remember where you came from."

Jordan remembers the first time he went back to Paul Hatcher Gym after his release, going to watch a basketball game. He remembers the smell the most. He said there was just something about that smell in the gym where he spent so much time. After the game, Jordan stepped on the floor and jumped just enough to touch the rim.

"It was a great feeling," he said. "I just kept staring up at the pictures. It was just a great feeling, but mostly that smell."

Jordan said he's blessed to have gotten a second chance and doesn't plan on wasting it. A couple of days a week during the 2015–16 season, Jordan helped out Jarrett Hatcher at practice. He wants to tell his story, maybe go to Jarrett's history classes at Lee High and let the students know how he screwed up and hopefully keep them from doing the same. Plus, he feels like he owes the Hatchers, owes the community that stood by him, owes his family. He knows what he did to them and wants to make it up.

"It hurts the people around you, it hurts your family," said Jordan. "That's who it hurts. You can do the time. They can sit you down and say they're going to give you a life sentence. It's not going to hurt you. You'll be sitting there every day, sitting there until you die wasting your time. That's what I came to realize. I was just hurting my family."

Paul Hatcher has spent a lot of time with Jordan since his release, talking with his former player on the screened-in porch in the backyard of his Staunton home. He's happy with the progress Jordan has made since getting out of prison.

"That's one of those, hopefully, success stories," said Paul Hatcher.

GET IT DONE

Lee got a late start with practice for the 2005–06 season because several of the players were on the football team that made the playoffs. It helped that nine players returned from the previous year's unbeaten state championship team, including four players—Eli Crawford, Ryan Crawford, Lawrence Lightfoot and Hosea Berkley—who had a pair of state championship rings. They wanted a third.

"That was kind of the center of attention during the offseason," said Paul Hatcher. "Everybody was 'Let's do it again, do it again.' But we had some big holes to fill."

One issue was that Paul Hatcher didn't think the Leemen had the depth they'd had previous years. Not only were Keary Bonner and Jason Jordan gone, but Ryan Knicely also graduated, and J.R. Ware had decided to focus on football instead of coming out for basketball.

Lightfoot joined the other two-time state champions in the starting lineup, while Logan Jones got the fifth starting spot coming out of preseason. Jones had come off the bench the year before for the Leemen. All the returning varsity players had gotten plenty of game time the previous year because of the blowouts, so experience wasn't an issue.

"Anything less than getting to the final game is going to be a colossal disappointment," Jarrett Hatcher said of the team's mindset before that season.

Lee opened with an easy 97–49 win over Fort Defiance, led by Eli Crawford's twenty-five points, seven rebounds, seven assists and three steals. Berkley added sixteen points, while Ryan Crawford got thirteen, and Keon Scott came off the bench to score twelve points in the win.

Lee then beat Rockbridge County, sandwiched between a pair of wins against Western Albemarle. Roanoke Catholic became victim number sixty, and Lee High was six wins shy of tying the state record. Whether they wanted it to be or not, the streak was a very real thing by this point.

The next opponent was the annual visitor from Down Under, marking the third year Lee High played an Australian touring team. Much like the first year, the team that arrived in the United States in December 2005—the Wombats—were no match for Lee High. The team arrived in the country on Wednesday and practiced one time together on Thursday before playing on Thursday night. One of the players, six-foot-ten Matthew Turner, told the *News Leader* that the team practiced for forty-five minutes and then, in the game, "just winged it."

That strategy didn't work. Of course, no strategy was working against Lee at this point, so winging it might have been as good as anything. Lee won 85–39 after leading 16–0. The Wombats turned the ball over seven times before getting a shot. Lee had seven dunks in the game, four by Lightfoot. Perhaps the only surprise of the night was Eli Crawford scoring just six points.

Crawford was passing up shots all night, and both Paul and Jarrett Hatcher asked him what was wrong. He said it was nothing the first few times he was asked but finally admitted he was close to one thousand points for his career and didn't want to score it against the Australians. He wanted it in the next game, against Spotswood at the MCI Center in Washington, D.C. The Leemen were playing during the afternoon of December 30, and that night the Washington Wizards would host the Miami Heat, who would win the NBA championship that season. Eli was hoping he would score his 1,000th point in front of Dwayne Wade, the Heat's star player.

No one has any record of Wade seeing Crawford's accomplishment, but when he did get the points, the game was stopped and Crawford was honored, however briefly.

Lee destroyed Spotswood that day 96–51, stretching the winning streak to sixty-two and improving to 7-0 on the season. Lee then beat Broadway, Turner Ashby and Harrisonburg, all easily. Then the Leemen tied the state record of sixty-six wins in a row with an 82–60 win over Miller School of Albemarle County.

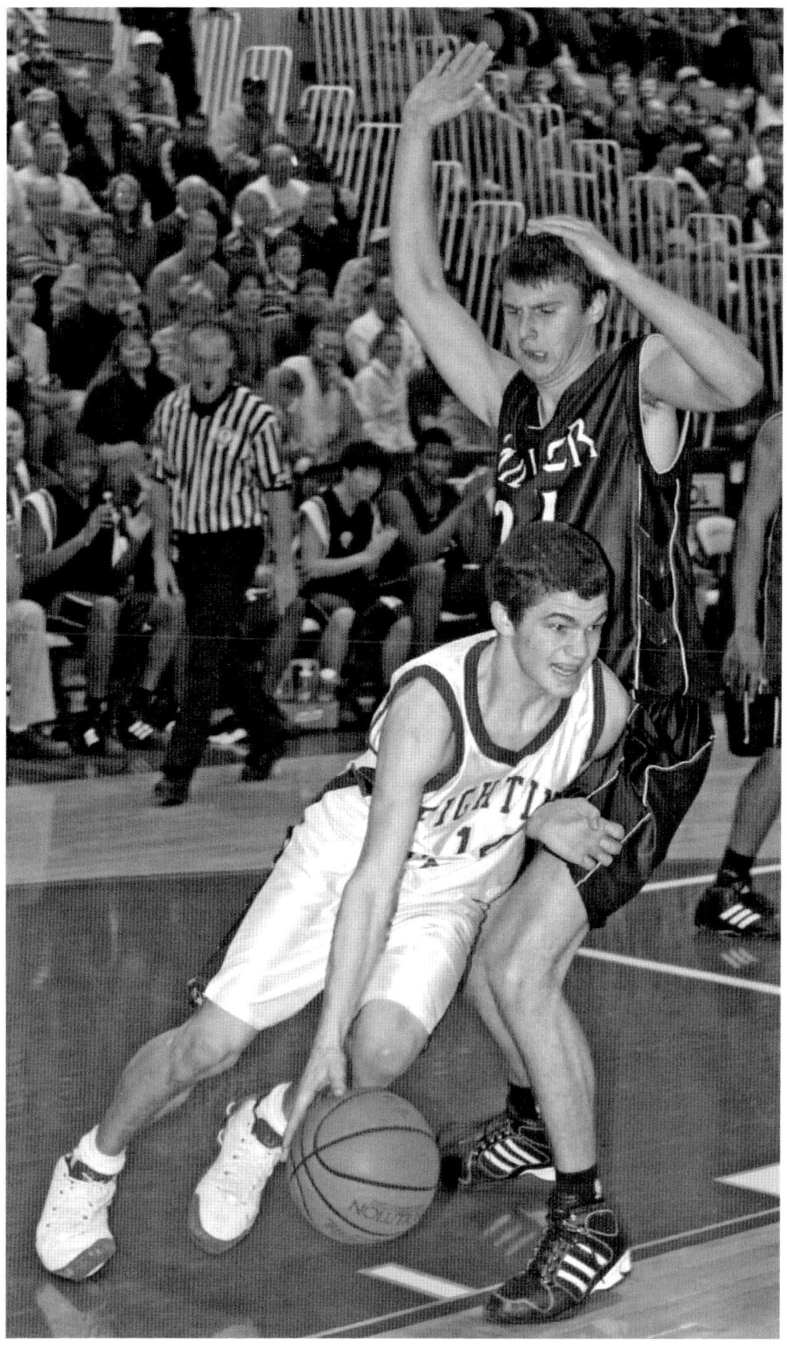

Keary Bonner helped lead Lee High past the Miller School to tie the state record of sixty-six wins in a row. *Vincent Lerz/the* News Leader.

Jarrett Hatcher always said winning streaks are only a big deal once they're over. Lee High had no plans on that streak being over with anytime soon. That being said, it was becoming a big deal, which made perfect sense.

"When you get that close," said Paul Hatcher, "you want to get it done."

9

Beginning of the End

Success and Paul Hatcher went hand-in-hand throughout the head coach's forty-three years at Lee High. By the time he retired, Hatcher had won 897 games, a staggering 84 percent of the games he coached, and never suffered a losing season. He won four state championships and, as of 2015, had been inducted into five halls of fame, including the Virginia Sports Hall of Fame and Museum and the National High School Athletic Coaches Hall of Fame. None of that, however, brought as much joy to him as did his 1970–71 team, Hatcher's third season as Lee High's head coach.

Lee High had not been immune to success before Hatcher's arrival. In fact, two years before Hatcher was the head coach, Lee won the state title by beating Northside to end the 1966–67 season. That was the school's second state championship, having also won in 1931.

Hatcher's first team in 1968–69 finished 11-10. It also marked the first year on varsity for Mouse Patterson, who recalled that a lot of the foundation of Lee's state championship team from two years prior had graduated. He said it was a rebuilding year for the Leemen. In Hatcher's second season, the rebuilding project must have been complete because Lee High had a twenty-win season and played in the 1B state championship game at Virginia Tech. Lee lost to John Langston 50–47.

"That year was a growing year for me," Patterson said. "I knew we could win ballgames, but we had to put it together. We put it together by playing more during the summer."

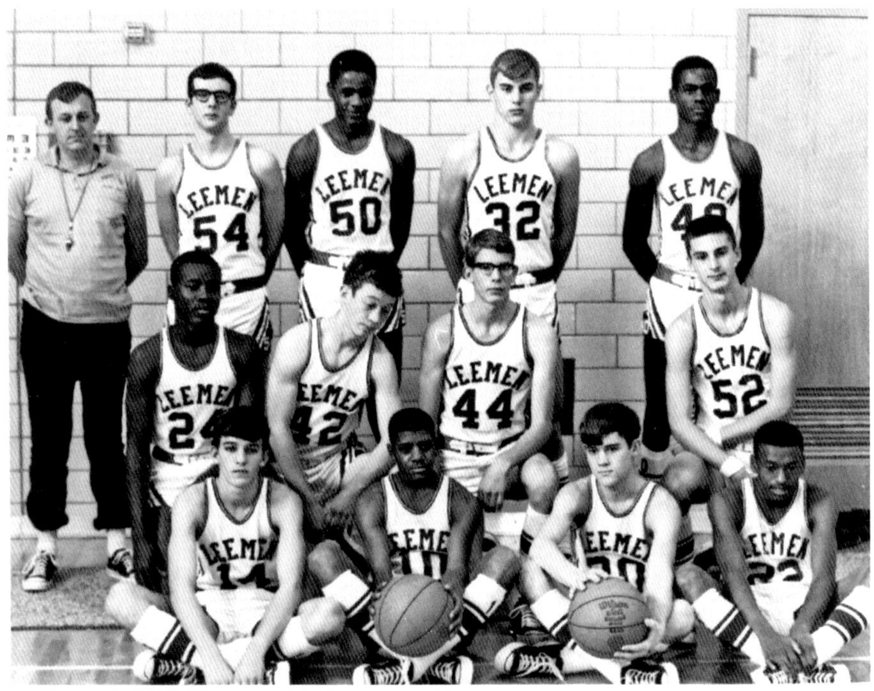

Paul Hatcher's first varsity team at Lee High finished the 1968–69 season 11-10. *Paul Hatcher's collection.*

The next season, the Virginia High School League went to three classifications, a format that remained until 2013. With 1,200 students, Lee High was placed in the highest classification: Group AAA.

Since no other area teams were large enough to be placed in Group AAA, Lee became the fourteenth member of the Western District, joining William Fleming, Cave Spring, Northside, Franklin County, Liberty-Bedford, E.C. Glass, Martinsville, George Washington–Danville, Patrick Henry–Roanoke, Halifax County, Andrew Lewis, Amherst and defending AAA state champion Jefferson Senior.

"Everyone was thinking, 'Lee won't be able to compete in triple-A because it's just a smaller school, and they just won't be able to handle the tougher competition from all the Roanoke schools,'" said Mark Newlen, a sophomore on that year's team.

In addition to tougher competition, Lee also faced much more travel. The closest school to Staunton was an hour and a half away.

"Long drives," Patterson said, recalling the only downside to that season. "I did a lot of sleeping going [to Roanoke], I know that."

The VHSL had considered forming two districts out of the fourteen teams but decided to leave it as one district. The players realized they were up against stiffer competition, but Newlen said Paul Hatcher had prepared them so well that they were confident they could succeed. More than anything, they wanted to prove to the naysayers that, even against bigger schools, Lee High basketball could be successful. And they did just that. Lee finished the regular season with a 15-3 record, good enough for third place behind Jefferson and Martinsville.

The postseason district tournament was held at the Salem Civic Center, just outside Roanoke. Lee just missed getting a bye that was given to the top two regular season teams, so it opened against Northside on a Wednesday afternoon.

After beating Northside, Lee played Fleming next. Late in the game, the score was tied, and Wayne Wymer drove the lane but was knocked to the floor and had to leave the game injured. He was replaced by Steve Sensabaugh, who hadn't played in the game before that moment. Sensabaugh made both foul shots to put Lee up by two with eight seconds left. Hatcher considered taking Sensabaugh back out of the game but felt it would make him look bad with so little time left. For a few seconds, Hatcher wondered if he had made a mistake. Sensabaugh fouled a Fleming player, but the entire Lee team breathed a sigh of relief when he missed the front end of a one-and-one. Sensabaugh got the rebound, and Lee held on for the win.

"He got a whole lot done in those seven or eight seconds," said Hatcher.

After the Northside game, the Lee High team went back to Staunton for the night, but after Thursday's win against Fleming, the Leemen stayed about a half hour outside the Roanoke area at Tinker Mountain. Hatcher felt it was far enough away from any activities that the players could focus on the task at hand—a semifinal game against Martinsville—but still close enough that travel the next day wouldn't be an issue. It would be the first time Hatcher had faced his old high school rival as a head coach.

The Bulldogs had beaten Cave Spring the night before, and Hatcher had scouted them. He said they "made everything they shot." In reality, they shot 67 percent—not everything they shot, but more than enough to worry the opposing coach. So Hatcher packed his players into a zone defense. It was a bit unorthodox to defend a team that could knock down shots from the outside with a zone, but Hatcher had a strategy.

"They're going to be so open that they're going to be thinking about it before they shoot," said the coach.

The Salem Civic Center was only four years old at the time, but the roof leaked during heavy rains. That was what was happening during the Lee-

Martinsville game. So arena officials put buckets on the floor during breaks in the action to catch the rain, and the coaches and officials agreed that if water got on the floor and caused someone to slip and fall, they would retain possession of the ball.

Martinsville struggled shooting, and Lee had just enough offense to edge the Bulldogs 63–60. That was three nights, three wins for the Leemen. The reward was a meeting with the defending state champion, Jefferson Senior, for the district championship. With the score tied late, Lee had the ball, and Hatcher thought about holding it but didn't do it. His team missed, Jefferson got the rebound and went down the court to score, holding on for the win. It was the third time Lee lost to Jefferson that season. The only other loss Lee had to that point was against Northside.

The good news for Hatcher and his Leemen, however, was that, with fourteen teams in the district, both Jefferson and Lee earned a berth in the regional tournament at the University of Virginia's University Hall. Hatcher swore that if he was ever again in the same situation as he had found himself against Jefferson, he'd hold the ball.

Lee beat Handley in the first round, earning a rematch with Jefferson for the regional championship. Patterson said he isn't sure what his teammates were feeling, but he was confident Lee could finally beat Jefferson in the fourth meeting of the season between the two, especially since they had come close in two of the three losses.

"I knew I was going all out," said Patterson. "Whatever I needed to do, all out."

Again, it was close down the stretch and, with 2:38 to go and the score tied, Hatcher told his players to hold the ball and, for the next two minutes, that's what they did. Newlen said it wasn't as if Jefferson went back in a zone and just let Lee hold it.

"They were guarding us pretty tight," said Newlen. "They were guarding us man to man. We had to hold it for a good while. We were going to hold it for the last shot, but we didn't have to. Mouse got fouled."

With twenty-seven seconds left, Patterson went to the free throw line and made both shots. Jefferson got one last shot but missed in the final seconds, and Newlen got the rebound and held on tightly to the ball as the game ended. Hatcher's plan to hold the ball worked. The coach is insistent that the win over Jefferson is the favorite game he ever coached. He still has a photo in his home of Patterson at the free throw line in those final seconds.

"We did everything right," said Hatcher. "And I didn't forget about what I thought about the last Saturday. I didn't wake up on Sunday, 'Oh darn, I was going to hold the ball.'"

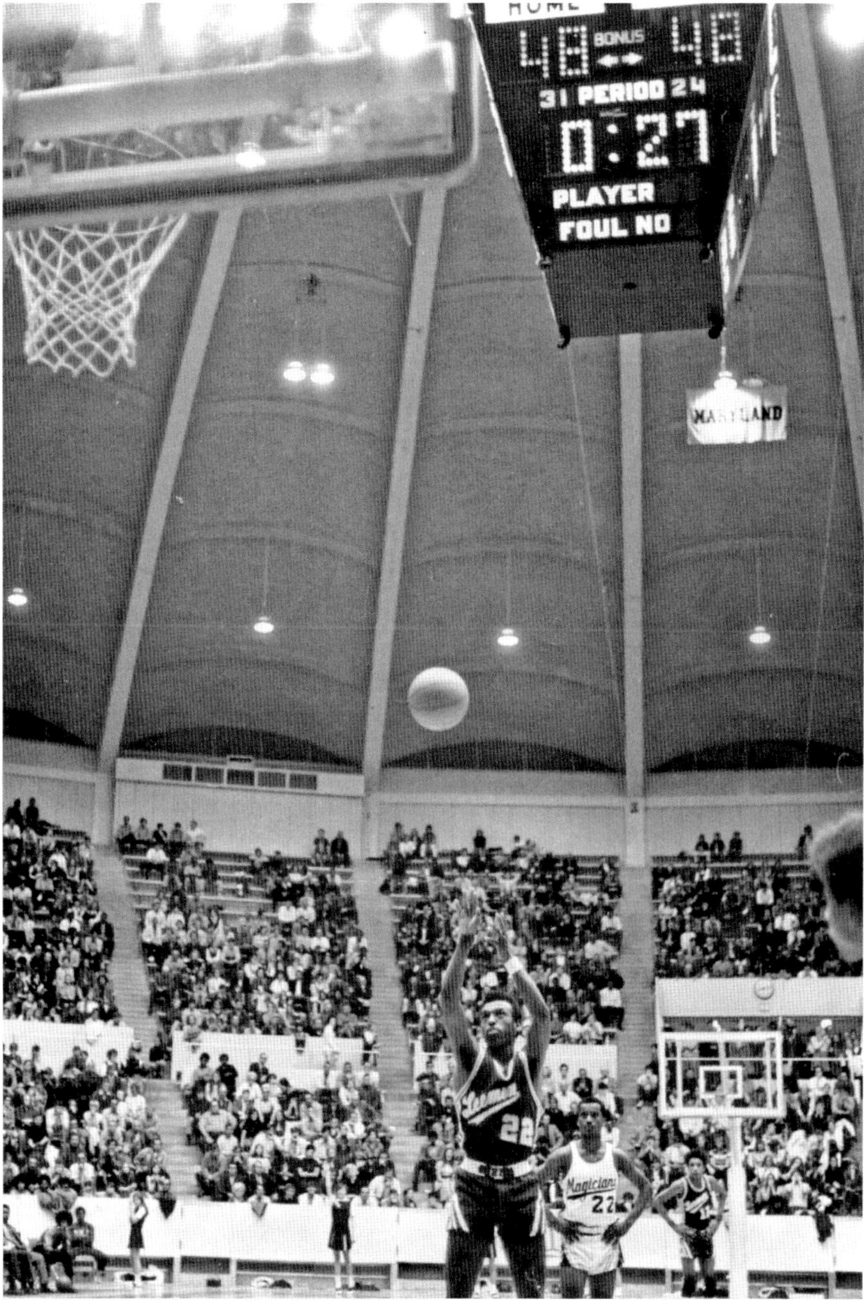

Mouse Patterson hit two free throws with twenty-seven seconds left to give Lee a two-point win over Jefferson in the 1971 regional championship. *Paul Hatcher's collection.*

Lee opened up state play against Newport News and trailed 24–9 in the second quarter. It looked like Hatcher's second state tournament appearance would end a game earlier than the year before. Now, looking back on the game, Patterson wonders if the team was overconfident. He said a lot of the Lee players felt like beating Jefferson was the championship. They didn't think they'd see a better team than the one they had just beaten.

Lee adjusted, though, and finished the first half on a 22–6 run. Lee scored twenty-three points in a row over the second and third quarters and ended up winning in a rout, 86–60. That set up Lee's second-straight state championship appearance, this time in Group AAA against Maggie Walker.

Lee started the game in a zone, according to Newlen, and Maggie Walker made it pay, hitting several early shots from outside. Lee fell behind but battled back to within one point late in the third quarter and had the ball with a chance to take the lead but couldn't do it. Maggie Walker gained control after that and won 80–63.

"Some things like that happen sometimes in life," said Patterson. "You learn, you live. You learn not to get behind."

Newlen said that's one game in his basketball career he'd like to have a chance to play again.

"To be with those guys who played on that team—it was such a great team, such a fun team to play on, and the competition was outstanding every night," said Newlen. "To get that far and just fall that short. If we'd played as well against Maggie Walker as we did [against Jefferson and Newport News], I think we would have won a state championship."

Despite the loss, Hatcher thought it was a great accomplishment just to reach the state championship game in the school's first year in Group AAA. The coach thoroughly enjoyed the season.

"This might have been the most fun year I ever had," said Hatcher. "It might have topped the state championships and all that stuff. Really."

Of course, enjoying the season didn't mean he has accepted the loss. Over the years, Jarrett Hatcher has heard his dad talk a lot about the loss to Maggie Walker. In 2014, Jarrett's Lee High team was in the same bracket with Maggie Walker in the regional tournament, but both lost in the first round. Jarrett wanted that game, wanted to avenge his dad's loss forty-three years before, but he knew, if he was honest with himself, that even if Lee played and beat Maggie Walker, it wouldn't make a difference. Wins never erase the losses.

"That doesn't ever go away," said Jarrett Hatcher. "Even success doesn't take it away. All right, back-to-back titles, but if I talk about Brunswick in '87, it doesn't make it any easier."

Patterson, along with brothers Phil and Donnie Darcus, all three members of the two-time state runner-up team, continued their playing careers at Ferrum, which, at the time, was a junior college in Virginia, about thirty-five miles southwest of Roanoke. They went on to play for the National Junior College Athletic Association championship in 1972 and lost. Three years in a row, the trio reached the final game of the season, only to come up on the short end of the score all three times.

Paul Hatcher could have been coaching that national runner-up. It was the only time in the forty-three years he coached the Leemen that Hatcher thought about coaching in college. He had been with those Lee players since eighth grade, his first year in the Staunton school system, so when they left, the coach thought about following them out of Staunton.

Hatcher interviewed for the Ferrum job but lost out to Bobby Watson, who eventually went on to coach Evansville. In 1977, Watson was on the airplane carrying the Evansville basketball team that crashed, killing all twenty-nine people on board.

Hatcher wasn't surprised he didn't get the Ferrum job. He had coached high school for only three years, although in two of those he had taken a team to the state championship game, losing both times. He might have had an easier time getting another job after a few more years of experience, but he never tested the waters again.

"I enjoyed high school, the challenge of every year," said Hatcher. "I didn't want, 'Boy, in three years we're going to be good.' I didn't want any of that. I wanted to be good all three years and then maybe great that fourth year."

What Hatcher enjoyed most in high school was that there was no recruiting like in college. He had to take the players who showed up for tryouts and form a team out of them. That was the challenge, to do that year after year and remain competitive.

Hatcher did just that, although after that game against Maggie Walker, Lee didn't get back to the state tournament until Kevin Madden's sophomore season. Still, in those eleven years without a state tournament appearance, Lee High went 210-47 and reached the regional tournament eight times. And once Hatcher made it to the state tournament in the 1982–83 season, Lee was there eight of the next ten seasons with a pair of state championships to show for it.

Record Setters

The official Virginia High School record had stood for fifty-four years. Clintwood's sixty-six-game winning streak was the best in the state for more than half of a century, although there was a one-hundred-game winning streak by Flat Gap in the 1930s that the VHSL doesn't recognize because the school played unauthorized games.

Now, Lee High had tied that official record and was set to face Fort Defiance on January 18, 2006, with a chance to own the record all by themselves. The outcome was never in question after Lee scored the first seventeen points of the game on the way to a 94–51 win.

Walking off the court, Paul Hatcher turned to Jarrett and said, "It's the longest streak in the history of Virginia. And that goes all the way back to Jamestown, and I have no idea what kind of team John Smith had."

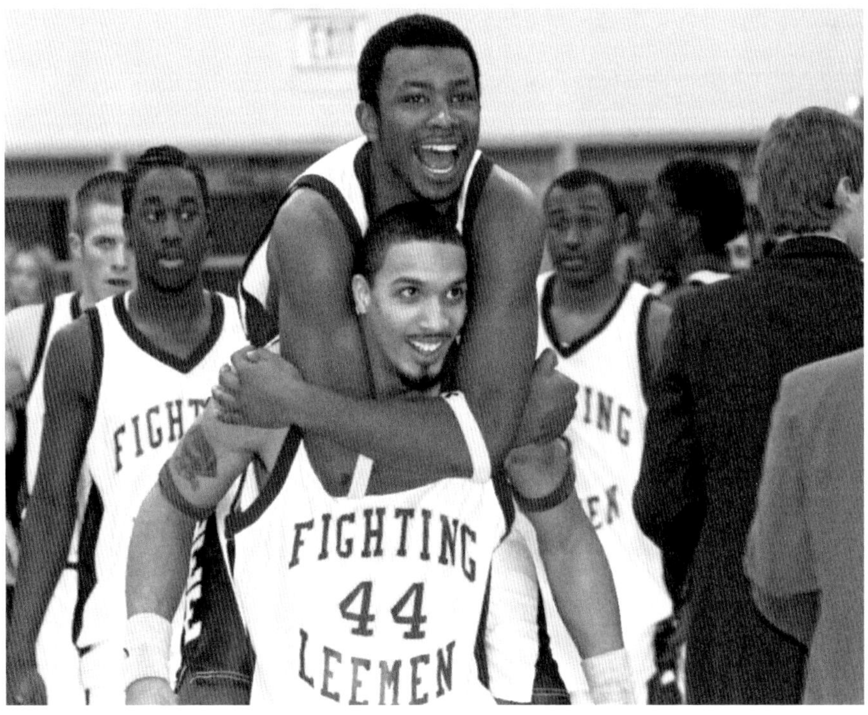

Lawrence Lightfoot jumped on the back of Hosea Berkley to celebrate Lee High's record-breaking win over Fort Defiance on January 18, 2006. It was the team's sixty-seventh win in a row. *Mike Tripp/the* News Leader.

For a history buff and basketball fanatic like Jarrett Hatcher, that comment still rings as one of the most amusing that his dad said during his coaching career.

The *News Leader* went big with its coverage, just as it should to honor a state record. The front page had a photo of Lee High fans cheering during the game and another of Lee players Lawrence Lightfoot and Hosea Berkley celebrating after the game. Both photos accompanied a story by staff writer Jennie Coughlin. Plus, there were "Lee Streak Facts" that ran down the right side of the page that included interesting tidbits such as Lee had beaten twenty-seven different opponents and won eighteen postseason games during the streak.

The sports section had another pair of stories and some more photos, plus a list of all the wins during the streak that started with an 86–55 win over Albemarle in December 2003 and was still going strong more than two years later.

"When we won that game, it was huge," said Eli Crawford. "You're breaking a state mark, something that hasn't been broken in years. You're putting your name in history, and it's not just your name, man. You're putting your team's name, your school's name, in history. We loved doing that. We wanted to break every record possible."

Two nights later, Lee scored 110 points in a 76-point win over Stuarts Draft. The point total matched the highest Lee had ever scored, equaling a 110–40 win over Spotswood in 1985. The scariest moment in the game came when Eli Crawford was fouled hard in the second quarter and remained sprawled on the floor for almost ten minutes. When Crawford returned to the game in the fourth quarter, the fans were relieved to see him. An injury to the star player could certainly mean trouble as the team pursued a third-straight state title.

The next game was an interesting mid-season contest at James Madison University's Convocation Center against Greensville, the team Lee had beaten for the state championship the past two years. It was the Fellowship of Christian Athletes Classic, an event that featured four games, including the nightcap featuring Lee and Greensville. Jarrett thought it was a great situation for the team.

"It's going to be a state championship atmosphere," said Jarrett Hatcher, thinking back on the game almost ten years after it was played. "It's going to be a game in the middle of the season. We've already set the record. Who cares?"

He then turned toward his dad as the two sat on the screened-in porch in Paul Hatcher's backyard and asked, "Right?"

"Wrong," said Paul Hatcher. Of course that would be his answer. He always cared. Always. There wasn't a game he coached in forty-three years that he didn't care about winning.

The Lee coaches also knew they would likely see Greensville again later that season, so this would be a good test. Paul Hatcher thought this might be the end of the streak, despite having easily beaten Greensville two years in a row. He had coached some of the Greensville players in an all-star game the previous summer and knew they were good. Plus, Greensville was ranked number two in the state, a spot behind Lee High, and had won thirteen-straight games after losing to a school from North Carolina to open the season.

Hatcher told his players before the game, "Upsets happen every day, gentlemen. Sometimes somebody gets beat that isn't supposed to get beat."

That, however, wasn't the case that Saturday night. Lee won 78–58, although Greensville led 51–50 with 2:41 left in the third quarter. Logan Jones and Keon Scott saved the Leemen though with three-point baskets that sparked Lee's 9–0 run. Jones finished with nineteen points, including five threes. Eli Crawford led the way with twenty-two points, but Lawrence Lightfoot added eighteen and Scott had fifteen in the win.

"We made them guard us, and they couldn't guard us," said Paul Hatcher. "I thought they took a lot of undisciplined shots."

The loss was just the eleventh in 124 games for Greensville's coach Randy Jessee. Three of those losses were to Lee High.

"Those cats are good, no doubt about it," Jessee told the *News Leader* after the game. "We weathered Lee's runs for three quarters, but not the fourth. They are like sharks that smell blood and go with it. We made a lot of adjustments, but Lee countered. That's the mark of a great team."

Things went rather smoothly for Lee over the next six games, as Lee improved to 20-0. Rockbridge came within six points of Lee, but none of the other five teams came any closer than fourteen points to the two-time defending state champion.

Logan Jones was in his first season starting for Lee. He had moved from Staunton and attended Spotswood, just northeast of Staunton, as a freshman before returning to Lee High. The junior had become a key contributor also. After his nineteen-point performance against Greensville, the guard averaged fifteen points a game over the next six, including scoring thirty against Stuarts Draft. He was the second-leading scorer on the team behind Eli Crawford.

But heading into the twenty-first game of the season at Spotswood, Jones was gone from the team. Years later, Paul Hatcher said he can't remember exactly what Jones did to get the boot, but what he does remember was Jones just being belligerent.

"You feel sorry for him," said Hatcher. "He couldn't conform, and he couldn't do what we wanted done, but as I've said many times, the group comes first."

Jarrett Hatcher said, 95 percent of the time, Jones was awesome to deal with, but sometimes he would get sideways. Jarrett wanted to keep him around, admitting now that maybe the winning streak was clouding his judgment. It didn't cloud Paul Hatcher's judgment, though.

"I don't know if many people would have the guts to do what dad did," said Jarrett.

Eli Crawford was worried what effect losing Jones would have, not only on the team, but also on him.

"That was my running mate," Eli said of Jones. "For years, man, running around in the park with this guy at Gypsy Hill, playing basketball, playing against him. We knew each other, we fed off each other. It was great to have that running mate. When we lost him, you got a little worried because he was the person, if I was off, he was going to have a good game. He was going to be able to pick up my slack. So a lot more went on my shoulders, which I loved having everything on my shoulders, but it became a factor where you say enough is enough."

With Jones gone, Lee junior Keon Scott earned the starting spot. His uncle, Keith Scott, was part of Lee's 1990 state championship team, and his brother, Daryl Taylor, had played on the 2004 state winner. So he had the genetics to succeed.

Paul Hatcher had called Scott his "sixth starter" that season, so Scott said he didn't feel too much pressure stepping into an actual starting role,

"I was more anxious than anything, but I knew I had talent around me," said Scott. "So I just played my game and tried to keep the team's chemistry clicking."

Scott had been hurt his sophomore year and missed eight or nine games with an ankle injury. That absence caused him to fall behind some of the other players in his skills, but he had talent. Jones could rebound and handle the ball better, but Scott was a better shooter.

"I don't know if either one of them was real interested in defense," said Jarrett. "Logan was probably the better defender."

Ryan Crawford said the loss of Jones hurt the team. Scott was a valuable asset off the bench—instant offense coming into the game—and now, with him starting, that was a piece of the puzzle that Lee was missing the remainder of the year.

"Whenever somebody got in foul trouble early, Keon would step in, and we'd pick up right where we left off," said Crawford. "We had a guard that could come in, and the train would still be moving with no problem."

Now, there was one less person to help keep that train on the tracks.

"Losing Logan shortened our guard rotation, and that was what made that team so dangerous," said Scott. "We had four guards that could've started on most high school teams in the state."

In his first game as a starter, an 84–52 win over Spotswood, Scott scored twelve points and had five assists. Lee then finished the regular season with an 80–54 win over Harrisonburg. Scott had only two points in that game, but Lee was still chugging along, finishing the regular season 22-0.

"Keon came in and played that role great after Logan left," said Eli Crawford. "It took him a game or two to get used to it, but I'll tell you something now, we didn't miss a beat. He knew how to run the offense. He had been on a state championship team. Unfortunately, he got injured my junior, his sophomore, year, so he didn't get to really play, but when he did get in there, he knew how to play. We didn't have no worry in him. He had control of the offense. We went as he went. He knew where to be and when to be."

FINAL ACT BEGINS

A surprising star helped Lee start off the Valley District Tournament with a 93–42 win over Stuarts Draft. Cody Hart hit five three-pointers and scored nineteen points in the win. Coming into the game, the junior had scored twenty-eight points all season. But just as Keary Bonner said, the guys coming off Lee's bench would have probably started as most area schools.

Waynesboro made Lee battle for a semifinal win, closing to within two points in the third quarter, but a dunk by Eli Crawford helped spark a Lee run. The reigning Group AA player of the year had eight points, two steals and an offensive rebound in a three-minute span as Lee pulled away for the 71–60 win.

Perhaps it was the lack of depth, but after surviving against Waynesboro, Lee fell behind 15–5 to Turner Ashby in the Valley District Championship game. Still, even without the bench power it had had for the previous two years, Lee had more talent than anyone. That showed as the Leemen responded with a 25–5 second-quarter run and won 69–56.

Lee had won eighty games in a row and hadn't lost a Valley District game in three years. But none of that mattered now. The senior-laden roster had one thing in mind: a third-straight state championship. The road to that championship had reached the Region II tournament and would next go through Broad Run.

Before the game, the players were quiet in the locker room, unusually so. Jarrett Hatcher asked Eli if they were nervous. Eli said no but that they were focused. They had to be. This was the first postseason opponent this season they were unfamiliar with and the first one that could end their season. Jarrett then asked Eli what he thought would happen.

"We'll win by fifty," he answered.

Almost. Lee won 99–57. Eli Crawford finished with twenty points, while Hosea Berkley had sixteen and Ryan Crawford and Keon Scott both added twelve points. Paul Hatcher was also able to get some quality minutes for Cody Hart, Thomas Nelson and Chris Tomlinson, who combined for fifteen points. With the lack of depth, those players might be needed to give the starters a rest.

"We really loved our bench," said Eli Crawford. "We wanted to see them get into the game and have an opportunity too, man. We wanted them to have everlasting memories and stuff like that on the court. We wanted to see them on the court. We took pride in going out there and putting teams away early."

Handley presented a challenge for the Leemen in the Region II semifinals, actually leading by two at halftime. But then Ryan and Tyler Crawford's mom, Angela Crawford, took over. She stood on her chair and started the chant that, for years, she had led for the Lee faithful. She was joined by the Lee fans in cheering, "Lee High, Lee High, Lee High," followed by Crawford's "One, two, three," with the crowd responding, "Whoa!"

"We do that last part to put the boogie in the opposing team," Angela Crawford told the *Washington Post*'s Angela Watts after the game.

Maybe it helped. Lee began the third quarter with a 6-0 run and never trailed again, although Handley would not completely surrender. Lee won 84–76, locking up a third-straight trip to the state tournament and improving to 27-0.

That win set up a meeting with the only other unbeaten team in Group AA: Orange County. Both teams were already in the state tournament, but a win meant one more game close to home. Leading by just a bucket heading to the fourth quarter, the Leemen went on a 23–6 run to put the game away, winning 72–53.

Lawrence Lightfoot finished with a career-high thirty points. Eli Crawford admitted after the game that, while there were a lot of Lee players who could score, he never thought Lightfoot could get thirty. It surprised Lightfoot also.

"I don't even know where that came from," he told Hubert Grim III of the *News Leader*.

Didn't matter. Another game, another Lee player stepping up, and Lee was now off to state play, needing three wins for the state title. Next up was Tabb in a state quarterfinal game at James Madison University. Lee easily won 68–44 behind Keon Scott's seventeen points and Lawrence Lightfoot's sixteen points.

The most significant thing to come out of the victory, other than keeping Lee's hopes of a third-straight title alive, was Paul Hatcher's 800th win. Fans held up signs with "800" written on them in the coach's honor. As usual, Hatcher didn't display much emotion when it came to his own accomplishment.

"If we didn't have eight hundred, we weren't going to be going to Richmond," Hatcher told Marcus Helton of the *Daily News-Record* after the game. "So that's the only important thing with that."

The other important thing, off the court, was that Judy Hatcher had just gotten out of the hospital after another stay to deal with a manic

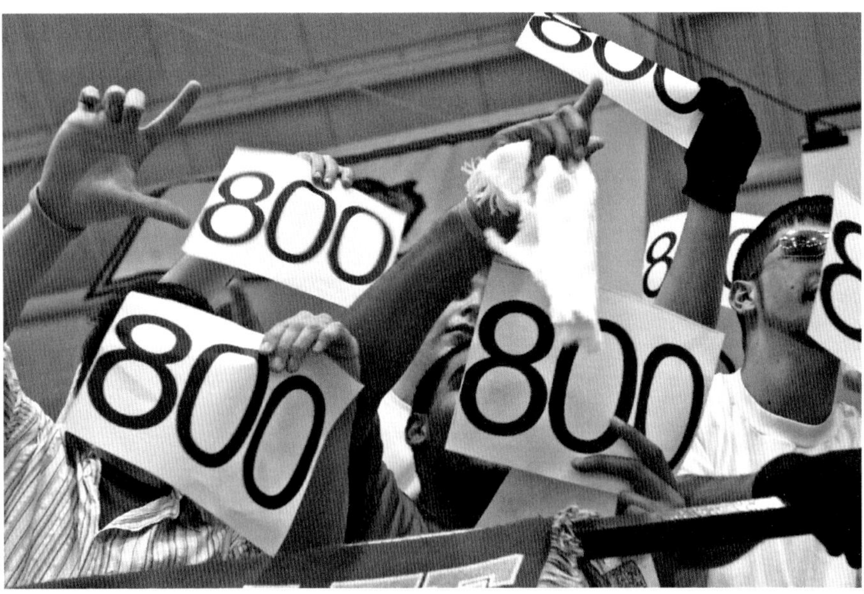

Fans cheer on Paul Hatcher as the coach closes in on his 800th win. *John Palmer Gregg/the* News Leader.

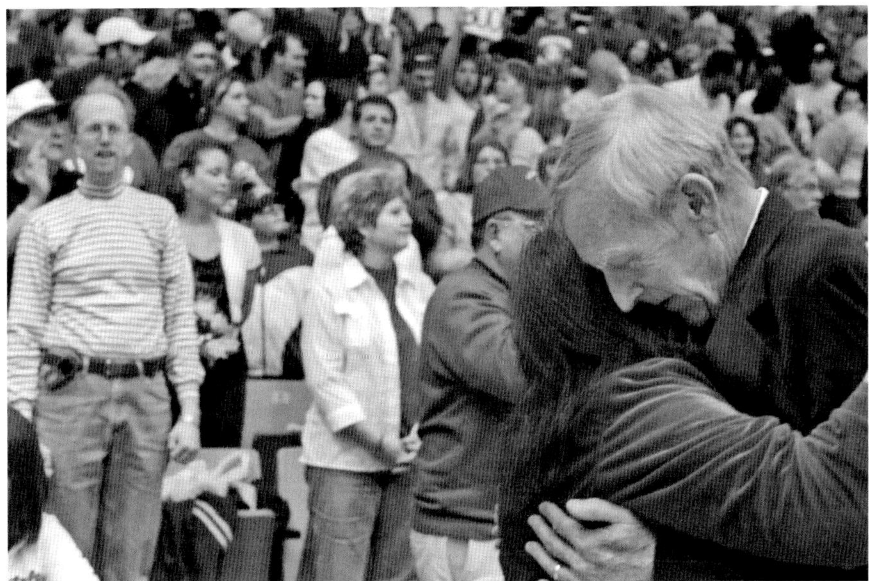

Paul and Judy Hatcher celebrate his 800th career victory on Saturday, March 4, 2006. *John Palmer Gregg/the* News Leader.

episode. It meant a lot for all of the Hatchers that she was there to see the milestone victory.

Lee was scheduled to play an afternoon game on Friday, March 10, in the state semifinals against Greensville. Yep, that Greensville. The same team Lee had beaten for the state championship the previous two seasons. After playing the final semifinal game of the day on Friday the two previous years, playing the afternoon game was different. Staunton City Schools even closed early that Friday so fans could travel to the game in Richmond.

Lee had beaten Greensville once that season, but at the time, Logan Jones was on the team. He scored nineteen points in that game. Since then, he had been dismissed, and Lee wasn't quite the same team. Greensville beat Orange County, the team Lee had crushed in the regional final, 64–63 in overtime.

On media day, held on the Sunday of state tournament week, Greensville's Randy Jessee told Paul Hatcher that he was happy Lee had beat Tabb. If anyone was going to beat the Leemen, Jessee wanted it to be his team.

That didn't happen. Greensville trailed by just four with 6:23 left, but an 18–6 run—Lee always seemed to have just such a run in them—ended any hopes that Jessee's team would pull the upset. Lawrence Lightfoot finished with twenty-seven points, two games after scoring thirty against Orange, and Eli Crawford had twenty-four points in the win.

Lee's group of four—Eli Crawford, Ryan Crawford, Lawrence Lightfoot and Hosea Berkley—would get a chance to play in one more state championship game, their third in a row. Now Lee just had to wait until later that night to see who the opponent would be, either Paul Hatcher's nemesis, Martinsville, or his alma mater, Bassett.

The teams had played four times coming into the game, with Martinsville winning three of those games, including one in double overtime and another on a buzzer-beating three-pointer. On this particular night, in the state semifinals, Bassett trailed by sixteen in the fourth quarter and then rallied, but not enough, to lose by three, 74–71.

Lee's winning streak stood at eighty-five, and Martinsville was in the way of not only number eighty-six but also a third-straight state title. The Bulldogs were 22-6 coming into the game, while Lee was 30-0, but anyone who knew the history of Lee High and Martinsville realized those records meant very little. The two schools had combined to win eighteen state championships, including four of the previous five. And they had split the last two times they met on the state tournament stage, with Martinsville winning in 2002 and Lee returning the favor in 2005.

At Lee's final practice that season, Jarrett Hatcher read "Casey at the Bat" to the players. Then he told them, "We want there to be joy in Mudville. We're not going to strike out."

10
Endings

A decade after the streak ended, Paul Hatcher reflected on it, saying the magnitude of it blew him away. The streak was not only the longest in Virginia High School League history, but also, at the time, the ninth-longest in high school basketball in the United States.

In 2006, Lee's eighty-five wins in a row were nineteen better than second-place Clintwood among boys' teams in Virginia. But by the 2013 season, Lee's streak was in danger of being toppled as the top basketball program in the state when the Millbrook girls' team was closing in on the record.

Millbrook won three-consecutive state championships from 2010 to 2012, the first two coming in Group AA, Division 3, and the third in Group AA, Division 4. The semifinal win in 2012 was the team's seventy-ninth in a row, breaking the girls' record, which had stood for sixty-two years. Millbrook then won the next game for a state championship and eighty wins in a row.

Paul Hatcher is nothing if not competitive. During the winning streak, he paid more attention to trying to win state championships, but once it was over, he enjoyed having coached the team that owned the record for most consecutive wins. And he didn't want that record to be just a boys' record.

"We were curious about the Millbrook streak," said Jarrett Hatcher. "I guess we watched it like the '72 Dolphins do undefeated NFL teams. You watch and hope your record stands. You don't cheer against the others, and you feel that awful feeling of it ending all over again."

When Millbrook finally lost, falling to Battlefield 44–42 five games into the 2012–13 season, the Hatchers breathed a sigh of relief. Millbrook's streak ended at eighty-four games, one shy of Lee High's.

As more years pass and the record remains standing, Paul Hatcher's respect for what his teams did in that three-year stretch continues to grow.

"I've thought more about it now that I've retired," Hatcher said in 2015. "I saw where [James Madison University] softball had thirty-six-straight wins this year. I thought, 'Well, win fifty more.' I mean, that's fantastic, thirty-six in a row, but you're not even close."

Lee prepared for win number eighty-six in a row and a third consecutive state championship on March 11, 2006, against Martinsville at the Siegel Center. Eli Crawford, Hosea Berkeley, Lawrence Lightfoot and Ryan Crawford had been part of the previous eighty-five wins, but the foursome would graduate that year. Unlike two years ago, when Lee lost three starters but had some talent to build around the following season, Jarrett Hatcher was realistic enough to know that, win or lose against Martinsville, the magical three-year run was over after the state championship game.

"The only time I had ever experienced it [before] was in drama or in musicals, this is the final show," said Jarrett. "We've had a great time. It does not matter what happens tonight. This cast is done. We're not going to be together ever [again]."

The team gathered for a dinner and then took a group picture—"It's probably like Custer's last group photo," said Jarrett Hatcher—then they got ready to play. The players and coaches weren't overly concerned; after all, they had been at this same place the previous two seasons and come away with wins. That will give a team confidence. At the same time, the guys knew Martinsville wouldn't be an automatic victory.

Troy Wells began his coaching career in 1970 as an assistant at William Fleming in Roanoke. Six years later, he got his first head-coaching job at Christiansburg but won just six games in three years before taking a job on Husky Hall's coaching staff at Martinsville. He remained Hall's assistant for sixteen years, and in 1995, when Hall retired, Wells was named Martinsville's head coach.

Wells had been head coach in two Martinsville–Lee High games, winning in 2002 and losing three years later. The 2006 state championship game would be the rubber match for the coach. Wells wasn't sure if his team would match up with the 30-0 Leemen.

"They were so talented," said Wells. "I tell people this all the time. If we played that bunch of Paul's that year ten times, they'd probably win nine out of ten, but fortunately we only had to play them one time, and we only had to win one time."

Wells's strategy was to run a deliberate offense to slow the tempo. On defense, he wanted to pack the lane to deny Lee any drives to the basket.

"The way they slowed the game down was really unexpected," said Keon Scott. "We knew they didn't want to turn it into an up-and-down game, but the strategy of holding the ball caused us to press a bit on the offensive end. [That is] part of the reason we played the worst we had all season in that game. Their strategy was smart, and they executed it really well."

The *Daily News-Record* in Harrisonburg also mentioned that Wells kept his players off the blocks on Martinsville free throws, sending four players back on defense to stop Lee's transition. That last bit of strategy, however, wasn't something implemented just for Lee High. Wells had done that for years against quicker teams.

"Most of the time, I'd say 90-plus percent of the time, those inside guys are going to get the rebound," said Wells. "I've always felt I don't want our guys making a silly foul four feet from the basket and going to the other end, putting them at the line when, to me, it's unnecessary."

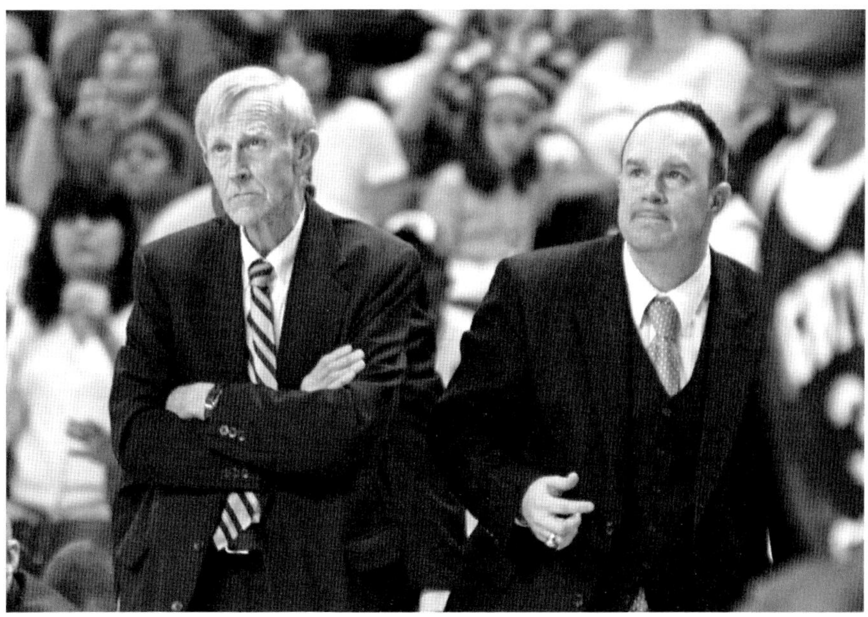

The realization that Lee High wouldn't win a third-straight state championship hits Paul and Jarrett Hatcher in the final minutes of a loss against Martinsville. *Mike Tripp/the* News Leader.

Wells also felt like high school teams playing in a college arena rarely shot well. The wide-open spaces make perimeter shooting difficult.

"We knew they were outstanding athletes," said Wells. "But we just felt like if we could play the 1-3-1 zone like we were capable of playing and make them shoot from the outside, that would be something that would at least give us a chance."

The strategy worked.

"The first thing I remember is how bad we shot from the field," Ryan Crawford said when asked about the Martinsville game a decade after it was played.

Lee High shot just 31.7 percent from the floor and hit only three of twenty-five from three-point range. Lee couldn't score and couldn't generate turnovers on defense. Lee's star Eli Crawford scored seventeen points in the game but was just six of twenty shooting, including two of nine on three-pointers.

"It was just an ugly game," said Jarrett Hatcher.

Ugly from Lee's perspective, at least. Martinsville shot 55.3 percent from the field in the game, making 68.8 percent of its shots in the second half. Jarvis Wimbush led Martinsville with nineteen points, and Shaquan Beamer added seventeen in the win. Paul Hatcher called it "typical Martinsville basketball," but this time they were even more deliberate on offense than Hatcher thought they would be. The Bulldogs were holding the ball for long stretches as they tried to find open lanes to drive to the basket.

"We should have probably collapsed in there," said Paul Hatcher, "but the problem of it is if you collapse in and don't go after them, then you're letting them control the game."

Despite the poor shooting, Lee led by one at halftime, but Martinsville went on a 22–13 run in the third quarter to lead 43–35 after three quarters. Lee got within four points in the final quarter but could never get it closer. Martinsville had just three field goals in the fourth but was fourteen of twenty-two from the foul line as it won 63–54.

Ryan Crawford, who finished with eight points, was called for a charge late in the game, his fifth foul. He walked to the bench, took a seat and started crying because he knew that was it for him. He couldn't contribute to his team anymore. Minutes later, the game ended.

"I remember the clock hitting zero and knowing it wasn't us running out in the middle of the floor, it was somebody else," said Ryan Crawford. "That's when it really hit. When the horn went off and I watched everybody run out to the middle of the floor."

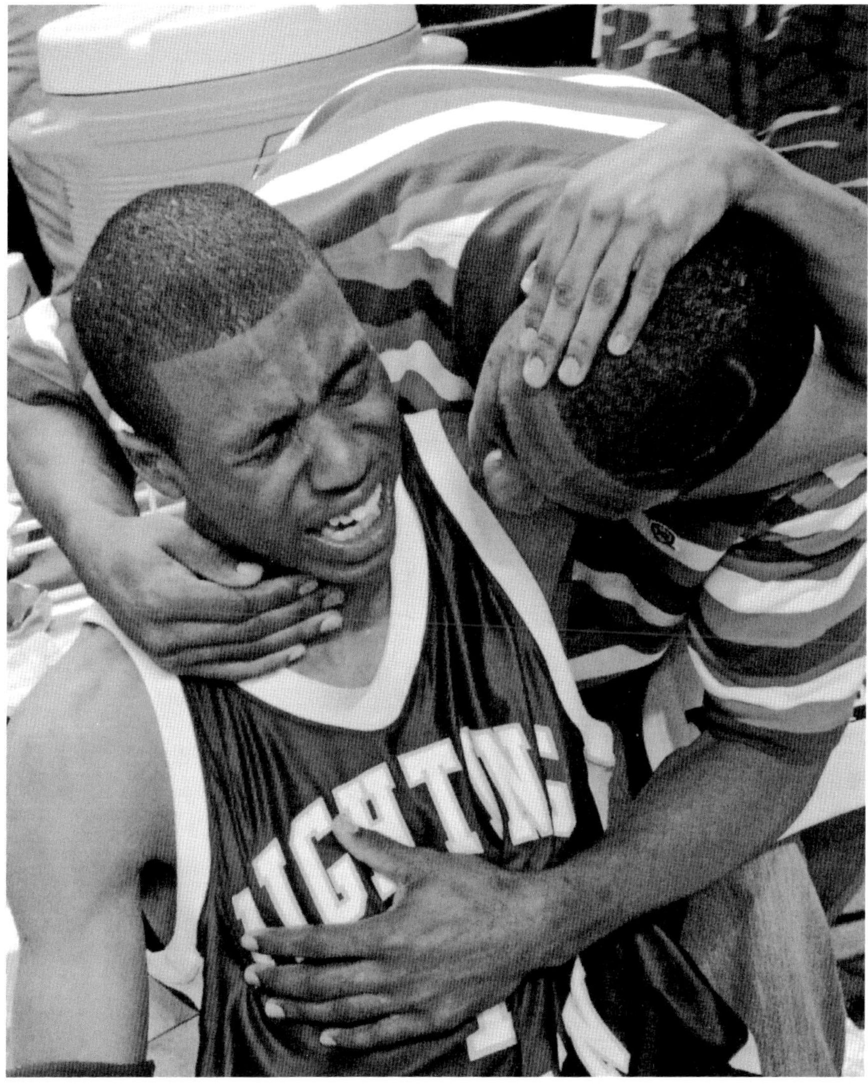

Ryan Crawford's final high school basketball game ended in tears as his big brother, Tyler, tries to console him. *Mike Tripp/the* News Leader.

Tyler Crawford, who had come to watch the game, came up behind his younger brother and tried to console him with a hug. Ryan Crawford remembers feeling disappointed, but he also tried to think back on what the team had accomplished. The senior had a pair of state championship rings, had played in the title game three times and was part of a record eighty-five wins in a row.

"You see teams that get to the state tournament and it's like, 'These guys had a heck of a year,' and they went twenty-five and four or twenty-five and five or something like that," said Ryan Crawford. "The fact that, in my high school career, me, Hosea, Eli and Lawrence, we went ninety-one and two. It's really hard to put it in perspective."

Paul Hatcher agreed. The state championship would have been great, but that winning streak, that's something special. After the loss, the Lee coach told reporters, "We're disappointed right now, but my God, somebody wins a state championship every year, but they don't win eighty-five games in a row every year."

Eli Crawford has put the loss in the very back of his mind. Like his coach, he chooses to focus on the positive.

"To be honest, I haven't really sat, cried, anything about it, man," he said. "I sat there and said, 'How many teams win eighty-five in a row? How many teams win back-to-back state championships?' And I looked at my individual standpoint and said, 'How many players have the opportunity to win not one but two state player-of-the-year [awards]?' Man, there is no doubt in my mind that I had the greatest time of my life."

A decade after that game, Troy Wells said as impressive as Paul Hatcher's record is, that may not be his true legacy.

"What he did off the floor was probably much more important than what he ever did on the basketball floor," said Wells. "To touch the lives that he's come in contact with over the years…that's what coaching is really all about. Hopefully you mentor young people and impact their lives in a positive way to give them some life lessons."

Perhaps that impact was never more evident than in the immediate aftermath of the Martinsville loss. Eli Crawford stood near midcourt as Martinsville accepted its winning trophy. He applauded the efforts of his opponent, something that impressed the *News Leader*'s photographer Mike Tripp enough that he wrote a column for the newspaper about the display of good sportsmanship a few days after the game.

Despite that display, Crawford isn't a fan of what happened that night in Richmond and doesn't care to be reminded about it.

"I never, ever in my life will watch that game," he said. "It's not because we lost but how we lost. I just pretty much look at it as it never happened."

Eli Crawford's tremendous high school career was over, but he found himself wishing it wasn't shortly after the loss to Martinsville, telling *Daily News-Record* reporter Mike Barber, "I wish this was the NBA and I could sign another contract 'cause I'd sign a lifetime contract to play for Coach Hatcher."

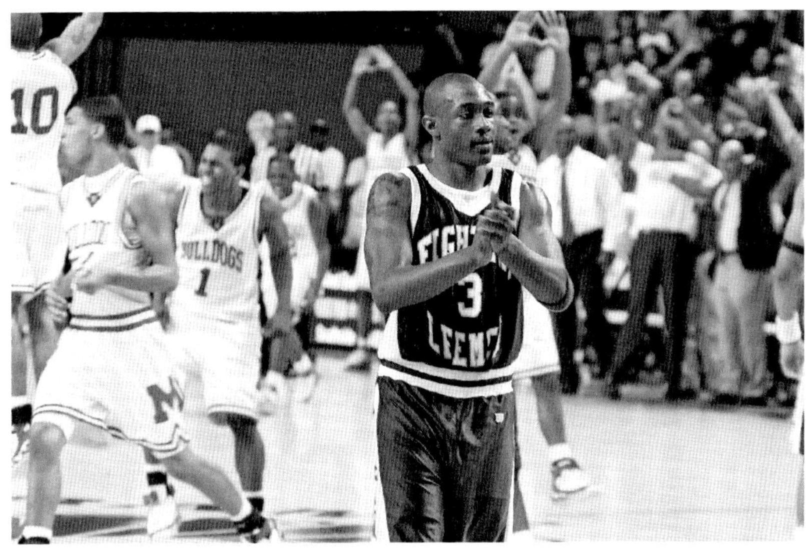

Eli Crawford displayed the sportsmanship taught by Paul Hatcher in the moments following Lee's loss to Martinsville in the 2006 state championship game. *Mike Tripp/the* News Leader.

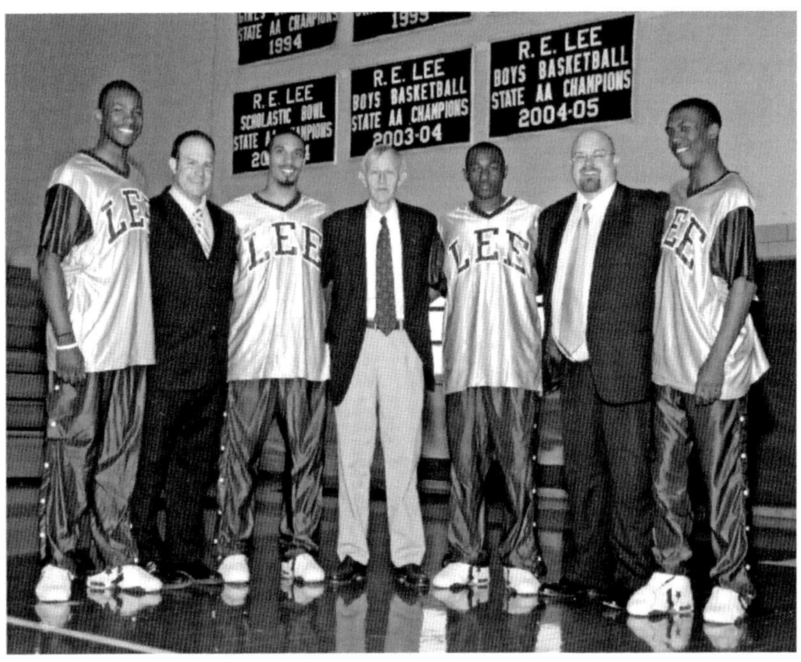

Lawrence Lightfoot, Hosea Berkley, Eli Crawford and Ryan Crawford were the only four players to be part of all eighty-five games in the winning streak. Here they are with Jarrett, Paul and Brandon Hatcher. *Paul Hatcher's collection.*

Years later, he would still like that chance to play for his former coach.

"I enjoyed playing for him," said Eli Crawford. "I wish I could do one more game for him. I don't care if it's an alumni game or whatever, I would love to just sit down beside him, man, and just like always have a talk with him and just enjoy the moment with him."

WINNER, WINNER, CHICKEN DINNER

Only two people appear in the team photo from all four of Paul Hatcher's state championships: Paul and Brandon. Jarrett was in college during the second state title in 1990 and not part of the staff. Brandon was hoping to make it five team photos, and even though his rational mind knows it isn't so, the younger Hatcher feels it is partly his fault Lee lost to Martinsville.

Early in the 2003–04 season, at the start of the streak, Brandon needed lunch on a game day. He had left his wallet at work, and he scraped together enough change from his car to buy two chicken sandwiches at Hardee's. Lee won that night. Brandon was so superstitious that he figured if eating two chicken sandwiches was good enough to get the win that night, he would eat that for lunch on every game day the rest of the season.

Lee won twenty-four games in a row that season and capped it with a state championship. When the next season began, Brandon couldn't risk jinxing the team with a different lunch, so he continued his tradition of two Hardee's chicken sandwiches. Lee went undefeated that season and won another state championship, so Brandon's game-day lunches in 2005–06 were again chicken sandwiches.

The first two years, Brandon drove separately to the state tournament. He would make it a point to get his chicken sandwiches, even walking more than a mile to a Hardee's before one of the semifinal games. In the third year, however, Paul Hatcher insisted the family all be together for the bus ride to Richmond. Brandon's hunch, and he still believes this is true, is that his dad would have retired if Lee won it all that third year. He feels that his dad wanted the family together to enjoy one last hurrah.

"He was really adamant about everyone being together, and I could tell it was really special to him and he didn't want to say it," said Brandon.

The day of the state championship game, Brandon told his dad he needed to stop at a Hardee's for his traditional lunch, but Paul Hatcher refused to do it. He said he wasn't going to make a special stop for one person. They ended up at another chain restaurant. Brandon at first refused to eat, fearing it would cause the team to lose, but the menu had a triple-play trio burger, and Paul told his son that maybe that was a good sign. Brandon gave in and ate the burger.

"For eighty-five games, I ate two chicken sandwiches," said Brandon. "The eighty-sixth game, I didn't eat two chicken sandwiches and we lost."

It wasn't Brandon's only superstition. There was a certain order the team had to shake hands before games, and Brandon handed out mints to the players in a very specific order.

"It got to the point where it was so consuming that by the end of the season, it's a relief [not to worry about it any longer]," said Brandon. "All players and athletes go through those habits and routines."

Brandon said he wasn't the only one who will say something was different about the routine that day of the Martinsville game. Even the statistician lost the pen she had used for the previous eighty-five wins and had to use a different one that day.

"[Dad] is famous for saying, 'Don't worry about that,' but then in the same breath he'll say, 'Well, we've got to go back out this door because this is the door we came in,'" said Brandon. "So the apple doesn't fall very far."

Brandon's girlfriend and future wife, Sarah, whom he started dating in February 2004, near the very beginning of the streak, worried that his superstitious habits might extend to her.

"We kept winning and winning, and we're going on two years of dating," said Brandon. "She honestly thought the only reason I was staying with her was because of my superstitions. I couldn't break up with her because that would ruin the superstition. She honestly said after that [loss in the] state championship game she was nervous because she didn't know what might happen. She thought maybe our relationship would end because we lost."

It didn't. The two eventually got married in 2010 and are still together and even have a young daughter now.

After the Loss

Sitting in his office after returning home following the state championship loss, Paul Hatcher laid his head on his desk. Jarrett Hatcher just sat in silence, watching his dad. Eventually, Paul raised his head and started talking about another loss in the state title game, this one thirty-five years earlier to Maggie Walker.

Losses always stuck with the coach longer than wins. Failures hurt more than successes felt good. That's one of the reasons that Maggie Walker game still bothered him. It was his favorite team, his team's first year competing in Group AAA and a painful loss in the championship game. But while losing the game still frustrated him all these years later, Hatcher knew he probably shouldn't focus on losses.

"There are people who would give their right arm to even get there one time," said Hatcher. "We got there sixteen times. …I shouldn't complain about anything. The way these kids responded and all they accomplished for forty-three years, I mean, my gosh, I should be thanking them every day for all they did, really."

The year after the streak ended, Lee High finished 18-7, losing in the regional tournament. By most standards, that would have been a good season, but Lee lost as many games that season as it had the previous four seasons combined. That was to be expected. A lot of firepower was gone from the previous three seasons.

"I'm actually happy that it was us that lost compared to the next team coming in," Eli Crawford said of the steak-ending game. "That's a lot of [pressure], eighty-six games on your mind all summer long, and it's not *if*, it's *when* it's going to happen. You knew if it went into the following year, they were going to lose. They lost a lot, not just me, but everyone over the years."

Over the next five seasons following the Martinsville loss, Lee made it back to the regional tournament every year, but was one-and-done in all but one of the seasons. That season was 2007–08, when Lee lost in the state quarterfinals, Paul Hatcher's only state appearance after the eighty-five-game winning streak ended.

By Lee standards, those years were mediocre at best. People still longed for the seasons when state tournament berths were almost guaranteed before the first game of the season tipped. Ryan Crawford still hears from those who loved watching those teams play.

"That brings a lot of pride and joy," said Ryan Crawford. "We used to pack the gym every night, and people would come from all over the place to watch us play."

Paul Hatcher knew it might be a struggle to find success in the years following the streak. And if Lee would have beaten Martinsville, perhaps it would have been easier to walk away from coaching. But Lee didn't beat Martinsville, and it wasn't the right time to retire.

"I guess I just wasn't ready to call it quits," said Hatcher. "Later in your career, at least I did, you evaluate things every year. Forty years is a long time, forty-one years is a long time, but I still enjoyed doing it. Naturally, it's a lot tougher."

Hatcher retired from teaching after the 2008–09 school year but kept coaching two more years. Since he taught two years before becoming head coach, the numbers worked out nicely—forty-three years as a head coach and forty-three years as a teacher.

In his final season, Hatcher guided his team to an undefeated regular season. Lee lost to Waynesboro in the district tournament championship game and then to Spotswood in the first round of the regional tournament.

"I just thought, at that point, I don't believe I want to do this anymore," said Hatcher. "And I thought about it, and I thought about it a lot."

He had considered retiring after tough losses before, but this time the thought remained with him throughout the summer as he was walking up and down the beaches in Cherry Grove, South Carolina, during his family's annual vacation.

"The difference was really seriously considering stopping versus some other years when you're mad and the next day you're drawing up Xs and Os," said Hatcher. "But I felt like I just didn't want to do it anymore."

Things had changed. Paul Hatcher still loved basketball. He still enjoyed the practices. Coaching games had become more difficult, but he still liked that part of his profession as well. He was sixty-eight, and the older he got, the more he found it difficult to recover after games. The hard work was still there, but the energy was lacking. Still, even that wasn't the main reason he decided to retire.

In the past, Hatcher had had more autonomy and input on decisions concerning the basketball program. That was starting to change, and there was a great deal of uncertainty surrounding not only the Lee High athletic program, but also the school and the school division in general. An embezzlement scandal involving the student activity fund had rocked the high school. Lee High's athletic director was placed on administrative leave, and the bookkeeper accused of embezzling the money committed suicide.

Inside the basketball program, more and more decisions regarding scheduling, practices and disciplinary measures involving players were taken out of Paul Hatcher's hands. Over the years, Hatcher had enjoyed working with Lee administrators who had been former coaches. As with other school divisions around the country, many of the new administrators had no coaching experience.

Paul Hatcher remembers one incident that kind of summed up the issues he dealt with in his final years as coach.

As had become an annual tradition, Lee was scheduled to play a traveling team from Australia. The team arrived in Staunton on a Monday after a five-hour drive. The teams were going to play on Tuesday night, but the weather forecast for that night was a wintry mix, and it was decided by the school administrators that the game should be cancelled.

"Here they are, they've come from Australia, they're here," said Hatcher, pounding on the table as he recalled the story. "They didn't say, 'Coach, the weather's going to be bad tonight, what do you think? Can we play maybe four or five o'clock?'"

Hatcher was thinking about moving the game to right after school and letting the students in for free, making it a special afternoon for them. But he was never asked his opinion so didn't get a chance to make that suggestion.

"Instead of saying let's see if we can work this stuff out since they're already here—any sensible person would have done that—but they just cancelled it and called me up and told me," said Hatcher.

The forecasted weather never happened, and neither did the game. The Australian team had another game the next night so had to leave Staunton.

"That's the kind of stuff, I just said, 'Heck with it,'" said Hatcher.

On October 10, 2011, he officially announced his retirement as the school's basketball coach. He was the winningest coach in VHSL history, with 897 victories, 142 wins ahead of Hopewell's Bill Littlepage, who retired in 2007. As of the end of the 2014–15 season, the closest active coach to Paul Hatcher's record was still 240 wins shy of breaking it.

Judy Hatcher said she thought her husband had another three or four years of coaching in him when he retired, but it was his decision, and she was okay with it.

"I think it was a little bit of an adjustment for us both," she said. "I still miss the people. I miss the kids, and I miss the fans and I miss the roar of the crowd, but I don't miss it enough to go back to it. Enough was enough. Forty-three years is a long time. That's a lot of ballgames to sit through."

Mark Newlen had become close friends with Paul Hatcher in the years since he graduated from Lee. By the early 1990s, the two were jointly running a basketball camp in Staunton. When Newlen was in Staunton every summer for the camp, he would always find time to join his former high school coach at his Staunton home, the two sitting on the screened-in porch in the backyard, talking.

"We would not only talk basketball, we would talk about life and family," said Newlen. "Any topic was open for discussion. That's kind of the neat thing through the years. I've gotten to know Coach Hatcher as a friend. He's so loyal. He's one of the most loyal, dedicated people I've ever met. He's a friend for life."

When Hatcher announced his retirement, just before the start of practice, it caught Newlen off guard at first, but as he thought about it more, it made sense.

"It didn't surprise me the way he retired," said Newlen. "He didn't want a lot of pomp and circumstance. He didn't want the farewell tour…he didn't want all the attention. That's just the way he is."

Perhaps the biggest surprise for everyone was that Hatcher retired three wins short of nine hundred wins. The coach claims it never bothered him.

"That's not what's important," said Hatcher. "Plus, we had 174 chances. If we couldn't win 3 in 174 chances, we don't need to stay around trying to [reach 900]."

After all, it's just a number, but there are those closest to him who wish he would have stuck around for nine hundred wins or more.

"I wish Coach Hatcher would have kept going until he got one thousand wins," said Tyler Crawford. "I was hoping he was going to do that. At the same time, I wish he would have left after Ryan and them, too. When you love something like you do, it's hard to give it up."

With the start of the season so close, Hatcher's retirement didn't give the administration too many options in finding a new coach. That's one of the reasons he decided on the time that he did.

"If I wait, there's a good chance Jarrett will get the job if he wants it," said Hatcher. "He'd always said he didn't want it."

Paul Hatcher tried to tell him it would be a tough job, a no-win situation especially at the start. Filling Paul Hatcher's shoes would be tough for anyone, much more so when the person trying to do it was his son.

"He had been a big part of the success," said Paul Hatcher. "But still, too, it's different."

Jarrett Hatcher was given the job, at first on an interim basis before it was made a permanent position.

In the years since, Paul Hatcher has mostly stayed away from the gym with his name on it—it was renamed Paul Hatcher Gymnasium in 1990—during games. He has gone to a few away games and, in recent years, served as a volunteer coach for his son.

"It was a whole lot tougher, really, watching Jarrett coach," said Paul Hatcher. "People raising Cain and carrying on, things I'm sure they did when I was coaching, but you get so involved in the game that you don't hear it."

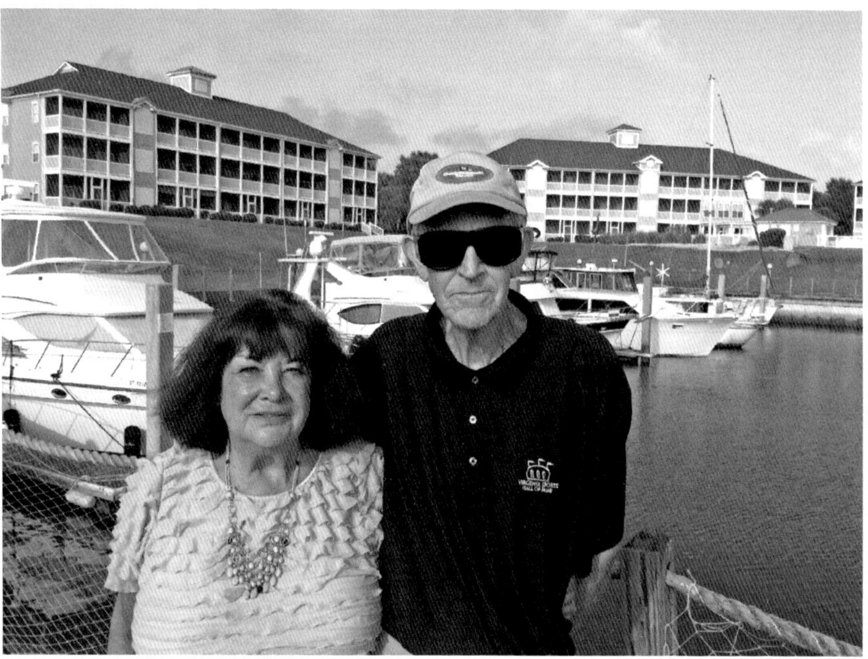

Judy and Paul Hatcher at Coquina Harbor in Little River, South Carolina. *Paul Hatcher's collection.*

Since Paul's retirement, the Hatchers have remained busy. Judy Hatcher refuses to let her mental illness define her, spending lots of time with community organizations, including Daughters of the American Revolution, the Staunton Senior Center, the Thursday Morning Music Club and her church. In addition, she enjoys playing the piano, reading and working in her flower gardens.

Judy also speaks to civic groups and patients at Western State Hospital about recovery and to local police about the best way to handle those with mental illnesses.

"Paul supports me in everything I do because he said I supported him so well for forty-three years," she said.

Meanwhile, Paul still keeps up with basketball, especially the Atlantic Coast Conference, and is a big NASCAR fan. He has converted Jarrett's old bedroom into a room to keep his NASCAR collectibles, of which he has many. His prized collectible? A poster signed by the late Dale Earnhardt, Hatcher's favorite driver.

He has never looked back. He hasn't regretted his decision to leave coaching in the least. He achieved everything he possibly could in his time at Lee High. There's no reason to regret anything.

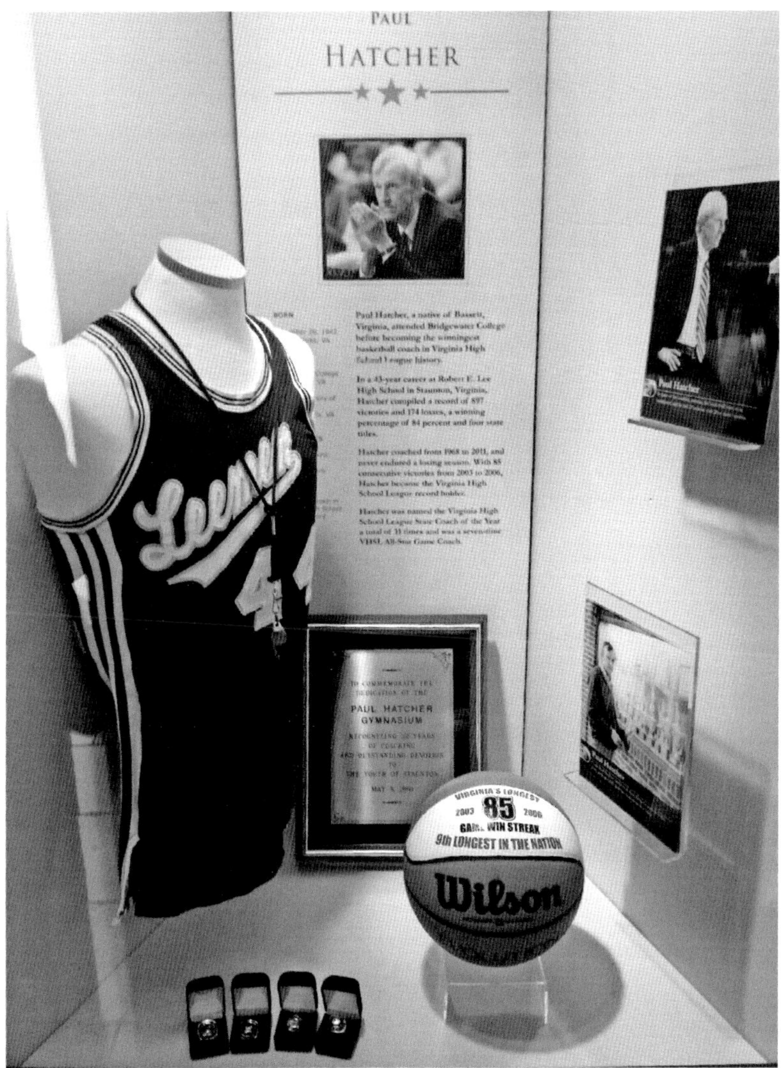

Paul Hatcher's display at the Virginia Sports Hall of Fame and Museum in Portsmouth. *Paul Hatcher's collection.*

"Paul is certainly a legend in the history of Virginia High School League basketball circles," said Troy Wells. "When you bring up basketball, he's one of the first names that you talk about. Paul is just a class individual and a super guy."

It's difficult to narrow down Paul Hatcher's list of accomplishments to the one most important, but if someone tried, it would be hard to argue if the answer was the eighty-five-game winning streak.

"It was one of the greatest feelings I think I've ever had in my life, just being part of something special," said Eli Crawford. "Not too many teams can win eighty-five. Going on a winning streak like we did, we had so much fun with it."

Keon Scott just felt blessed to be part of the streak.

"To do it with the group of guys and coaches we did it with made the achievement even more special for me because we all grew up playing with and against each other," said Scott.

For Paul Hatcher, the streak came as close to what he considered perfection as anything he did in forty-three years of coaching.

"He's always talked about a perfect game would be we score every possession and the other guy doesn't score," said Jarrett Hatcher. "And until that happens, he's not going to be happy. So he's wired to 'I'm going to win every game.' So the streak was what he wanted to do all along. Just wanted to win every game."

Epilogue

By Jarrett Hatcher

My friend and mentor Mike Cartolaro always says, "We all lose our last game." He is right, very few of us ever go out on top. Michael Jordan did, yet the desire to play again landed him in Washington, D.C., and his game-winning shot against the Utah Jazz in Game 6 of the 1998 NBA Finals turned out not to be his last shot.

Mike Cartolaro knows a thing about winning. His Altavista team won three state titles from 2013 to 2015. I had hoped that Dad would win his last game against Martinsville in 2006 and then retire after three-straight state titles. We took pictures of Dad getting on and off the bus for the last time that night. I sat across from him on the way to the 2006 championship game and thought that it would be the last time.

As it turned out, our last trip together was to the district title game at Wilson Memorial High School to play local rival Waynesboro. We were 22-0 and rolling along in our season. We lost the game when a foul was called with no time remaining on the clock. The Waynesboro kid missed the first shot, giving us a false sense of hope, but he ended Dad's last win streak with a free throw. It was a heartbreaking loss for all of us.

The regional tournament was the next week, and we had to face Spotswood. Spotswood was extremely familiar with our program. Their coach, Chad Edwards, was my best friend, college roomie and golf partner, and I was the best man in his wedding. When he decided to get into coaching, my dad spent many hours sharing his ideas on basketball with Chad. Much like Anakin Skywalker eliminated Obi-Wan Kenobi, Chad would end my father's career.

Since Dad's retirement, Chad has elevated his program to not only the class of the Valley District but also of the state. I don't remember much about that loss, but I do remember Chad apologizing for beating us. The best thing about losing at home is there is no bus ride. It is still just as painful, but you get to go home sooner.

In the parking lot after the game, I told Dad I did not want to coach anymore. I said it always ends in tears, it always ends in frustration, it was just not worth it. I had gotten married a year before and realized that I wanted to spend more time with my family. We stood in the parking lot and talked about all of the pluses and minuses facing us. The climate of high school sports was changing, the VHSL and sports in Virginia were changing, the administration at Lee was different and we had been informed that our freshmen team was being eliminated. Most alarmingly, it seemed that our talent was dropping off. I had run the YMCA youth program since 1999 and noticed that there were fewer outstanding players. There were some kids with potential in the sixth and seventh grades, but that was a long way off. We talked at length, and then my dad agreed and said he was going to retire.

That spring and summer, Dad retired and returned what seemed like a million times. It consumed every conversation. It had a profound impact on me. I alternated between being bereaved and relieved. During our annual beach trip, Dad said he wanted to coach again. He wavered until the fall, before finally deciding he would retire.

On the Thursday of our homecoming week, there was a scheduling conflict with the gym. Homecoming at Lee is a pretty raucous affair, and the highlight is the male cheerleading assembly. It is an old tradition where male athletes become cheerleaders and do elaborate routines and comedy sketches. The gym had been reserved for the cheerleading practice. Five minutes into our open gym, we were informed we had to leave. Dad just looked at me and said, "I guess that is it."

We went back to the office, and Dad told our jayvee coach Kevin Madden and me what I already knew. It was an emotional conversation, and we both told Dad how much we loved him. We all agreed we would retire together. After several group hugs and more tears, we walked out of the office. My dad turned toward me and said, "If you want the job, you should take it." I was stunned. We had always agreed that I would never follow him. He said for years that he did not want to come to games or hang around after he retired. He wanted to ride off into the sunset and let someone else coach.

I went home and talked to my wife, Kristi, and she encouraged me to take the job. She and my stepchildren all insisted that I would regret never doing it. I went to Waynesboro to watch my stepdaughter in a jayvee volleyball match, and my head was reeling.

The next morning, Dad told the players that he was going to retire. Malachi Crawford, a junior who had been in our program since the seventh grade as a manager, began to cry. By the end, we were all crying. My dad's hiring was a small two-inch story in the *News Leader*. His retirement made *USA Today*.

Our principal offered me the job on an interim basis in the hallway during lunch. That weekend was unreal, with the story all over social media and the newspapers and television. I was rumored to be the head coach on Twitter and on message boards. I accepted the offer on Monday and tried to go about teaching and having a normal day. I logged on to the *News Leader* website and saw a story about me accepting the job on the front page. I nearly threw up. I thought, "Oh my, what have I done? I am not ready for this." I had been training eighteen years for this, and I was mortified.

I started that season's first practice overwhelmed by the absences of my father and brother, who had also retired from coaching. About ten minutes in, I noticed a head sticking around the corner, watching the practice. It was my dad. He came to watch his son on his first day as a coach.

Our season began with a loss to William Fleming, and the *News Leader* ran a headline above the banner that I had lost my debut game. My second foray as a head coach was no better, losing on the road at Western Albemarle. I wondered if taking the job was the dumbest thing I had ever done.

Our third game was against a very good Broadway team that was a season removed from a state title game appearance. My team made a steal on the final play and gave me my first win as head coach. I was very emotional and just lost it when Eli Crawford walked into the Blue Room to congratulate me. The Blue Room is the holy room of Lee basketball. Only varsity members and former players are allowed in the storage room that is converted to our dressing room. Eli hugged me, and I began to cry.

The next person who walked through the door was my father, who had watched the game from outside the gym, through the door windows. He never wanted to be in the next coach's way, so much so that he stood in the cold to watch the game. We hugged, and I sobbed. Everyone was cheering and crying at the same time. It was the best moment I have ever experienced as a head coach.

These days, my father attends our games infrequently because he says it makes him nervous. He said he was never nervous as a coach, but he and Mom can't handle listening to or watching my games. Dad keeps up with scores from games through Twitter or by texts from our jayvee players. He is giddy when we win, but I can hear the disappointment in his voice when we lose. We talk every night at the same time, and he comes to practice most days to walk the gym and watch. Occasionally, he will ask if he can interrupt and say something. Those times are magical for me. I am a young boy, a player and a young coach again. It is as things are supposed to be, my dad in the gym teaching life and basketball.

Every day I coach, I am amazed at what my dad accomplished in his career. It is hard to win basketball games. It is really hard to win them all for three years.

Appendix 1

List of Wins During the Staunton Streak

Game 1 (12/30/03) Lee High 86, Albemarle 55 (UVA University Hall, Charlottesville)
Game 2 (1/2/04) Lee High 89, Australia HSE 27 (Robert E. Lee HS, Staunton)
Game 3 (1/6/04) Lee High 70, Harrisonburg 53 (Robert E. Lee HS, Staunton)
Game 4 (1/10/04) Lee High 65, Western Albemarle 45 (Western Albemarle HS, Crozet)
Game 5 (1/13/04) Lee High 70, Fort Defiance 29 (Fort Defiance HS, Fort Defiance)
Game 6 (1/16/04) Lee High 83, Spotswood 58 (Robert E. Lee HS, Staunton)
Game 7 (1/20/04) Lee High 92, Broadway 45 (Broadway HS, Broadway)
Game 8 (1/23/04) Lee High 95, Turner Ashby 39 (Robert E. Lee HS, Staunton)
Game 9 (1/24/04) Lee High 76, Rockbridge 25 (Rockbridge HS, Lexington)
Game 10 (1/30/04) Lee High 106, Waynesboro 31 (Waynesboro HS, Waynesboro)
Game 11 (2/4/04) Lee High 91, Stuarts Draft 32 (Stuarts Draft HS, Stuarts Draft)
Game 12 (2/6/04) Lee High 76, Harrisonburg 67 (Harrisonburg HS, Harrisonburg)
Game 13 (2/10/04) Lee High 75, Rockbridge 36 (Robert E. Lee HS, Staunton)
Game 14 (2/12/04) Lee High 90, Fort Defiance 40 (Robert E. Lee HS, Staunton)
Game 15 (2/13/04) Lee High 95, Ridgeview 27 (Robert E. Lee HS, Staunton)
Game 16 (2/17/04) Lee High 84, Broadway 42 (Robert E. Lee HS, Staunton)
Game 17 (2/20/04) Lee High 65, Rockbridge 43 (JMU Convocation Center, Harrisonburg)

Game 18 (2/21/04) Lee High 72, Harrisonburg 51 (JMU Convocation Center, Harrisonburg)
Game 19 (2/24/04) Lee High 67, Western Albemarle 50 (Robert E. Lee HS, Staunton)
Game 20 (2/27/04) Lee High 69, Liberty-Bealeton 39 (JMU Convocation Center, Harrisonburg)
Game 21 (2/28/04) Lee High 71, Loudoun Valley 49 (JMU Convocation Center, Harrisonburg)
Game 22 (3/6/04) Lee High 78, Spotsylvania 68 (Spotswood HS, Penn Laird)
Game 23 (3/12/04) Lee High 52, Salem 50 (VCU Siegel Center, Richmond)
Game 24 (3/13/04) Lee High 96, Greensville County 57 (VCU Siegel Center, Richmond)
Game 25 (12/1/04) Lee High 74, Western Albemarle 44 (Robert E. Lee HS, Staunton)
Game 26 (12/3/04) Lee High 79, Spotswood 38 (Robert E. Lee HS, Staunton)
Game 27 (12/10/04) Lee High 62, Turner Ashby 42 (Robert E. Lee HS, Staunton)
Game 28 (12/11/04) Lee High 64, Jefferson Forest 32 (Liberty Vines Center, Lynchburg)
Game 29 (12/14/04) Lee High 72, Stuarts Draft 46 (Stuarts Draft HS, Stuarts Draft)
Game 30 (12/17/04) Lee High 91, Waynesboro 31 (Waynesboro HS, Waynesboro)
Game 31 (12/21/04) Lee High 88, Ridgeview 30 (Robert E. Lee HS, Staunton)
Game 32 (12/29/04) Lee High 56, Melbourne Australia 50 (Robert E. Lee HS, Staunton)
Game 33 (1/4/05) Lee High 57, Harrisonburg 54 (Harrisonburg HS, Harrisonburg)
Game 34 (1/7/05) Lee High 69, Rockbridge 22 (Robert E. Lee HS, Staunton)
Game 35 (1/8/05) Lee High 61, Western Albemarle 53 (Western Albemarle HS, Crozet)
Game 36 (1/13/05) Lee High 72, Fort Defiance 28 (Robert E. Lee HS, Staunton)
Game 37 (1/14/05) Lee High 86, Spotswood 52 (Spotswood HS, Penn Laird)
Game 38 (1/18/05) Lee High 76, Broadway 54 (Robert E. Lee HS, Staunton)
Game 39 (1/21/05) Lee High 63, Turner Ashby 60 (Turner Ashby HS, Bridgewater)
Game 40 (1/25/05) Lee High 79, Stuarts Draft 32 (Robert E. Lee HS, Staunton)
Game 41 (1/28/05) Lee High 79, Waynesboro 27 (Robert E. Lee HS, Staunton)
Game 42 (2/2/05) Lee High 73, Broadway 46 (Broadway HS, Broadway)
Game 43 (2/4/05) Lee High 71, Harrisonburg 56 (Robert E. Lee HS, Staunton)
Game 44 (2/8/05) Lee High 88, Rockbridge 43 (Rockbridge HS, Lexington)

Game 45 (2/10/05) Lee High 85, Fort Defiance 44 (Fort Defiance HS, Fort Defiance)
Game 46 (2/11/05) Lee High 69, Miller 53 (Robert E. Lee HS, Staunton)
Game 47 (2/14/05) Lee High 90, Waynesboro 49 (Robert E. Lee HS, Staunton)
Game 48 (2/17/05) Lee High 83, Stuarts Draft 38 (JMU Convocation Center, Harrisonburg)
Game 49 (2/19/05) Lee High 66, Harrisonburg 45 (JMU Convocation Center, Harrisonburg)
Game 50 (2/22/05) Lee High 97, Handley 64 (Robert E. Lee HS, Staunton)
Game 51 (2/25/05) Lee High 74, Potomac Falls 68 (JMU Convocation Center, Harrisonburg)
Game 52 (3/2/05) Lee High 72, Millbrook 48 (JMU Convocation Center, Harrisonburg)
Game 53 (3/6/05) Lee High 86, Brunswick 55 (Spotswood HS, Penn Laird)
Game 54 (3/11/05) Lee High 72, Martinsville 62 (VCU Siegel Center, Richmond)
Game 55 (3/12/05) Lee High 74, Greensville 55 (VCU Siegel Center, Richmond)
Game 56 (12/6/05) Lee High 97, Fort Defiance 49 (Fort Defiance HS, Fort Defiance)
Game 57 (12/10/05) Lee High 76, Western Albemarle 51 (Western Albemarle HS, Crozet)
Game 58 (12/13/05) Lee High 65, Rockbridge 49 (Robert E. Lee HS, Staunton)
Game 59 (12/14/05) Lee High 65, Western Albemarle 57 (Robert E. Lee HS, Staunton)
Game 60 (12/21/05) Lee High 61, Roanoke Catholic 50 (Robert E. Lee HS, Staunton)
Game 61 (12/29/05) Lee High 85, Australia HSE 39 (Robert E. Lee HS, Staunton)
Game 62 (12/30/05) Lee High 96, Spotswood 51 (MCI Center, Washington, D.C.)
Game 63 (1/3/06) Lee High 69, Broadway 41 (Broadway HS, Broadway)
Game 64 (1/5/06) Lee High 92, Turner Ashby 51 (Robert E. Lee HS, Staunton)
Game 65 (1/10/06) Lee High 81, Harrisonburg 45 (Robert E. Lee HS, Staunton)
Game 66 (1/14/06) Lee High 82, Miller 60 (Robert E. Lee HS, Staunton)
Game 67 (1/18/06) Lee High 94, Fort Defiance 51 (Robert E. Lee HS, Staunton)
Game 68 (1/20/06) Lee High 110, Stuarts Draft 34 (Robert E. Lee HS, Staunton)
Game 69 (1/21/06) Lee High 78, Greensville 58 (JMU Convocation Center, Harrisonburg)
Game 70 (1/24/06) Lee High 71, Rockbridge 65 (Rockbridge HS, Lexington)
Game 71 (1/26/06) Lee High 99, Stuarts Draft 62 (Stuarts Draft HS, Stuarts Draft)

Game 72 (1/27/06) Lee High 82, Waynesboro 68 (Robert E. Lee HS, Staunton)
Game 73 (1/31/06) Lee High 99, Turner Ashby 77 (Turner Ashby HS, Bridgewater)
Game 74 (2/1/06) Lee High 74, Waynesboro 56 (Waynesboro HS, Waynesboro)
Game 75 (2/3/06) Lee High 83, Broadway 44 (Robert E. Lee HS, Staunton)
Game 76 (2/7/06) Lee High 84, Spotswood 52 (Spotswood HS, Penn Laird)
Game 77 (2/9/06) Lee High 80, Harrisonburg 54 (Harrisonburg HS, Harrisonburg)
Game 78 (2/14/06) Lee High 93, Stuarts Draft 42 (Robert E. Lee HS, Staunton)
Game 79 (2/16/06) Lee High 71, Waynesboro 60 (JMU Convocation Center, Harrisonburg)
Game 80 (2/18/06) Lee High 69, Turner Ashby 56 (JMU Convocation Center, Harrisonburg)
Game 81 (2/21/06) Lee High 99, Broad Run 57 (Robert E. Lee HS, Staunton)
Game 82 (2/24/06) Lee High 84, Handley 76 (JMU Convocation Center, Harrisonburg)
Game 83 (2/25/06) Lee High 72, Orange 53 (JMU Convocation Center, Harrisonburg)
Game 84 (3/4/06) Lee High 68, Tabb 44 (JMU Convocation Center, Harrisonburg)
Game 85 (3/10/06) Lee High 83, Greensville 67 (VCU Siegel Center, Richmond)

Appendix 2

Paul Hatcher's Coaching Record, Year by Year

1968–69	11-10	1990–91	25-5
1969–70	20-3	1991–92	22-4
1970–71	21-5	1992–93	21-2
1971–72	17-4	1993–94	20-3
1972–73	22-2	1994–95	19-5
1973–74	18-3	1995–96	15-10
1974–75	18-6	1996–97	22-3
1975–76	19-7	1997–98	22-5
1976–77	20-3	1998–99	20-3
1977–78	24-3	1999–00	16-5
1978–79	17-7	2000–01	20-6
1979–80	16-7	2001–02	22-6
1980–81	21-1	2002–03	22-5
1981–82	18-4	2003–04	30-1
1982–83	23-3	2004–05	31-0
1983–84	27-0	2005–06	30-1
1984–85	25-1	2006–07	18-7
1985–86	25-1	2007–08	23-5
1986–87	24-4	2008–09	22-3
1987–88	16-6	2009–10	11-6
1988–89	14-7	2010–11	22-2
1989–90	28-0	**TOTAL**	**897-174**

Appendix 3

List of Coaches Who Assisted Paul Hatcher

Joe Cochran
Timmy Crawford
Jim Digges
Jim Goodloe
Mike Guertler
Frank Hamilton
Brandon Hatcher
Jarrett Hatcher
Ron Herr
Jim Hodges
Ernie Holley
Kevin Madden
Joe O'Donnell
Warren Tetley
Larry Thornton
Steve Walk
Charlie Wymer

Bibliography

Anderson, Robert. "Martinsville Can't Stop Lee's Winning Streak." *Roanoke Times*, March 12, 2005.

Associated Press (ESPN.com). "Frosh Williams Caps Rally for Outright ACC Title." March 6, 2005.

Barber, Mike. "It's Time for Round 2." *Daily News-Record*, February 4, 2005.

———. "Leemen Slam Spotsy." *Daily News-Record*, March 8, 2004.

———. "With Class, Lee Bows Out." *Daily News-Record*, March 13, 2006.

Bergeron, Tom. "The Most Hyped Basketball Recruits of All-Time." Rivals.com, May 31, 2011.

Britt, Jim, and Karl Magenhofer. "Lee vs. Brunswick Group AA Quarterfinals." WSVA, Harrisonburg, Virginia radio. March 6, 2005.

———. "Lee vs. Greensville Group AA Championship." WSVA, Harrisonburg, Virginia radio. March 12, 2005.

———. "Lee vs. Salem Group AA Semifinals." WSVA, Harrisonburg, Virginia radio. March 12, 2004.

Button, Bod, ed. VHSL Basketball Tournament, 2004.

Colon, Bob. "Panhandle Set for NAIA Opener for Two Players." Newsok.com. March 15, 1983.

Dailypress.com. "Mclean Is All-State in AA Basketball." April 22, 2004.

El-Bashir, Tarik, Angela Watts and Jon Gallo. "Update." WashingtonPost.com. February 28, 2004.

Graham, Chris, and Patrick Hite. "Mad About U: Four Decades of Basketball at University Hall." 2006.

Griffin, Mark. "Leemen's Late Rally Falls Short." *News Leader*, February 25, 2015.

Grim, Hubert F., III. "Another Milestone Victory." *News Leader*, January 8, 2005

———. "Change Doesn't Slow Leemen." *News Leader*, February 8, 2006.

———. "Coaches' Parallel Careers Finally Intersect." *News Leader*, November 26, 2003.

———. "Desperate Rally Saves Leemen." *News Leader*, February 6, 2004.

———. "Eagles Land with a Thud." *News Leader*, January 22, 2006.

———. "Eli Boosts Leemen." *News Leader*, February 29, 2004.

———. "Experienced Leemen Shoot for State Tourney." *News Leader*, December 2, 2003.

———. "Giants Pay after Eli's Big Plays." *News Leader*, February 17, 2006.

———. "The Greatest: '90 Lee." Newsleader.com. March 19, 2006.

———. "Lee Climbs Valley Peak." *News Leader*, February 5, 2005.

———. "Lee Makes Escape." *News Leader*, January 22, 2005.

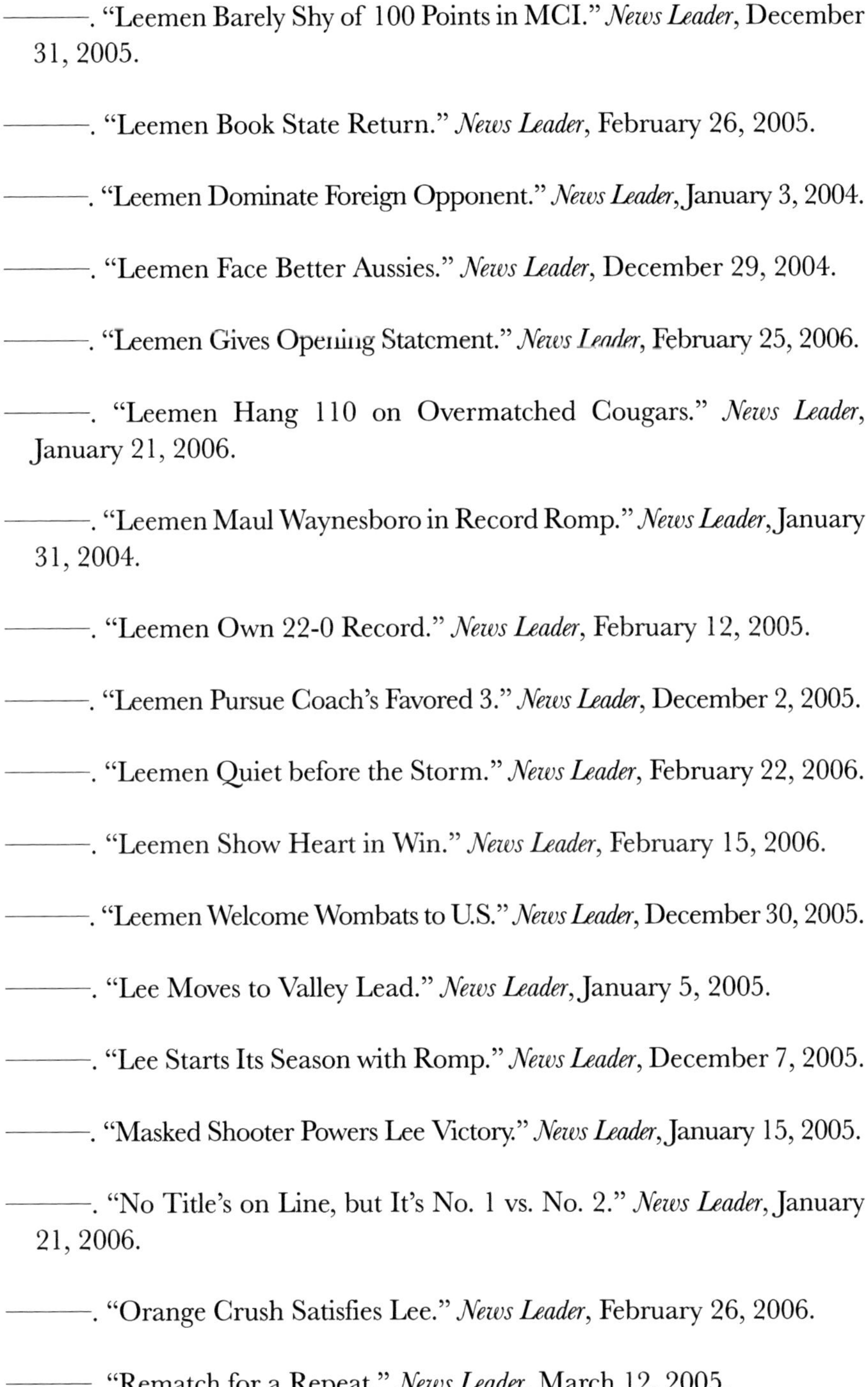

———. "Leemen Barely Shy of 100 Points in MCI." *News Leader*, December 31, 2005.

———. "Leemen Book State Return." *News Leader*, February 26, 2005.

———. "Leemen Dominate Foreign Opponent." *News Leader*, January 3, 2004.

———. "Leemen Face Better Aussies." *News Leader*, December 29, 2004.

———. "Leemen Gives Opening Statement." *News Leader*, February 25, 2006.

———. "Leemen Hang 110 on Overmatched Cougars." *News Leader*, January 21, 2006.

———. "Leemen Maul Waynesboro in Record Romp." *News Leader*, January 31, 2004.

———. "Leemen Own 22-0 Record." *News Leader*, February 12, 2005.

———. "Leemen Pursue Coach's Favored 3." *News Leader*, December 2, 2005.

———. "Leemen Quiet before the Storm." *News Leader*, February 22, 2006.

———. "Leemen Show Heart in Win." *News Leader*, February 15, 2006.

———. "Leemen Welcome Wombats to U.S." *News Leader*, December 30, 2005.

———. "Lee Moves to Valley Lead." *News Leader*, January 5, 2005.

———. "Lee Starts Its Season with Romp." *News Leader*, December 7, 2005.

———. "Masked Shooter Powers Lee Victory." *News Leader*, January 15, 2005.

———. "No Title's on Line, but It's No. 1 vs. No. 2." *News Leader*, January 21, 2006.

———. "Orange Crush Satisfies Lee." *News Leader*, February 26, 2006.

———. "Rematch for a Repeat." *News Leader*, March 12, 2005.

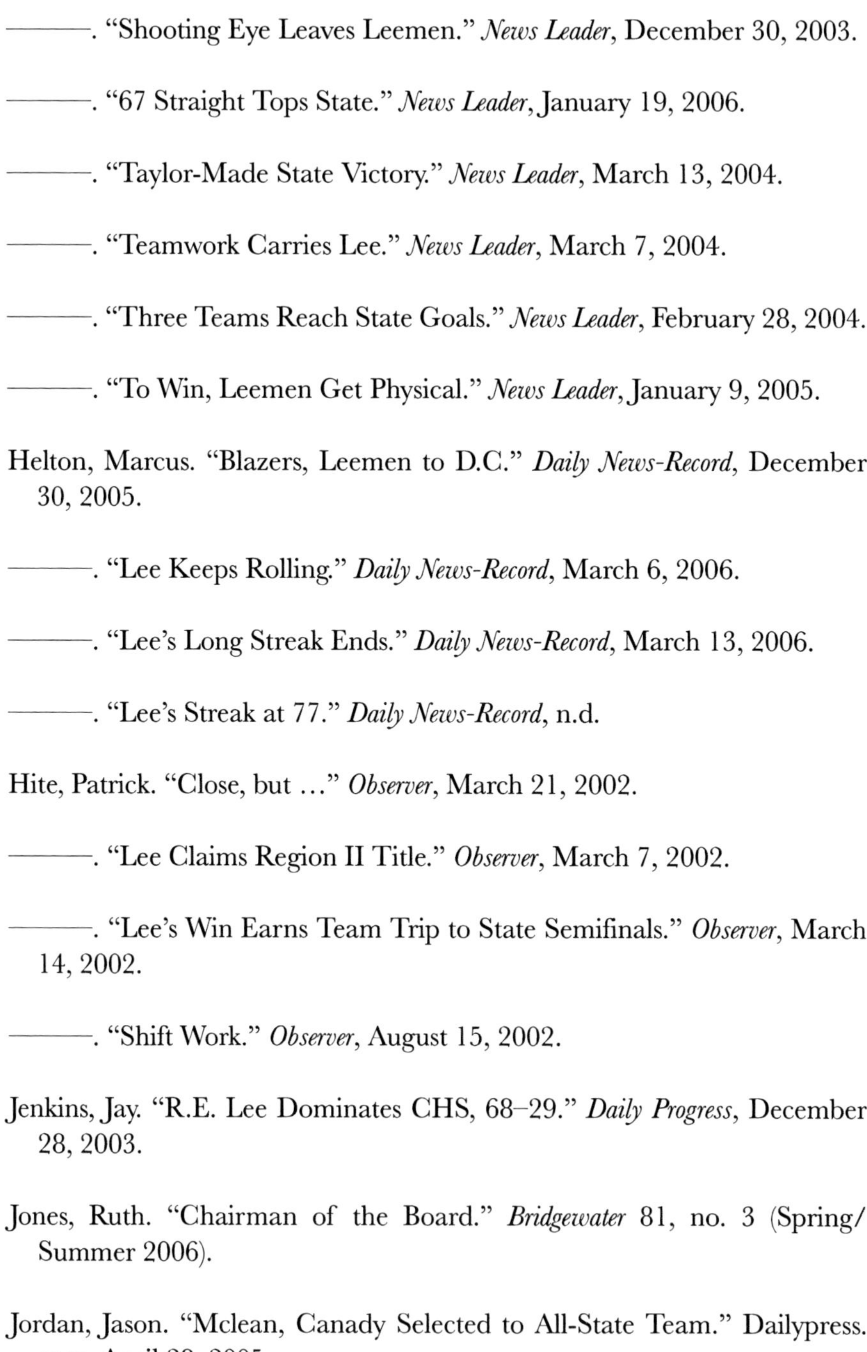

———. "Shooting Eye Leaves Leemen." *News Leader*, December 30, 2003.

———. "67 Straight Tops State." *News Leader*, January 19, 2006.

———. "Taylor-Made State Victory." *News Leader*, March 13, 2004.

———. "Teamwork Carries Lee." *News Leader*, March 7, 2004.

———. "Three Teams Reach State Goals." *News Leader*, February 28, 2004.

———. "To Win, Leemen Get Physical." *News Leader*, January 9, 2005.

Helton, Marcus. "Blazers, Leemen to D.C." *Daily News-Record*, December 30, 2005.

———. "Lee Keeps Rolling." *Daily News-Record*, March 6, 2006.

———. "Lee's Long Streak Ends." *Daily News-Record*, March 13, 2006.

———. "Lee's Streak at 77." *Daily News-Record*, n.d.

Hite, Patrick. "Close, but …" *Observer*, March 21, 2002.

———. "Lee Claims Region II Title." *Observer*, March 7, 2002.

———. "Lee's Win Earns Team Trip to State Semifinals." *Observer*, March 14, 2002.

———. "Shift Work." *Observer*, August 15, 2002.

Jenkins, Jay. "R.E. Lee Dominates CHS, 68–29." *Daily Progress*, December 28, 2003.

Jones, Ruth. "Chairman of the Board." *Bridgewater* 81, no. 3 (Spring/Summer 2006).

Jordan, Jason. "Mclean, Canady Selected to All-State Team." Dailypress.com. April 28, 2005.

Joyner, Andrew. "Leemen Blast AHS." *Daily Progress*, December 31, 2003.

Krider, Dave. "Millbrook Runs to 80th Straight Win, Third Title in a Row." MaxPreps.com, March 11, 2012.

Lassiter, Chris. "Former Player: Keon's Success No Surprise." *News Leader*, March 4, 2006.

———. "Leemen's Foe Makes History." *News Leader*, February 25, 2005.

———. "Lee, Miller School Is Battle of No. 1s." *News Leader*, February 10, 2005.

Meade, Bill. "R.E. Lee Way Too Much for Giants." *News Virginian*, January 31, 2004.

Meade, Bill, and Carl Holcomb. "Taylor Lifts Lee to Finals." *News Virginian*, March 13, 2004.

Mendlowitz, Andy. "Can Anyone Beat Lee?" *Daily News-Record*, February 17, 2004.

———. "HHS, Lee Flexing Muscles." *Daily News-Record*, December 28, 2004.

———. "Lee Alone Atop Valley." *Daily News-Record*, January 5, 2005.

———. "Leemen Edge Knights." *Daily News-Record*, January 22, 2005.

———. "Leemen Little but Loaded." *Daily News-Record*, n.d.

———. "Lee Roars Back." *Daily News-Record*, February 6, 2004.

———. "No. 1 Lee Wins." *Daily News-Record*, March 13, 2004.

———. "Showdown in the Valley." *Daily News-Record*, January 6, 2004.

Merritt-Benton, Sage. "End Game." *News Virginian*, February 17, 2006.

Murphy, Christina. "Hoops Fever to Close Schools Early." *News Leader*, March 7, 2006.

National Institute of Mental Health. http://www.nimh.nih.gov.

NBC29.com. "Staunton School Board in Favor of Building New Lee High School." March 20, 2015.

News Leader. "Lee's Paul Hatcher to Join Virginia Hall of Fame." January 22, 2015.

O'Brien, Marty. "Sports League in Violation of Discrimination Laws." Dailypress.com. July 22, 2000.

Pearrell, Tim. "Bassett Surge Fails." *(Richmond) Times-Dispatch*, March 11, 2006.

———. "Lee Extends Streak, Heads to Title Game." *(Richmond) Times-Dispatch*, March 11, 2006.

Rhoden, William C. "Baldi in the Middle for Redmen." *New York Times*, June 7, 1985.

Roth, Beth Ford. "USS *Carl Vinson* Continues Airstrikes in Campaign Against ISIS." KPBS. November 25, 2014.

Slack, Ken. "Reported Suicide Linked to Staunton Embezzlement Case." NBC29.com, August 30, 2011.

TheSabre.com. "Sampson's Best Hall of Fame Worthy." September 5, 2012.

Tilley, Ken. VHSL Basketball Championships, 2012.

———. *Virginia High School League Book of Records*. 19th ed. N.p.: Ken Tilley, 2015–16.

Tripp, Mike. "True Sportsmanship." *News Leader*, March 15, 2006.

Turner, Bill. "Well's Legendary Coaching Career Comes to a Close." TheRoanokeStar.com, January 7, 2015.

Utley, Arthur. "Taylor's 12-Footer Propels Leemen." *(Richmond) Times-Dispatch*, March 13, 2004.

Washington Post. "ROUNDUP; Shelton's 26 Lead Louisa in Region II." March 5, 1994.

Watts, Angela. "Lee-Staunton Gets Some Winning Support." *Washington Post*, February 25, 2006.

Wilbon, Michael. "Chaminade: 'Amazing' in Va. Upset." *Washington Post*, December 25, 1982.

Williams, Preston. "A, AA Girls Basketball May Face Change of Season." Washingtonpost.com. September 9, 2000.

WinchesterStar.com. "Millbrook Girls Basketball Coach Debby Sanders Resigns." April 11, 2013.

Wolff, Alexander. "The Greatest Upset Never Seen." si.com. December 24, 2007.

WEBSITES

https://casetext.com/case/us-v-jordan-58.

www.BigBlueHistory.net/bb/ralphsampson.html.

www.Bridgewatereagles.com.

www.navy.mil/local/cvn70/index.asp.

www.SiegelCenter.com.

www.sports-reference.com/cbb/schools/virginia/1983-schedule.html.

www.tarheeltimes.com/schedulebasketball-1982.aspx.

INDEX

D

E

F

G

H

J

K

L

M

N

O

P

R

S

T

U

V

W

About the Author

Patrick Hite has spent more than twenty-five years working for newspapers and radio stations in the Shenandoah Valley and Piedmont regions of Virginia. He has won seven Virginia Press Association awards, including ones for his column writing. His dream is to one day be a skipper on Disney World's Jungle Cruise. He lives in Staunton with his wife, Kari, and daughters, Alexa and Ainsley. This is his second book.

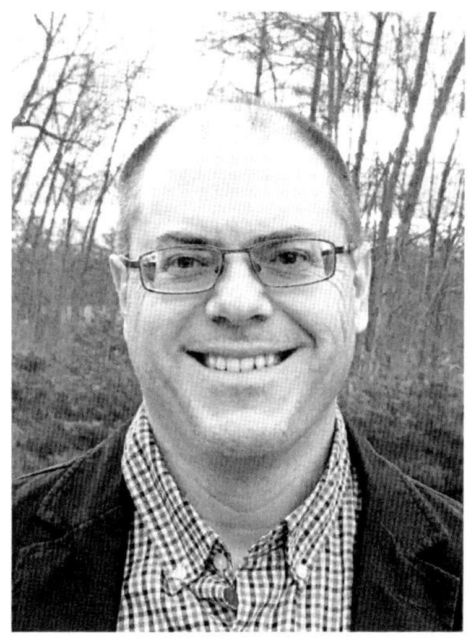

Visit us at
www.historypress.net

This title is also available as an e-book